THE
PHANTOM
MAJOR

*The Story of David Stirling and
the S.A.S. Regiment*

VIRGINIA COWLES

Pen & Sword
MILITARY

ublished in Great Britain in 1958 by William Collins & Sons Co Ltd
and reprinted in this format in 2010, 2015 and 2016 by
PEN & SWORD MILITARY
An imprint of
Pen & Sword Books Ltd
47 Church Street
Barnsley, South Yorkshire
S70 2AS

ISBN 978 1 84884 386 8

A CIP catalogue record for this book is
available from the British Library

Printed and bound in England by
CPI Group (UK) Ltd, Croydon, CR0 4YY

Pen & Sword Books Ltd incorporates the Imprints of Aviation, Atlas,
Family History, Fiction, Maritime, Military, Discovery, Politics, History,
Archaeology, Select, Wharncliffe Local History, Wharncliffe True Crime,
Military Classics, Wharncliffe Transport, Leo Cooper, The Praetorian Press,
Remember When, Seaforth Publishing and Frontline Publishing.

For a complete list of Pen & Sword titles please contact
PEN & SWORD BOOKS LIMITED
47 Church Street, Barnsley, South Yorkshire, S70 2AS, England
E-mail: enquiries@pen-and-sword.co.uk
Website: www.pen-and-sword.co.uk

THE PHANTOM MAJOR

David Stirling

ACKNOWLEDGMENTS

Needless to say the S.A.S. did not keep detailed records of their operations in the Western Desert. Most of the information in this book has been gathered from eyewitness accounts which have involved much painful searching of memory. Dates and names have been checked, as far as possible, through the few diaries that exist.

I am grateful to Colonel David Stirling who told me all that he could remember, and racked his brain to try and place the details of the raids in their correct chronological order.

I am also grateful to Mr. Alexander Scratchley for putting me in touch with many former members of the S.A.S., and I would like to thank Mr. Gordon Alston, Major Michael Sadler, Mr. Stephen Hastings, Brigadier Vivian Street, Brigadier Sir Fitzroy Maclean, Mr. Peter Oldfield, Colonel David Sutherland, Colonel David Lloyd-Owen, Major Carol Mather, Major Cooper, Captain Hillman, Captain Riley, Lieutenant Timpson and Sergeants Du Vivier, Bennett, Seekings and Lilley for letting me see and use their private papers and diaries, or for giving me first-hand accounts of the raids I have described.

It may be interesting to the reader to know that many of the private reports were written not long after the war ended, at Colonel Stirling's request, for his own files. Others were written to give me the necessary information in compiling this book.

M. Augustin Jordan, of the French Foreign Office, supplied me with a detailed description of the raids which he led in June, July and December 1942; and gave me an account of the expedition to Crete led by Colonel Bergé, who is now head of the French helicopter forces.

I have also to thank Generals Reid, Hackett, Sir John

Marriott, Sir Robert Laycock for providing me with background information, and Mr. Douglas Mayne who sent me the scrapbook assembled by his brother Paddy.

Except for short excerpts to which acknowledgment is given in footnotes, none of the material quoted in this book has been published before.

19 *Chester Square,*   *Virginia Cowles*
*London, S.W.*1   *January, 1958*

CONTENTS

1.	The Beginning	*page*	11
2.	Kabrit		26
3.	Action		39
4.	On the Run		52
5.	The Long Walk		71
6.	At the Waterfront		86
7.	Benghazi Harbour		111
8.	The Malta Convoy		132
9.	Evening Out		147
10.	Desert Rendezvous		167
11.	Qattara Depression		185
12.	The Jeep Attack		196
13.	The Trip Home		209
14.	Disaster		226
15.	The Tide Turns		243
16.	The Road		254
17.	Rommel and the S.A.S.		267
18.	To the First Army		282
	Afterwards		305
	Appendix		309
	Index		313

LIST OF MAPS

Area of Operations: November 1941—January 1943   *page* 10

From Jalo to the coast: December 1941—January 1942   56

From Jalo and Siwa to Bouerat and Benghazi: Spring 1942   94

Route taken to establish base for raiding: July 1942   173

Kabrit—Kufra—Benghazi: September 1942   234

Sectors for A and B Squadrons: November—December 1942   257

Through the Gabes Gap en route to First Army: January 1943   287

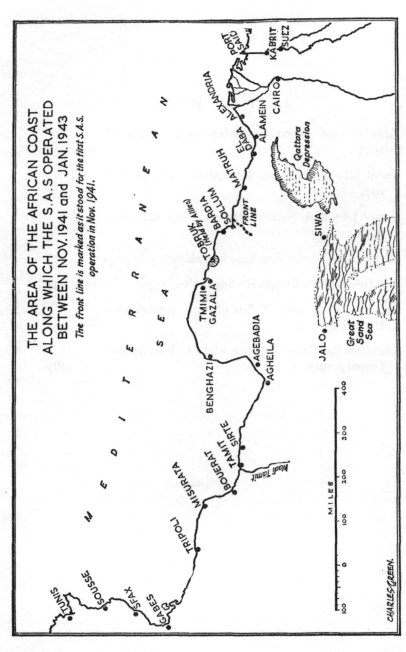

THE AREA OF THE AFRICAN COAST
ALONG WHICH THE S.A.S OPERATED
BETWEEN NOV. 1941 and JAN. 1943

*The front line is marked as it stood for the first S.A.S.
operation in Nov. 1941.*

The section of the coast along which David Stirling's S.A.S. operated between November 1941 and January 1943

CHAPTER ONE

THE BEGINNING

It was nearly a week before the German High Command in the Western Desert became aware that the notorious British soldier, whom their radio referred to as " the phantom major " because of his persistent night raids behind their lines, had at last fallen into their hands.

It was enough of an event for Field-Marshal Rommel to write in his diary: " During January, a number of our A.A. gunners succeeded in surprising a British column . . . in Tunisia and captured the commander of the 1st S.A.S. Regiment, Lieut.-Col. David Stirling. Insufficiently guarded, he managed to escape and made his way back to some Arabs, to whom he offered a reward if they would get him back to the British lines. But his bid must have been too small, for the Arabs, with their usual eye to business, offered him to us for eleven pounds of tea—a bargain which we soon clinched. Thus the British lost the very able and adaptable commander of the desert group which had caused us more damage than any other British unit of equal strength." [1]

This tribute to Stirling's leadership from such a distinguished soldier as Rommel was high praise; even so, it was an understatement. The truth was that Stirling's outfit had done more damage to the enemy than many units, not of equal, but of far greater strength. During the fourteen months that Stirling was in command his forces had destroyed over two hundred and fifty aircraft; they had blown up car parks and ammunition

---

[1] *The Rommel Papers:* edited by B. H. Liddell Hart. Rommel's account of Stirling's recapture is not accurate.

depots, hijacked lorries, mined roads, derailed trains, set fire
to petrol dumps, and killed many times their own number.
Not only had they struck fear into the hearts of German and
Italian soldiers who should have felt themselves safe hundreds
of miles behind their own front lines, but they had forced
Rommel to divert troops to protect his rear, and at important
times had disrupted his use of the coast road at night, which
meant that his convoys were subjected to air attacks by day.

Stirling became almost a legend to the men who served him.
They felt he led a charmed life; that there was no trap from
which he could not fight his way, no occasion on which he could
not outwit the enemy. He fascinated them, not only because
of his daring and ingenuity, but because of his odd, paradoxical
personality. If you met him in a Cairo restaurant you would
be struck by his gentle voice and modest demeanour. Six feet
six inches tall, he stooped slightly, as though apologising for his
unusual height. His immaculate clothes and his perfect
manners seemed to suggest another century, and perhaps you
would be reminded of Sir Percy Blakeney, vague, soft-spoken,
aristocratic and a bit of a dandy. But if you met him at a
forward base in the desert Blakeney had become the Pimpernel;
you were aware of a blackbearded giant with inexhaustible
energy and a loving and extensive knowledge of explosives.
The gentle voice was still there, but the vagueness was gone.
The dark, shrewd eyes shone with a cold determination which
had escaped your notice in Cairo.

*   *   *

David Stirling's private army was born on paper in a
hospital bed in Cairo. And it was brought to the attention
of Middle East Headquarters one blisteringly hot morning in
July 1941 by unusual means. A car drove up to the main
entrance of the Headquarters compound, and a young man
wearing battledress with one pip on the shoulder and the
insignia of No. 8 Commando on the sleeve, climbed out. He
adjusted a pair of crutches and swung himself up to the
entrance. A stream of officers and staff personnel were moving
through the gates, and two sentries were busy checking passes.

The young lieutenant had an absent-minded expression and was half-way through the gate before the peremptory voice of the guard bade him show his pass. " Oh, yes, of course," he replied, fumbling in his pockets. Then: " I'm sorry, but I must have left it behind. I've got an important appointment and I'm late. You couldn't overlook it just this once, could you? " He gave a charming smile but the sentry was not open to persuasion and the answer was an unqualified no.

The lieutenant moved a few yards away and leaned up against a tree. His eye swept along the barbed-wire fence that enclosed the compound. There was a small break in the wire next to the guard post. A staff car had just driven up and half a dozen officers were spilling out. The sentries were occupied. The lieutenant removed his crutches from under his arms and stood them against the tree. With astonishing adroitness he moved his long, lean body through the narrow gap a few feet behind the preoccupied sentry. Lurching precariously he hurried as fast as he was able toward the asphalt path that led to the main building.

It was not until he was nearing the steps that the sentry's eye caught the tall, dark haired figure so like the officer on crutches. Where had the officer on crutches gone? The sentry looked down the street. No officer, but leaning against the post were the crutches. It was quite clear. " Sir," shouted the sentry. He ran after the tall figure which seemed to be accelerating. " Stop that man! " The people on the path looked around in surprise but by this time the culprit was disappearing through the front door.

The lieutenant saw that there was no time to lose. He did not, in fact, have an appointment with anyone, but his intention was to pay a call on the Commander-in-Chief of the British Forces in the Middle East. Now it was obvious that he could not afford to be particular, for the commotion outside was growing louder. He lurched down one corridor and around another. Then he came to a door marked Adjutant-General. This, he decided, must do. He pushed it open and walked in.

The small, red-faced major was sitting at a desk, writing. He looked up in surprise, then an expression of indignation crossed his face as he noticed the single star on the intruder's shoulder.

"What the devil do you want bursting in like this? Even in the army it's customary to knock."

The lieutenant saluted smartly. "I'm sorry, sir, but I had to see you on urgent business."

The major was too annoyed to be impressed, and without asking the lieutenant to be seated replied coldly, "Are you sure you can spare the time to explain ? "

The lieutenant advanced a few paces and told the major that his name was David Stirling; that he was an officer in the Scots Guards; that he had transferred to No. 8 Commando in 1940 and come out to the Middle East with Layforce which, as the major of course knew, was now being disbanded because of the unfortunate arrival of the Germans in Africa and the British Army's urgent need for replacements. But Lieutenant Stirling had a scheme of his own. He was certain, he said, that if he were given a small command of hand-picked men and officers he could parachute behind the enemy lines and destroy the whole of the German air-force on the ground. His plan was designed to coincide with the next major offensive.

The major listened, his anger swelling visibly. Stirling can still recall the conversation that followed, which went something like this. "Do you remember me, Stirling? "

"No, sir."

"And do you know *why* you don't remember me? And *why* on the other hand I remember you only too clearly? "

"No, sir."

"Because in 1939 I was temporarily attached to the Scots Guards and gave a series of lectures to the Second Battalion at Pirbright on tactics. And when I came to question you, Stirling, I found you in a deep sleep. The reason? Because I was told you made a habit of going to gay parties in London every night and not returning until 6 a.m. Frankly, I regarded you even then as one of the least desirable officers in your regiment. I'm not at all surprised to find that you soon left, and joined the first crack-pot outfit you could find. Now you have the presumption to come to me and suggest that you be given your own private command, in charge of your own private strategy with your own private hand-picked men. In my whole military career I've never heard such insolence. The answer is no, Lieutenant Stirling, a flat, unqualified no. And before you leave let me say I'm sorry that you found your way to this office, for I assure you I will use my influence to see that you are posted to the battalion of your regiment now serving in the desert at the earliest possible moment. I am not sanguine about the advantage they will reap from your company, but in my report on you I will recommend that drastic steps be taken to lick you into shape. Good day."

Stirling saluted. As he retreated towards the door the telephone rang and he just had time to hear the major say: " The sentry wants to make a complaint? Broke past the guard post? Send him up to my office. Yes, right away . . ." By this time Stirling was hurrying unsteadily down the corridor. As he turned a corner he saw the sentry approaching from the far end. He retreated rapidly, then paused at a door marked D.C.G.S. The letters meant nothing to him, but it looked a useful port in a storm. This time he knocked and walked in. He found himself facing a man he knew well by photograph; General Ritchie, Deputy Chief of Staff, Middle East Forces.

Ritchie looked up from his desk with the same surprise as the major. David apologised for his unconventional call but insisted that he had " vital business " to bring to the general's attention. There was a moment's pause then Ritchie asked him to have a seat. David introduced himself and pulled a pencilled memorandum out of his pocket.

Ritchie began to read. The writing was bad, and every now and then his brow knitted into a frown but he read for ten minutes without moving. Then he looked up and said brusquely, " I think this may be the sort of plan we are looking for. I will discuss it with the commander-in-chief and let you know our decision in the next day or so."

Stirling was not prepared for such a cut and dried reply, and did his best to hide his astonishment. He began murmuring his thanks but Ritchie cut him off. The report would be studied in detail. Stirling would be summoned when a decision had been made. However, there was one person that David should meet before he departed. That was Major Smith[1] from the A.G. branch. He picked up the telephone, and summoned the same major who had given David the dressing down. When he put down the receiver he explained to David that Smith was the man who would have to work out the organisational side if the commander-in-chief decided to go ahead with the project.

Major Smith obeyed Ritchie's summons at once. He had just finished interviewing the sentry who had furnished him with the details of Stirling's outrageous behaviour, and felt that he was now in a position to prefer charges against the insolent young man. When he opened Ritchie's door, and saw Stirling sitting in the general's arm-chair, he was so taken aback he could find no words. Ritchie did not seem to notice his surprise; nor did he listen to David's murmur, " We've met before. We were chatting about old times only this morning . . ." He told Smith that Stirling had an interesting proposition which might be " just what we're after "; and to be prepared to see him and help him if his plan was approved.

A moment later Ritchie dismissed the two men. When they found themselves together in the corridor with the door closed behind them, the major gave David a withering look. " I will do my duty no matter how disagreeable," he said. " But I trust, Stirling, you will not be expecting any favours."

*   *   *

During the next forty-eight hours Ritchie not only studied David Stirling's plan in detail, but made a few inquiries about the character and capabilities of his unexpected visitor. He learned that David came from an old well-to-do Scottish family, whose ancestors had often distinguished themselves in the border wars of other days. David had two sisters and three brothers; one of the brothers, Peter, was third secretary at the British Embassy in Cairo; two others, Bill and Hugh,[2] were officers with the Scots Guards. His cousin, Lord Lovat, was

---

[1] This name is fictitious.
[2] Hugh Stirling was killed on patrol duty in the spring of 1941.

the commander of the Scottish Commando. The Stirlings lived at Keir, in Stirlingshire, and were passionately fond of all the Scottish pursuits; shooting, stalking, mountain climbing. As a family they were known for their energy, good-looks and sociability. But Ritchie probably did not discover that before the war David Stirling, the middle member, was regarded as something of a problem child. Like his brothers he was sent to Ampleforth and Cambridge. He did not do badly at public school but by the time he reached the University his interest in study had waned. He was a gambler, and he spent too much time and lost too much money at Newmarket.

His mother was anxious for him to settle down but David could not make up his mind what to do. The idea of office routine and fixed hours appalled him. He passed some months in idleness then told his mother that he had settled upon a course. He had decided to be the first man to climb Mount Everest. He had worked out a long term plan. It would require five years' training, and he was starting at once. Mrs. Stirling did not regard this scheme as a sensible ambition and did her best to dissuade her son, but her arguments beat futilely against the stubborn persistence for which he was known. For the next two years he spent most of his time in Switzerland and America. He was in the Rocky Mountains when war was declared in 1939.

He came home and joined the Scots Guards. His battalion was in training and he longed for something more exciting than routine duties. When Major Robert Laycock raised No. 8 Commando from the Brigade of Guards, recruiting many of his officers in the bar at White's, Stirling was among those who joined. At the end of 1940 this commando, plus four others, set sail from the Middle East with instructions to capture the island of Rhodes and prevent the German Air Force from setting up a base there. Laycock was promoted to the rank of full colonel and given command of all five commandos, which totalled two thousand men, and became known as " Layforce."

*   *   *

When Layforce disembarked at Suez at the beginning of February 1941 the war was going well for the British Army in the Mediterranean. General Wavell was in the midst of a full scale offensive against the Italian Army in the Western Desert. By 7th February the British Army had advanced five hundred miles from Sollum to Agheila, on the border of Tripolitania, and had captured 130,000 prisoners, 400 tanks and 1,290 guns. Cyrenaica had been swept clean of the enemy and Wavell's prestige had reached its peak.

Then the Germans stepped in. For some days reports had been coming in that German armour and reinforcements were moving into Tripolitania; and that a general named Rommel had arrived to take charge of a new phase of desert operations. At the same time there were indications that German troops were massing in Bulgaria for an attack on Yugoslavia and Greece.

General Wavell was not pessimistic. He was convinced it would take some weeks for the Axis to regroup its forces to launch a counter-offensive against the British Army's vital coastline position at Agheila. In the meantime he reluctantly agreed that a number of British troops and tanks should be diverted to Greece to help meet the new threat.

The enemy's blows fell in April and May. The new general, Erwin Rommel, performed a lightning stroke which took Wavell by surprise and succeeded in outflanking Agheila. Within ten days he had driven the British Army back to the Egyptian frontier. Only Tobruk held fast with twenty-five thousand British troops ringed inside. When Churchill heard the startling news he murmured, " Rommel has torn the new-worn laurels from Wavell's brow and thrown them in the sand."

At the same time that these battles were being fought the German Army struck at Yugoslavia and Greece. Yugoslavia capitulated after eleven days of fighting on 17th April; and Greece, despite the help of British troops, surrendered on the 24th. This was not all. At the end of May German parachute troops successfully invaded the British-protected island of Crete, inflicting still another defeat on the Middle East Army. And in June Wavell's final offensive, Battle-axe, designed to relieve the Tobruk garrison, fizzled out in failure.[1] The tables had been completely turned, and the New Year that had promised so well had offered little but disaster. In July General Auchinleck succeeded General Wavell as Commander-in-Chief of the Middle East.

* * *

While the war blazed fiercely during those spring months of 1941, and the Germans scored their relentless string of victories, Brigadier Laycock's small unit found itself buffeted about from plan to plan. By April it was obvious that it was no longer possible to attempt an invasion of Rhodes. Instead, a contingent of commandos, led personally by Laycock, fought a valiant rear-guard action in Crete; a second contingent made a landing in Syria and a third force was sent to hold a section of the line at Tobruk—and was still there.

These operations were only stop-gaps. What role could Layforce play? The High Command decided to employ it along the African coast, where it would land on enemy beaches and move up to wreck airfields and lines of communication. Three times expeditions were launched, but since every British ship was needed in the bitter Mediterranean struggle the Navy was instructed to run no unnecessary risks. The men were landed only once; on the other two occasions they were brought back to port without going ashore.

Headquarters then decided that Layforce must be disbanded. The Navy could not spare the vessels to provide a ferry service; besides it looked as though Rommel was well guarded against small-scale invasion from the sea. Some of the men would be used as replacements for the badly mauled divisions; others would be sent home to join their parent units.

David Stirling sat in Alexandria fuming. He refused to accept the fact that there was no place for " special operations " in the desert battle. The trouble with Layforce, he argued, was that it was too immobile. Because the Navy could not " lift " it was no reason to abandon the raids. Commando

[1] In this same month of June over a hundred divisions of the German Army attacked Russia. Britain was no longer alone.

troops should be dropped by parachute, not landed by sea.
The Germans had demonstrated the practicability of the
technique by their successful onslaught on Crete. However,
in the spring of 1941 there were no parachute schools in the
Middle East. Indeed there was not a single parachute expert.
A training centre had been opened in England, but neither
instructors nor equipment had found their way to the
Mediterranean.

While Stirling was pondering these problems, he heard that
a fellow officer in No. 8 Commando, Jock Lewis, had laid his
hands on fifty parachutes which had been intended for India
but had been unloaded in Alexandria by mistake. Lewis had
received permission and encouragement from Brigadier Laycock to experiment with them. David at once asked if he might
join the group. Lewis replied that he had only been able to
get hold of an old Valencia aeroplane, wonderfully unsuited
for parachute jumping, so that a certain amount of risk was
involved. Stirling said that he was willing to take the chance,
and on the appointed day the two officers and six other ranks
conducted their trials from an airfield near Mersa Matruh.
The static lines of the parachutes were fastened to the chair
seats of the aeroplane and it looked a very hazardous operation; but on the whole the experiment was successful. Stirling
was the only unlucky one. When his parachute ripped away
from the static lines it caught on the tail structure of the plane
and tore a hole in the top. He fell much too fast and hit the
rocky ground so hard that he severely injured his back. For
some days both his legs were paralysed, and for some weeks
he was unable to move from his bed at the Scottish Military
Hospital in Alexandria.

This period of idleness was not wasted. He began to work
out his own scheme for special operations. The commandos,
he decided, were not only too immobile but too large. This
was an original conclusion for up until now military critics had
used the inverse argument. Stirling pointed out, however,
that commando parties usually contained a minimum of
200 men because they were designed to approach their targets
from the sea and at least a third of their force had to remain

on the beach to keep the bridge-head secure. These numbers, he said, meant that the element of surprise often was lost soon after the landing began.

He felt that the conception was wrong. Surprise, he was certain, was the key to success. Much better to drop half a dozen men, use every one of them, and to retain surprise until the demolition fuses went off.

Soon his hospital bed was strewn with maps and pencilled notes. The desert was ideal for his scheme. The fighting between the two armies was concentrated along the coast road. On one side lay the Mediterranean, and on the other the vast expanse of empty desert. All along the coast road the armies pitched their tents. From the air it was a strange sight; the blue sea glistening and shining in the sun; the miles of rocky white waste; the thread of winding road and the little dots nearby that meant airfields, supply dumps, car parks, and repair shops and camps. It was obvious that if a handful of men could be dropped by parachute miles behind the enemy lines, they could hide in the desert waste by day, then at night creep on to the unguarded and exposed airfields and place their bombs on the aircraft. Still under cover of darkness they could make off again across the desert, join up with a patrol, and find their way back to their own lines. No troops would be needed to defend anything; they would just do their job and fade away.

Stirling's ' military appreciation ' suggested that a force of sixty men be raised ; and that his experiment be tried out on the night preceding the next big Allied attack. The sixty men would be divided into five groups of twelve men each, and they would attack the five advanced German airfields. If each man carried twelve bombs, they would have enough ammunition to blow up the whole of the enemy's African air force.

*   *   *

It was not surprising that David Stirling's plan appealed to the High Command. It was wonderfully economical. It promised much and risked practically nothing. The new Commander-in-Chief, General Auchinleck, was an efficient, thorough, cautious Scot. His temperament would not allow him to take chances that involved whole divisions, but here was a proposal that required only a handful of men.

At this time Auchinleck was having difficulties with Winston Churchill. The Prime Minister was pressing for an early offensive, arguing that Germany's gigantic operations in Russia had greatly increased her difficulties in supplying the North African theatre, and that British forces should strike as rapidly as possible. But Auchinleck was refusing to comply. Although he realised the necessity of relieving Tobruk, he needed time, he said, to get his armour repaired, his men trained on new tanks, his supply depots thoroughly stocked, and his divisions brought up to strength. " It is clear . . . that there were serious divergencies of views and values between us," wrote Churchill in *The Second World War*. " Generals are often prone, if they have the chance, to choose a set-piece battle, when all is ready, at their own selected moment, rather than to wear down the enemy by continued unspectacular fighting. They naturally prefer certainty to hazard. They forget that war never stops, but burns from day to day with everchanging results, not only in one theatre but in all . . ."

Auchinleck could not fail to detect the critical undertone in Churchill's messages. The daring stroke was not in his nature. He did not pretend to be a gambler, and set his face firmly against anything that involved heavy risk. This did not mean that occasionally he was not willing to take a flutter, provided the stakes were low and fixed. In this light he regarded Stirling's venture. Something might be gained and nothing could be lost.

Thus, three days after David's interview with Ritchie, he found himself in the presence of the commander-in-chief. Auchinleck had a masterful personality, and no matter whether his decisions were affirmative or negative, always took them quickly. Stirling's requests were granted. He could recruit six officers, and sixty non-commissioned men and other ranks from the depot at Geneifa where the remnants of Layforce were encamped. He could set up a training camp in the Suez Canal Zone and prepare his men for a raid on the advanced

German airfields on the night preceding the major offensive in November. His unit, as he had particularly specified, would come under the direct authority of the commander-in-chief. Henceforth Stirling would bear the rank of captain and his force would be known as 'L Detachment' of the S.A.S. Brigade.

The S.A.S. stood for the Special Air Service, which, the general explained, did not exist. A staff officer by the name of Brigadier Dudley Clarke had invented it in order to make the enemy believe that the British parachute troops had arrived in the Middle East. For some months Clarke had been busy dropping dummy soldiers near the prisoner-of-war cages so that the matter should receive wide circulation; he had also built dummy gliders which had been left on airfields for the benefit of enemy air reconnaissance. "Whatever comes of your project," said Auchinleck shaking hands, "your presence will greatly relieve Clarke's burden."

Before David left the building he was taken to meet the Director of Military Information. Here he thought he detected a faint note of hostility, and he was glad his new authority stemmed directly from the commander-in-chief. Then he went to the adjutant general's department where he had to deal with his old foe, Major Smith. The major greeted him with pursed lips. He had to allow him to recruit the number of men Auchinleck had authorised. "But," he said with relish, "you may find the Q side a bit sticky."

David suspected that the major had a friend at Q, and had already given him advice on how to deal with 'L Detachment's' requests. He was not surprised, therefore, to find that Q regarded the supply difficulties as insurmountable. "At the moment," said the officer in charge, "I'm afraid we can only lay our hands on two tents and not much else. There's a tremendous shortage, you know. We lost everything in Greece and Crete not to mention the recent set-back here. Of course we'll find the stuff in time, but I wouldn't count on anything for the next six months. You see most of it will have to come from England."

David argued that he was asking for very little; and that

his operation was scheduled to take place in three months'
time. But the officer was adamant. " I see your problem, but
there's nothing I can do about it. I'm snowed under with
requests and everyone must take their turn. I'm afraid," he
ended merrily, " you have to queue at Q."

David thought it a poor joke. Hang the supplies; what
mattered most was the men.

*   *   *

The recruiting took only a few days. First he went from
Mersa Matruh to Tobruk by ship and contacted Jock Lewis
who was in the beleaguered town with a detachment of
commandos, carrying out night patrols. This was the officer
he wanted most. Lewis was not only a daring soldier but a
scholar as well. He had taken an honours degree in science at
Cambridge. He had the sort of mind that David needed to
organise the training school and to thrash out the problems
involved in a new enterprise. Lewis listened to David's proposals with interest. But would this operation really come off?
Or was it like the raids planned by Layforce that would be
cancelled at the last moment? David's earnestness finally
persuaded him, and he promised to turn up in the Canal Zone
at the end of the week.

Then David hastened to Geneifa. The men were assembled
in a large tent and he told them his proposition. At the end
of his speech he had so many volunteers that he could pick
and choose. He interviewed each one individually and, as one
of the sergeants wrote, the S.A.S. ' appealed to us more than
bashing the square with the Guards.' His first recruits included
non-commissioned officers Cooper, Seekings, Rose, Lilley and
Bennett, all of whom were to prove invaluable stand-bys in
the days to come.

Stirling selected four more officers. An Irishman by the
name of McGonigal, two Englishmen, Bonnington and Thomas,
and a Scot named Bill Fraser. Fraser had a solid army tradition, for his father and grandfather had both been sergeants
in the Gordon Highlanders. His family were proud of the fact
that he had been commissioned a lieutenant. Fraser was quiet

and resourceful, and so desperately keen to join that he was almost the first on Stirling's list.

Last came an interview with the fifth officer, a Northern Irishman by the name of Paddy Mayne. He was a close friend of the Southern Irishman, McGonigal. He had been an international rugger player of the top rank before the war but had acquired new fame in the last few months by settling an argument with a superior officer by knocking him out. He had been under close detention for some weeks but had been released to hear Stirling's proposals.

Mayne was a huge, broadshouldered man with a quiet, almost docile manner. It seemed impossible that he could pick a quarrel with anyone. Most of the time he was gentle and reserved; only once in a while did his temper flash out, and when this happened it was a shattering explosion. He regarded David with reservation. Stirling was some years younger than Mayne and it was plain that the latter was not convinced that he cared to throw in his lot with an unknown, untried leader. Besides, he too was sceptical. He did not want to take part in any more plans that might not come off. He made no attempt to keep the doubt from his voice as he plied David with the same sort of questions Lewis had asked. Was this just another hare-brained paper scheme. "What in fact," he demanded, " are the prospects of fighting? " David returned his appraising stare. " None," he said briskly. " Except against the enemy." There was a moment's silence, then Mayne grinned. " All right. I'll come."

By the end of the afternoon the recruitment was complete.

CHAPTER TWO

KABRIT

THE NEW CAMP was pretty forlorn. It was set up at Kabrit, a village in the Suez Canal Zone on the edge of the Great Bitter Lake about a hundred miles from Cairo. The flat, bare landscape, the heat and the flies were bad enough. Even more trying was the fact that except for a wooden sign which said '" L " Detachment—S.A.S.' one would not have known it was a camp at all. There were only two small tents for personnel and one large supply tent; inside was nothing but a table and a few chairs.

The major in the adjutant-general's office was following David's vicissitudes closely. He told his friends triumphantly that the Q side could not find much for the S.A.S. at the moment. The rest would come in time, perhaps a long time; no one could say.

However, Captain Stirling had his own plans. He greeted the new recruits, who arrived in half a dozen army trucks, over fifty strong, and told them to make themselves at home, then explained how ' home ' could be improved. First he described the resistance he was encountering from the adjutant-general's office, then added that he had completed a reconnaissance of the neighbourhood, and discovered a splendid New Zealand camp, luxuriously furnished, which at the moment stood empty. The inmates were out on manœuvres and it was guarded by Indian sentries. The New Zealanders, David went on to explain, had no difficulty with equipment. Unlike ' L Detachment ' they had friendly relations with their supply departments, and could easily lay their hands on replacements.

So the first operation of L Detachment would take place that night. A dozen men would be detailed to remove any equipment which might prove useful.

One of the sergeants was put in charge of the sortie. About ten o'clock L Detachment's one and only 3-ton truck rattled down the narrow macadam road until it reached its destination two miles away. The New Zealand camp was at the far end of a large compound which also housed Indian, Australian and British units. At the entrance was a guard post patrolled by Indian sentries.

The sergeant decided that the only hope of success was to brazen things out. The driver started through the entrance, barely slowing down as he leaned out and said, " Major Jones —New Zealand Division." The Indian guard apparently saw nothing unusual in this procedure for he nodded and saluted. A second later the truck was bumping along an uneven path which ran through the centre of the compound. On either side the tents were spread out, hundreds of them, like shadowy feluccas on a black sea. Many of the men had not gone to bed. An occasional sliver of light shone through the tent openings, and shadowy forms and the crunch of footsteps were reminders that life was still stirring.

The sergeant consulted his map and gave orders for the truck to swing to the right. A few more yards and he said, " This is it." The truck stopped before a large tent; behind it were two more large tents and a dozen small ones. Everything was quiet and deserted. Taking four men with him, the sergeant made his way into the first tent. He flashed his torch around the interior. There was a whistle of approval. It was a recreation room. In one corner stood a piano, in another a bar. There was a polished table in the middle, half a dozen wicker chairs, a long table with magazines at the far end, even a grass-matted carpet. " All the comforts of home," said the sergeant. " Guess this would come under the heading of useful—particularly the bar and the piano. We better move the whole lot out."

The group then made a quick recce of the other tents; chairs, tables, hurricane lamps, wash-basins, kitchen utensils;

all were deemed ' handy.' " And of course the tents," said the sergeant. " We need at least fifteen small tents. Come on, boys, we'd better get cracking."

It was not easy working in the dark. " Don't use your torches unless absolutely necessary," instructed the sergeant. " We don't want anyone coming along to tick us off. It might prove fatal." For the next four hours the men sweated, stumbled and cursed in the dark as they unfastened the tent pegs, or strained under the weight of the piano, or carried precariously balanced basins full of glasses and crockery. The truck made four trips back to Kabrit.

In the meantime, passers-by gave them casual glances. No one seemed to find their exertions in the least strange. A man in the next tent, stripped to the waist, poked out his head but, perhaps not wanting to be asked for a helping hand, did not speak and soon disappeared.

As the last load was being secured, one of the men said in a low voice, " Look what's coming." By this time it wasn't difficult to see in the dark. The sergeant was aware of a tall figure approaching, and as it came closer made out the authoritative red band on the sleeve with the letters M.P. There was a moment of tense silence, then the M.P's voice broke the stillness. " Got a light? " he asked in a friendly voice, " What you chaps up to this time of night? " " Plenty," said the sergeant producing a light. " And we don't get paid overtime either."

The sergeant recognised the danger. The M.P. had only stopped for a light and a chat, but if he began asking questions his friendliness might change to suspicion. The load was nearly complete now, so it was essential to keep talking. " Won't half be glad to get back to Civvy Street and get a night's sleep," said the sergeant. " Our C.O. isn't a bad bloke but he's just not human. Thinks you ought to be on the job twenty-four hours out of twenty-four. He's only got one song running through his head. ' Night and day, you are the ones.' " The men were climbing up on the truck, and the sergeant jumped in the front seat. " The trouble with the army," he said as the engine started up, " is they're just not satisfied with an

honest day's work." A second later the 3-tonner was on
its way.

*   *   *

The next day the S.A.S. boasted the smartest camp in the
Canal Zone.[1] When the last tent was pegged down, and the
bar in the recreation tent was functioning to everyone's
satisfaction Captain Stirling gathered the men together. " We
have a fine camp," he said, " and we want to keep it in as
good order as it is now. The standard in this unit is going to
be on the same level as in the Brigade of Guards. Spit and
polish and a high grade performance on parade is absolutely
essential. When we are operating we won't be so formal. And
one more point. When anyone is on leave in Cairo or
Alexandria, please remember that there's to be no bragging
or scrapping in bars or restaurants. Get this quite clear.
In the S.A.S. all toughness is reserved exclusively for the
enemy."

Captain Stirling left out only one thing; the toughness
required in the training course. There were all the normal
activities such as rifle practice, map-reading, and weapon
training which included stripping down anything from Italian
Barettas and German Schmeissers to English tommy-guns.
There was also P.T. with the sergeant major's voice ringing out
relentlessly from the big tent, " One, two, one, two, touch
your toes, I said your TOES! "; and at night mock raids in
which the recruits were required to identify objects and shoot
toward sound. Although the men never knew it, these night
tests were made progressively easier, for David believed a
soldier's success in the dark depended largely on self-
confidence.

This part of the training course, however, was soon regarded
as child's play compared to the marches into the desert that
the unit was required to undertake, or even to the daily
routine of the ground parachute practice. Despite the fact
that nearly all the men had been through rigorous commando

[1] The New Zealanders never traced the culprits. There had been many Arab
thefts in the Zone, and they no doubt attributed the pillaging of the camp to
this source.

courses before arriving in the Middle East, Stirling and Lewis decided that S.A.S. training must be even more exacting. First they believed that physical endurance and quick reflexes were more essential in this new type of warfare than in the massed attacks of the commandos; second they felt they must set severe standards in order to eliminate inferior material.

Certainly the parachute course provided this. David's plan was to have wooden platforms mounted on rollers which would run down a sloping trolley line. When the platforms were at full speed the recruit would jump off, land with both feet together and do a forward roll; when he had mastered this he would turn his attention to backward rolls. However the Q side was unable to produce the wood for the platforms so David decided that the unit would have to make do with lorries moving at thirty miles an hour. Backward rolls from trucks at this speed was a true test of determination. But they proved costly. Scarcely a man survived the ordeal without a fracture of some kind which put him out of training for weeks at a time. Luckily the wood arrived for the platforms before the entire detachment was laid low.

Even the platforms exacted their toll. The training took place at the far side of the grounds which bordered on the naval camp known as *H.M.S. Saunders.* The naval ratings found it amusing to come out and watch. At the end of an hour the soldiers resembled war veterans rather than fresh young reinforcements, with bruised shoulders or wrenched backs. This used to delight the Navy and as the S.A.S. hobbled away from the wooden stands they were mocked by shouts of " Up the paratripes! Germans beware! "

The ground practice was a preliminary to the actual jumps. Since there were no parachute instructors in the Middle East, Stirling contacted Ringway, the parachute school in England, asking for advice and instruction. Despite several urgent signals he received little help, so there was nothing to do but go ahead as best he could.

The R.A.F. agreed to " lay on " a Bombay for several hours a day. The type of parachutes provided were not the same as those used by Air Force pilots. They had no rip cords but opened automatically as the parachutes pulled away from static lines, fastened to a steel rail inside the plane.

David took part in the first two trials. Both were successful. The third time he stayed on the ground to watch. Twelve men were taken up. A red light flashed which was the two-minute signal, and the doors on the side of the plane were opened. Then came the green light. The first man jumped. To the dispatching sergeant's horror he saw the ring break away from the clip which was attached to the rail. The static lines disappeared into space and the soldier fell with closed parachute. The men were jumping in such quick succession number two had already gone before he could stop him. The same thing happened. The sergeant shouted a warning and held the third man back. He signalled the aircraftman to close the doors. Everyone soon knew what had happened and there was a numbed atmosphere of shock.

When the plane landed the occupants climbed out silently. David had witnessed the appalling drama and hurried up to meet the men. "The trials are cancelled for the rest of the day," he said briskly. "We will find out exactly what went wrong, and we ought to be able to resume at five-thirty to-morrow morning."

The mechanics soon discovered the fault. The angle of the pressure from the slipstream had caused the ring fastened to the static lines to twist; all the force came against the clip and the ring slipped out. Other types of clips were available and were substituted. Some months later David learned bitterly that Ringway had already had a similar accident. He felt that if they had bothered to reply in detail to his cables and co-operate with him the S.A.S. tragedy might easily have been avoided.

The next day the men were taken up again. Their faces were strained and their fingers yellow from too many cigarettes. This time David was the first man to jump. The others followed in quick, orderly succession. The tests were successful.

* * *

Meanwhile David was busy planning the November opera-

tion. Until early September he had had the help of Lieutenant
Ian Collins of No. 8 Commando, who had agreed to act as
his P.A. for a few weeks before returning to the Coldstream
Guards in England. Now Ian had departed and the work was
left to David and Jock Lewis. Together the two men spent
long hours studying maps and intelligence reports, made endless
trips to G.H.Q. to arrange air co-operation, worked out complicated calculations about supplies, ammunition and explosives. David's plan was to attack five German forward
aerodromes at the same time. It was believed that these fields
contained the bulk of the enemy's fighter force.

However, there was a snag to David's scheme. How could
so few men carry enough ammunition to blow up the forty
or fifty planes they might find on an airfield? If they took
only high explosive with them they could destroy the airframes
but the engines might be left intact. If they tried to take both
high explosive and incendiary bombs the weight would be so
heavy they could only carry enough to destroy four of five
planes each.

" There's only one answer," said Jock Lewis firmly. " We
must get the sappers to make us a better bomb. It must be
both an explosive and an incendiary. And it must be light.
I'm sure it's possible, and it's absolutely vital if our plan is
to work."

David agreed. The next morning he got into touch with
the engineers at G.H.Q. and persuaded them to send a sapper
to Kabrit. A few days later an explosive expert arrived in the
person of a tall, aggressive major. Lewis and Stirling explained
their dilemma, but the major announced flatly that there was
no way out of the difficulty. The following is the gist of the
conversation that passed between them.

" It's impossible," he said. " The combination you want
doesn't exist. We've tried all sorts of experiments with thermite
and gelignite and ammonal and a half-dozen other substances,
and we can't get the sort of bomb you're after. They either
explode or ignite but they won't do both."

" It *must* be possible," argued Lewis. " Surely it's a question
of striking the right balance. The explosion ought to light the

thermite—or whatever incendiary you use—and both substances work together."

"You fellows want the moon," said the major sarcastically.
"Perhaps it ought to work but the answer is it just doesn't.
Of course I can package you a double barrelled-bomb, half-
explosive and half-incendiary, but it won't operate on the
same fuse. It will take at least ten minutes to set up and it
will weigh five pounds. It won't have any advantage over the
bomb you have now. My advice is to make the best of what
you've got. Carry both explosives and incendiaries and stop
dreaming about the impossible. When we get something better
we'll let you know."

"I suppose that will be in time for the third world war,"
fumed Lewis when the major had left. "I still think it can
be done, David. And I'm going to have a go myself. We were
sent a new plastic high explosive last week and it's good stuff
to experiment with; safe and easy to handle and it doesn't
give you a beastly headache like gelignite—or for that matter
like the major."

"Which major?" asked David caustically. "At the
moment I'm allergic to all majors everywhere."

*   *   *

The next day Lewis set up a chemistry shop near the rifle
range. He began mixing different combinations of plastic and
thermite together. He had a row of four-gallon oil drums into
each of which he poured half a pint of petrol. He tried out
his experiment by exploding his bombs on top of the drum
which was reinforced with a second lid. The object was to get
a combination that would not only blow through the two lids
but ignite the petrol at the bottom.

He tried endless experiments. For hours at a time the sound
of periodic explosions rent the air. The bombs would blow
holes in the top of the drum, but they never managed to set
the petrol alight. At the end of two weeks he was despondent
but he refused to give up. He went down to the work-shop
and sat on a chair thinking. He put his hand on a lump of
plastic. It felt like dough. He played with it idly, staring

through the tent opening at the rifle range. Perhaps the thermite was failing to ignite the petrol because it wasn't being distributed evenly enough through the plastic. There must be an ingredient missing—the sort of ingredient that would give a truer mix. It was like making bread; what knitted the different materials in the dough together? Some form of liquid. Suddenly Lewis became aware of the fact that he was staring at a bottle of oil that someone had left on the rifle range. Liquid. Oil. Lubrication. Perhaps this was the answer.

He hurried out, brought the bottle back, and poured some of the oil into the plastic. Then he added the thermite and kneaded the material together. It was wet and sticky. He rolled it into a lump about the size of a tennis ball, put a fuse into it and laid it on top of the oil drum. He ran back and watched. A moment later there was a loud explosion, then a flash as the petrol blazed into fire. " I've got it, David, I've got it," he cried as he ran toward Stirling's tent.

" Got what ? " asked David, rising from his desk.

" The bomb. The explosive incendiary bomb. The Lewis bomb! " he added joyfully. " Come and see for yourself. It's as light as a feather. Can't weight as much as a pound. Every man can carry twenty or thirty of them. And one's enough to blow up and burn a whole ruddy plane! "

The two men hurried down to the work-shop and Jock showed David how he made up the bomb. Once again he laid it on an oil drum, once again the reinforced top was blown in and the petrol caught fire.

" I think the major would be very hurt if we failed to inform him of our discovery," David said with a grin. " I think it's only polite to invite him back for a demonstration."

This event took place the following week. The sapper watched silently as Lewis blew up and set alight three oil drums in succession.

" A very interesting combination," he said clearing his throat. " Wouldn't have thought it possible. Quite a handy little bomb you've got."

" And since it hasn't got a name," said David, " we propose
to call it the Lewis bomb. Any objections? "

" Not at all," said the major. Then with an effort at
heartiness. " We've got a Lewis gun. Why not a Lewis
bomb? "

" Why not," said David with a laugh. " Now let's all have
a drink."

*   *   *

General Ritchie regarded L Detachment as his particular
toy. He visited Kabrit on several occasions and frequently
sent other high-ranking officers to watch the parachute jumping. One day a group captain appeared from G.H.Q. David
took him out to the airfield and stood by him as he watched
a Bombay circling above, and finally saw the posse of little
white mushrooms appear like magic and float toward the
ground.

David remembers the group captain saying, " Of course the
parachuting is the least of your worries," and the pattern
of the argument that followed. " I'll be quite frank with
you, Captain Stirling. I admire your determination, but I
can't say I would like to put my money on your chances of
success once you're on the ground. How you managed to
convince the high-ups that you could get on to enemy aerodromes and destroy their aircraft is something of a mystery
to me."

David was nettled by the group captain's tone. It was
plain that he belonged to the band of snipers at G.H.Q. who
regarded L Detachment as a waste of time and effort.

" I think you're wrong, sir," said David. " We believe
access to the airfields will be the easiest part of our task. Our
difficulty is making sure that your people get us to the right
spot, and finding our way back to our lines again—not
destroying our targets."

" What makes you think it's going to be so easy to get on
to the airfields? "

" Because the enemy won't be expecting us. And airfields
are always badly guarded."

The group captain laughed, a little derisively David thought.

" You certainly take a sanguine view. I hope the enemy is as careless as you imagine. I'm sure a raiding party wouldn't find it very easy to gain access to *our* airfields undetected."

" I don't agree with you," said David stubbornly. " I am sure it wouldn't be difficult to get on to our own—or perhaps I should say—your airfields. Perhaps you would like to put some money on it. I'll bet you ten pounds that we can get on to Heliopolis[1] any night we like. It will be all right," David added mischievously, " because we'll leave labels on the planes instead of bombs."

" Of course I'll take the bet," snapped the group captain. " If only to prove that you're underestimating the task you've set yourself."

" And what's more I don't mind in the least if you warn Heliopolis," added David. " Tell them we'll be paying them a visit around the end of October."

Nearly forty men took part in the exercise. They were divided into four groups of about ten each. The route they chose to Heliopolis aerodrome, which lay a few miles outside Cairo, was straight across the desert, a distance of 90 miles. Each man had to carry his own supply of food and water; he was given the usual army ration of bully beef and biscuits and had four water bottles containing one pint of water each.

The men marched by night and ' lay up ' by day. The groups moved off independently and soon lost sight of each other. The ground over which they walked was mainly flat and rocky, and stretched out on all sides as far as the eye could see. During the whole three days they never saw another human soul; no life of any kind except for the endless swarms of flies which seemed to come from nowhere.

Although it was October, the sun was still fiercely hot. The group led by Paddy Mayne covered their thirty miles the first night easily, and the following day camouflaged down under Hessian sacks and tried to sleep.

At the end of twenty-four hours every man began to ex-

[1] Heliopolis is the main Cairo aerodrome.

perience the pain of thirst. They had been given precise instructions concerning their precious water supply; no man must share his bottle with another; each man should drink only at prescribed times, morning, noon and night. At the end of forty-eight hours, the craving for water was so acute, and throats so parched and sore it was an effort to talk. At last, as dawn was breaking after the third night, they reached a point only a few miles from the Cairo road. This meant they were nearing the end of the journey. Only one more day of lying up, and a few hours for the raid; then back to civilisation.

One of the sergeants with Mayne's group says that as he lay on the hard desert that last day, covered with sacks, he could see nothing in his mind's eye but a tap of running water. As darkness fell he heard Mayne's order to move forward with infinite relief. About midnight the group approached the outskirts of Heliopolis aerodrome. A barbed wire fence surrounded the two mile perimeter.

No one seemed to be expecting them. Compared to the march it seemed a simple business to get on to the field. They learned later that the commanding officer had sent planes out to do a reconnaissance of the desert. Not spotting any men, he had assumed the raiders must be coming by the main road. For several days he had ordered a double check on all vehicles entering the aerodrome, believing they might attempt to smuggle themselves in.

Mayne's group worked noiselessly in the dark. They cut their way through the wire. They put forty-five labels on the aircraft, then slipped out again, and headed for the army barracks at Abassea. They reached them at first light. With their four-day beards and their Italian haversacks (part of an allotment of captured material) the British soldiers took them for prisoners-of-war. None of the S.A.S. argued until he had drunk his fill of water. Then the men made their identity more than plain and the commanding officer arranged to send them back to Kabrit by truck.

All the groups were successful. They reached Heliopolis at various times during the night, and some planes bore not one, but four labels. The success of L Detachment's operation was

brought to the attention of the group captain, who sent
Stirling a cheque for ten pounds and a handsome letter saying
that "steps would be taken to remedy the defence system of
Heliopolis." David learned that heated reprimands disturbed
the serenity of the Air Branch of G.H.Q. for some weeks to
come.

CHAPTER THREE

ACTION

EXCITEMENT WAS mounting at Kabrit. David had told his men that they would have the privilege of striking a telling blow at the enemy some time in November. That was all the information he gave them, but it was enough. By the end of October the spirit of the camp was rising with each day that passed.

David's officers knew the full details of his plan. General Auchinleck's first major offensive, designed to relieve Tobruk and push Rommel out of Cyrenaica, was scheduled to open at dawn on the 18th of November, 1941. The S.A.S. attack on the enemy's five advanced airfields in the Gazala-Timini area would take place the night before; therefore the men would be parachuted down on the evening of the 16th. David gave his officers explicit instructions. Air Transport would fly the unit to 216 Squadron's forward base on D minus 2. The same night the five groups would be dropped near their targets. Under cover of darkness they would make their way to the rocky escarpments that ran south of the coast road where they could ' hide up ' and observe their targets during the following day. On the second night they would creep on to the airfields and place their bombs. When their work was done they would set off for an established rendezvous about forty-five miles inside the desert, where a patrol of the Long Range Desert Group would be waiting with trucks to carry them across the wilderness to Siwa Oasis. From here planes would fly them back to Kabrit.

The day before the opening move David took the men into

his confidence. As he unfolded his scheme , the murmurs of admiration and approval revealed that the response was even more enthusiastic than he had imagined. " Very few soldiers in the British Army will ever have such a chance as we've got," he said. " With luck we'll polish off Rommel's entire fighter force." This drew whistles and cheers. Then David told them that he would meet them at 216 Squadron's forward field the following afternoon; in the meantime he was going to 8th Army Headquarters, which was only a few miles from the aerodrome, to complete the final arrangements.

During the next twenty-four hours David worked closely with the brigadier on the General Staff who was responsible for the undertaking. His raid would mark the first operational parachute jump in the Middle East. Because of its novelty it was not only arousing great interest but causing considerable concern. Everything depended on organisation and perfect timing. All day long David studied the latest intelligence reports and checked and re-checked map positions with the experts. Then there was the supply problem. Bombs, fuses, grenades and Thompson sub-machine guns were packed in containers and would be parachuted down at the same time as the men jumped. So would food, water and sleeping bags.

On the morning of the 16th the weather reports were disturbing. A wind was rising and it looked as though there might be rain in the next forty-eight hours. By five o'clock that evening the wind had increased to gale force and was blowing at thirty-five miles an hour. The brigadier broke the news to David glumly. The odds against the operation, he said, were lengthening drastically. Parachuting on a moonless night was hazardous enough, but with such a gale the chances of David's party landing intact would be practically nil. They would be scattered all over the desert. Frankly he felt that David should call off the operation. Then seeing the disappointment in the young man's face he added, " That is only my advice. We'll leave the decision to you." David thanked the brigadier, told him he would consult his officers and give him a decision within the next hour.

He then got into his car and drove to 216 Squadron which

was only fifteen minutes away. He felt, himself, that it would be disastrous for morale to cancel the operation. Most of his men had been recruited from Layforce and had sorry memories of the three raids that had been called off at the last moment. He gathered his six officers together and told them what the brigadier had said. " Personally," he said, " I would like to go ahead regardless of the risk. I think it would shake the men's confidence in the unit if we chucked in our hand at this late hour."

Jock Lewis smiled. " I'm with you. Conditions are never perfect. If we sit around waiting for the ideal moment we'll spend the duration on our backsides."

Fraser, and the other three officers nodded their assent. Then David turned to Paddy Mayne. " Don't look at me," said Paddy, " you know what I think. I joined this unit to *fight*, and if I don't get a crack at the enemy soon I may have to indulge in a few practice rounds with some of the chaps at Headquarters."

" That settles it," said David. " The operation's on. I'll signal the brigadier and we'll take off at 7.30 as scheduled."

In the meantime David's men were enjoying a splendid repast in the mess. The pilots had never before been asked to take a human cargo over enemy territory and slough it off into space. They regarded L Detachment as a suicide squadron. Of course they did not refer to the night's work but the way they hovered around the tables, insisting on waiting on the men themselves, was an indication of their feelings.

At 7.15 the engines of the five Bombays were revving up. The men divided into their various groups. Stirling, Mayne, Lewis, McGonigal, and Bonnington were each in command of a plane. The remaining two officers, Fraser and Thomas, served as seconds-in-command. Soon the men had fastened on their parachute harnesses and taken their seats. On the dot of 7.30 the first machine was slipping down the runway. The rest followed in quick succession.

Once in the air David's hopes began to rise again. Supplies were stacked up at one end of the plane, the men were crowded together on the floor, and it was cold and uncomfortable.

Nevertheless, he felt a sense of relief. At least the plan that had been conceived so long ago was being brought to fruition. And it might succeed in its purpose. After all, desert weather was changeable. Winds could drop as quickly as they rose. There might be a sudden lull ; and if not, perhaps the jump would not prove as hazardous as people thought. The unit certainly had had a good deal of practice in breaking the impact of falls.

The pilot had instructions to fly out to sea and approach his target from the north for nearly an hour and a half. Time seemed to drag interminably. No one was talking and some of the men sat with their eyes half-closed as though sleep might come to blot out the unpleasant business of waiting. An hour passed, then two hours, and still no signal. The flight sergeant came back and murmured to David that they were ' having difficulty in locating the position ' which would give them a correct bearing. Bomber Command had agreed to drop powerful flares over the coastline to enable the five Bombays to chart their courses. However, the gale was blowing so hard that it had raised a heavy sandstorm and all landmarks were blotted out.

The plane was flying quite low now for David could hear the crackle of anti-aircraft guns. The pilot banked sharply in evasive action, then flew straight, then banked again. It seemed that they were flying in an endless circle. Another twenty minutes passed and the flight sergeant came out again. " According to our reckoning we'll be over the dropping zone in six minutes."

He signalled the aircraftman to open the doors of the plane. The rush of air made everyone sit up, and the men began to test their harnesses. No one spoke. Each man knew the order of his jump and exactly what he had to do. Then the red light came on. Two minutes to go. There was complete silence as the seconds passed. At last the green light flashed, and in quick succession the men disappeared into the blackness.

David was the first to jump and once he felt the jerk of his parachute opening, he was amazed at the smoothness of the descent. He could feel no pressure against his body and he wondered if there really was a high wind blowing or whether by some miracle it had stopped. After a minute he began to prepare for the landing. It was so black there was no prospect of seeing the ground. He would not know the earth was near until he hit it. But if the pilot had dropped them from an altitude of five hundred feet, as he had said he would, it should come at once. He braced his body expectantly, but he continued to drift through space. Now his whole being was keyed up. Each second he expected to feel the impact of the ground, but it never came. It was almost as though the laws of gravity had stopped working and he was floating away from the earth through infinity.

Then a smashing blow obliterated his senses. He must have been unconscious for two or three minutes. He awoke to find himself being dragged very fast over rough stony ground. He knocked the release harness and rolled over on his back, free. For a moment he lay in a daze. He felt blood trickling down his face but he moved his arms and legs and was relieved to find that no bones were broken. When he stood up he had to brace himself against a raging wind. The air was thick with dust and sand which almost choked him. He could see nothing through the black, noisy night. He shouted but the gale carried his voice away. He flashed his torch. Still he saw nothing. He began to walk waving the torch. After a few minutes a light blinked in the distance; then off to the right was another and yet another. The group was starting to converge.

It took nearly an hour to assemble the men. One was missing and the remainder presented a sorry sight. There was a broken arm, a sprained wrist, and two badly wrenched ankles. All of them had gashes and cuts. Apart from this, only two out of ten supply parachutes had been found. These contained six blankets, twelve water bottles, one day's food for all, and half a dozen tins of Lewis bombs—but no fuses. The fuses had been packed in separate containers. Live and learn, thought David to himself. It's the last time we ever send down parachutes with essential parts dispersed.

For the next two hours the men searched down the line of

wind for the missing soldier and the missing supplies. They did not even have any weapons except for the revolvers they carried on them. Finally David decided to give it up. The soldier had probably been knocked unconscious on landing. " By this time he must have been blown miles into the desert."

The same thing applied to the supplies; there was no use searching any longer. With no fuses the unit was non-operational. David decided to take one man with him, however, and proceed to the coast road. He could not do much damage to the enemy but he might gain useful knowledge from a reconnaissance. The rest of the unit would have to set out for the rendezvous. Since they were short of food and water, and in poor condition, the sooner they started the better. " If we've been dropped in the right place you should be only thirty miles away," he said. He picked Sergeant Tait to accompany himself and put Sergeant Yates in charge of the returning party. Although three of the men were limping badly they were confident they could reach their destination. The meagre rations were divided and the two groups set off.

The gale had begun to die down, but it was still cold. The coast should have been only ten miles away. As first light broke David and Tait saw that they were in a huge expanse of featureless desert. Although they reckoned that they had walked well over thirteen miles there was no sign of the escarpment. The escarpment was a high ridge that ran for many miles along this section of the coast. Below it was a rough plain leading to the Mediterranean. " This means that we were dropped well outside the zone," said David. " There's nothing to do but keep going. We have to hit the coast sometime."

It was not until ten o'clock that the sky-line began to change. Through field-glasses David could see a rough, uneven line. " Looks as though we're nearly there. About four miles, I should think. We'd better stop and hide up until it gets dark."

They found a dip in the hard sand and settled down. The sky was a sullen grey. It was plain there was going to be no sun to warm them. They only had two water bottles, so they drank sparingly, and munched a few biscuits and pieces of

chocolate. Tait had two sacks which they used as mattresses
and they tried to keep warm under one blanket. They slept
fitfully until three o'clock when they noticed dark clouds
beginning to gather.

David was restless and wanted to move on. By half-past
four they reached the escarpment. They approached it
cautiously, taking cover behind a cluster of rocks that stood
near the edge. In the distance lay the Mediterranean, and
below them ran the coast road. Traffic was moving along it.
Near the road stood a few scattered huts and on the far side a
group of tents. It was windswept and forlorn. David studied
the map but he could not make out his position. Finally he
said, " I think we must be east of Gazala. Not far from
Tobruk."

The sky was growing darker with storm clouds, and now
that the afternoon was fading, visibility was poor. At half-past
five the rain began. Rain is a rare occurrence in the desert
and when it comes it is something to remember. The clouds
opened and water poured down in the most torrential outburst
David had ever seen. Soon the wadis were raging rivers. The
two men were sodden. David's store of cigarettes, packed
away in a haversack, were ruined. " At least," said Tait
cheerfully, " we don't have to worry about quenching our
thirst."

The storm gave cover from aircraft so the two men started
along the coast. The 8th Army offensive would open in a few
hours' time and they wondered anxiously how it would fare.
It was bitterly cold and time and again they found themselves
up to their knees in water. It was impossible to carry out a
reconnaissance for the elements had once again blotted out the
landscape. There was nothing to do but head for the rendezvous.
This lay along an old desert track, known as the Trig el Abd,
which, at this point, ran parallel to the coast road about forty
miles inland. Near the track was a small hill; the Long Range
Desert Patrol had arranged to shine a hurricane lamp from
the top of it which could be seen a long way. David figured
that they had a walk of fifty miles ahead of them.

All night long the rain came down, and all night they

tramped toward their destination. David had long ago abandoned any hope of the unit's success. His chief concern now was for its survival. How many of them would find their way to the rendezvous? Having been dropped miles from the correct position how would they get a bearing to lead them to a pin-point on a barren expanse of desert? If Yates continued to assume that he had been dropped in the right place, he would turn left instead of right when he hit the Trig el Abd and walk into wilderness.

At seven in the morning the rain stopped. The two men were so tired they lay down in their wet clothes and slept for four hours. Then they started off again. They were moving very slowly now. Tait's ankle was beginning to swell; he must have hurt it on landing. At five o'clock in the afternoon David surveyed the desolate unchanging scene through field-glasses. Suddenly he saw something move on the horizon. It was a group of men. " Must be of our own," he said eagerly. " Perhaps it's Yates." There was no possibility of catching them up, for they were nearly four miles away. But he watched them as long as he could and with relief saw them turn to the right. " They're going in the right direction," he said. " They ought to make the rendezvous to-night."

When darkness came the sky presented an innocent and wonderful array of stars, as if to make up for the ruthless behaviour of the past two nights. At midnight David's attention was caught by a star, low on the horizon. It was so clear and steady that for a moment he thought it might be the light of the Long Range Desert Patrol. He put the idea out of his mind, for fear of disappointment, but as the miles passed and the star continued to return a bright, unfaltering gaze he began to hope. At last came the joy of recognising the shadowy outline of a hill.

At two o'clock in the morning they reached the rendezvous. Behind the hill, in a small ravine, were trucks covered with camouflage nets. Fires were burning and tea brewing up. The smiling face of the Long Range patrol leader, Jake Eason-Smith, looked up in the darkness. Then he saw Fraser and Lewis.

. These two officers had arrived together earlier in the night, with eight of their ten men. Their experiences were similar to David's. Their unit had been scattered and they had spent hours searching for their supplies. They found their primers and fuses but not their bombs, so they, too, were non-operational. They had collected enough of their rations to walk to the coast and get their bearing. One of the men had a broken leg and could not be moved, and a second must have been knocked out and carried away for he was never found.

David drank tea and whisky and refused to go to sleep. He was convinced that the men he had seen through his glasses must have been Sergeant Yates and his own group. " They can't be far away. They were heading in the right direction at five o'clock yesterday evening."

At dawn Eason-Smith sent out a truck to search for them, but it returned empty after scouring the desert for hours. It was not until the end of the war that David learned that Sergeant Yates had turned right at the track; that the others had insisted he was wrong and finally persuaded him to double back and turn left. They had walked all night. Next day they saw what must have been Eason-Smith's vehicle but had taken cover presuming it to belong to the enemy. After three days of wandering about the desert they had been spotted by an enemy patrol and picked up.

The only gratifying event that daylight brought was the arrival of Paddy Mayne and nine men. Mayne had reached a point a mile away from the rendezvous the night before; but he had decided to wait until daybreak to make sure. He, too, had been non-operational and had walked to the coast for his bearings. Two of his men had been so badly injured that he had had to leave them behind.

Of Lieutenant Bonnington's and Lieutenant McGonigal's two groups there was no sign. All that day and the next night David waited at the rendezvous hoping more men would come in. McGonigal's party was never seen again. Every member of it must have been killed.

A few days later he learned what had happened to Bonnington. The pilot who transported the group had been unable to find his bearings for the dropping zone. Finally, in desperation, he had wirelessed to the ground saying he was lost and asking for a beam to land on. The Germans had picked up his signal. In perfect English they had beamed him in to their own landing field. The occupants were all taken prisoner.

After thirty-six hours David gave up any further hope of salvaging more of his unit. Out of the fifty-five men and seven officers who had taken part in the venture only eighteen men and four officers were left. His operation was not merely a failure; it was a debacle.

*   *   *

David had a hard, resilient spirit which was not easily depressed. His experience, far from raising doubts in his mind, had made him more certain than ever that his strategic concept was right. The very fact that he had wandered about the enemy's desert flank for the last few days, unhindered and unnoticed, had strengthened his conviction that his basic idea was sound. Of course, he reproached himself for mistakes. He never again would allow essential parts to be packed separately from one another; and he was coming to the conclusion that parachuting was not the best way to reach targets in the desert. If the Long Range Desert Patrol could lead his men home, why could it not take them to a rendezvous in the first place ?

David's immediate problem was how to strike again. Would Middle East Headquarters let him have another try? Judging by the hostility in the adjutant-general's office, he thought not. Although Auchinleck and Ritchie were staunch friends they would be fully occupied with their offensive. He must avoid returning to the base at all costs. Yet this raised another difficulty. He could not recruit new strength to his unit without the adjutant-general's consent. He came to two conclusions. First, he must plan and execute his next raids with the remaining eighteen men and four officers; second he must try and attach himself for supply purposes to one of the

fighting brigades at the front. He would go to 8th Army
Headquarters and see what sort of a *sub rosa* arrangement he
could fix up.

The L.R.D.G. patrol drove the unit across the desert to
Siwa Oasis, a distance of two hundred and fifty miles. David
told his three officers to try and lay on air transport to fly the
men back to Kabrit, to pack up all useful supplies and weapons
and to return to Siwa within the week. By that time he hoped
to have L Detachment's forward base established.

*   *   *

David arrived at 8th Army Headquarters to find that General
Auchinleck's offensive, which was now a week old, was
not going so well. The wireless reports he had heard at Siwa
had stated that British troops were making rapid and substantial gains. Now, it seemed, they had suffered a sudden
reverse. Rommel had pulled one of his surprise tricks out of
the bag. He had regrouped his army with lightning speed and
sent it round the allied flank. One of his columns had penetrated twenty miles into Egypt at Maddalena. The 8th Army
commander, General Cunningham, was deeply depressed. He
believed that his troops were in danger of being cut off.
Unless he ordered an immediate withdrawal he might lose
the bulk of his own precious armour.

General Auchinleck, on the other hand, was convinced that
Rommel's thrust was only a desperate gamble. He was sure
that the enemy had no reserves with which to exploit the
break-through. Whatever happened, the 8th Army must not
retreat. On 24th November Auchinleck flew from Cairo to
the desert headquarters and ordered the bewildered and shaken
Cunningham to stop talking in defensive terms and to continue
his attack. The following day Auchinleck instructed his Chief
of Staff, General Ritchie, to take over the command of the
8th Army.

David witnessed a slice of this high drama. The morning
after his arrival he was approached by a staff officer and told
that Cunningham would like to see him. The general had
heard that Stirling had observed the coast road between Gazala

and Tobruk and thought he might be able to learn something about enemy dispositions. David was ushered into a small tent and found Cunningham sitting at his desk. He was struck by the strain and fatigue in the general's face.

" I understand that you were on the escarpment overlooking the Gazala-Tobruk road a few days ago. Can you give me any idea what reinforcements were coming up? I'm particularly interested in the enemy's tank strength."

David could tell him very little. " I watched the road for about half an hour," he said. " I saw no armour. Only supply trucks."

The interview lasted less than five minutes. That afternoon David was approached by another staff officer who told him that the 8th Army Commander would like to see him. " But I've already seen him," said David.

" No, you haven't," replied the young man cheerfully. " We've got a new one. Ritchie."

Once again David was ushered into the tent. This time he found a confident, smiling general. " I hear you were scuppered by the weather," said Ritchie genially. " Rotten luck. Heavy losses? "

" Not too bad," said David warily. Ritchie then asked him the same questions as Cunningham, and after an equally brief interview David escaped, relieved that the new commander was too pre-occupied with the battle on his hands to issue any precise instructions about L Detachment.

*   *   *

It took David several days to organise his next move. It was not until Brigadier Marriott arrived at Headquarters, fresh from the fighting front, that David saw the way ahead. Marriott was in command of the 22nd Guards Brigade. He was a charming, warm-hearted man whom David had known in Cairo. He was amused and impressed by his young friend's activities and listened sympathetically to his problems. David made a clean breast of his difficulties. " I must attach myself to a fighting unit which will be willing to supply me and give me a fairly free hand. Something a little off the beaten track if possible, because if I'm based too close to Headquarters I may get tied up in red tape."

Marriott thought for a minute. " I think I know just the man for you. Brigadier Denys Reid. I hear he's just captured Jalo with a Flying Squadron. And I'm told he plans to operate from there for the next few weeks. He's a fine soldier. Jolly and enterprising, and I'm sure you'd get a good welcome. And Jalo is conveniently remote," added Marriott with a twinkle.

Jalo sounded like the most delectable spot on earth. It was an oasis, and at the moment was many miles behind the enemy's fluctuating lines. Most of the fighting in the desert took place on a narrow strip along the coast. Jalo was a hundred and fifty miles inland, and therefore, except for short, sharp onslaughts, when one side or the other decided to capture it, was out of the main stream of the battle. It was close enough to the enemy to provide a good jumping-off place for David's raids, and far enough away from 8th Army Head-quarters to offer him independence.

" It sounds perfect," he said. " I'll push off to Jalo in the morning."

Marriott smiled. " Reid's a great friend of mine. Tell him I hope he'll do everything he can for you."

CHAPTER FOUR

ON THE RUN

JALO WAS not a beauty spot. Although it was described as a
' Saharan oasis ' the water was charged with salt and almost
undrinkable. Hundreds of years earlier it had been a centre
of the Majabra, an Arab tribe which wandered through the
desert as merchant caravaneers; now it was a poor, sandswept
spot which could boast only a few mud villages, a fort, some
Italian buildings and a mass of scraggly palm trees.

Nevertheless it was ideal for David's purposes. It offered a
perfect base from which to strike at the enemy's airfields dotted
along the Mediterranean. And Brigadier Reid was as welcom-
ing as Marriott had predicted. A massive, ruddy-cheeked man
with an iron handshake, he was an adventurous and skilful
soldier. He had attacked Jalo from Jaghbub, along a route of
three hundred miles. He had been able to carry enough petrol
with him for only a one-way journey, so if his offensive had
failed, there would have been no means of withdrawing. But
this was the sort of gamble that increased his zest, and on the
afternoon of 25th November, after a series of adroit manœuvres,
he entered Jalo in triumph. It was not surprising that a man
of Reid's stamp should find David a sympathetic character.
He at once put L Detachment on his ration strength, and
promised whatever help he could give and whatever ammunition he could spare.

But Jalo was a key point for still another reason. A day or
two after David's arrival Major Don Steele, the commander
of A squadron of the Long Rang Desert Group, arrived from
Siwa to set up a forward base. He had a force of thirty men

and fifteen or sixteen trucks carrying guns, maps, wireless sets and supplies of every kind. This was the organisation upon which David was basing his hopes. He told Steele that he intended to carry out a series of raids on enemy airfields and asked if he would provide the ferry service.

Steele listened with interest. The Long Range Desert Group was a quixotic English invention which had come into being only sixteen months previously, and whose primary job was reconnaissance and intelligence. This was accomplished by sending patrols in thirty-hundredweight lorries hundreds of miles behind the enemy lines to ' lay up ' near the coastal road and keep a careful road check. Most of the 8th Army's information about the enemy's supply lines and movements came from the wireless trucks of these little groups.

The idea for such an organisation had come from a distinguished scholar. After the first world war R. A. Bagnold, a Fellow of the Royal Society, began working on a book entitled *The Physics of Blown Sand and Desert Dunes*. Since little had been written on the subject he decided that his research must be done on the spot. At that time large parts of the Libyan desert were unmapped and unknown. Bagnold began to organise expeditions with week-end trips from Cairo to Siwa or the Sinai. During the thirties these trips gradually expanded into large scale explorations, involving journeys of five or six thousand miles, and covering most of the desert from the northern Sudan to the Mediterranean. They were financed privately and the enthusiastic amateurs who took part in them paid about £20 a head for each thousand miles. Meanwhile Bagnold took notes for his book and in between times managed to perfect the sun compass and to invent rope-ladders and steel channels for ' unsticking ' cars bogged in soft sand.

When war broke out the erudite Bagnold put up a scheme for a unit that would operate in the great wastes behind the enemy lines. It was perfectly possible for them to live for weeks in the desert without returning to base, and to send back reliable reports on enemy equipment and movements. The idea was accepted by General Wavell in the summer of 1940 and the Long Range Desert Group came into being.

Bagnold collected as many pre-war desert trippers as he could; then he got permission to recruit thirty volunteers from the New Zealand forces. The qualifications for the job were brains and stamina. The Libyan desert was roughly the same size as India, about twelve hundred miles by one thousand. In places it was hard and flat and stretched out with a terrifying sameness for hundreds of miles ; in other places there were shelves or escarpments, that fell away like huge steps, or rocky ground that gave way to sudden depressions, or treacherous soft sand.

All members of the Long Range Desert Group were specialists. They had to learn how to handle their thirty-hundredweight trucks in all types of going, carrying food, petrol, and ammunition for weeks at a time, across desert tracts which hitherto had been regarded as impassable. They had to know how to keep their machines in repair, their guns from jamming with sand, their wireless sets in perfect order; they had to know the technique of taking vehicles down treacherous ravines or through soft sand, and how to measure distances with theodolites. Above all they had to know how to navigate perfectly. In miles of featureless desert their knowledge had to be as wide as that required of a sailor at sea.

Bagnold had to create his unit from scratch. He was aided by an able second-in-command, Colonel Prendergast, who later succeeded him ; and he had the firm support of General Wavell. Middle Eastern Headquarters co-operated willingly, although at times they regarded his requests as strange. " We asked, for example, for sandals while everyone else wore boots "; wrote Kennedy Shaw, " for an Egyptian shop-keeper's whole stock of trouser-clips, because there was nothing else to be had for holding maps to map-boards; for Nautical Almanacks, yet we were not sailors; for ten-ton Diesel lorries, but we were not R.A.S.C.; for a 4.5 howitzer, usually given only to gunners; for Arab head-dresses; for an apparently scandalous quantity of tyres (most Army vehicles ran on roads or passable tracks); for two aircraft; for a paraffin-worked refrigerator, to preserve the M.O's vaccines in the heat of Kufra.

" Once we had occasion to seek some new theodolites to replace losses in action. The officer who controlled them was indignant. What on earth did we want theodolites for? Were we sappers? He himself had made a march of twenty miles in the Sinai Desert and using a prismatic compass had been only four hundred yards out at the end of his ' plot.' When we said that he would still have been five miles out at the end of four hundred he began to see the point."[1]

This, then, was the Long Range Desert Group. In the sixteen months of their existence they had built up an enviable reputation, not only for brilliance and efficiency, but for adventure. It was only natural that Don Steele should find David's plans exciting and feasible. " Of course we'll help," he said. " We'll take you wherever you want to go—and bring you back again."

*   *   *

David's headquarters were in a dilapidated storehouse. At night, with a hurricane lamp on a rickety table, he worked over his plans. The war map was changing every day. Auchinleck's personal intervention at the crucial stage of the 8th Army offensive had turned the scales and Rommel was now in full retreat to Gazala.

Reid told David that he had orders to proceed to the Antelat-Agedabia area and join up with Brigadier Marriott. He was held up by lack of petrol and supplies, and it did not look as though he could reach the area until the 22nd of December, which was in three weeks' time. If David's men could knock out the aircraft on the Agedabia field on the night of the 21st, before the final lap of the journey, it would be infinitely helpful. His unit feared lack of cover during the last miles of their advance. This move, he explained, would be part of a general assault on Benghazi and an attempt to trap Rommel's forces when they started to retreat southwards.

David was delighted to support Reid; at last someone accepted the fact that his force was capable of useful work. He would send one party of raiders to attack Agedabia field

[1] *Long Range Desert Group:* W. B. Kennedy Shaw.

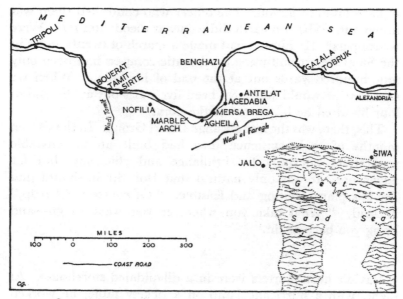

*Operations from Jalo oasis against the enemy coastline in
December and January 1941-42*

on the night of the 21st; other groups would carry out preliminary operations on the night of the 14th. That would be
phase one. Phase two would consist of more visits to the
advance airfields between the 25th and the 28th of December
when the attack on Benghazi was approaching its climax.

During the next few days the three men consulted each other
freely. By nature they had much in common. They were all
adventurers in so far as they would not hesitate to use unconventional methods to achieve results. But whereas ' E ' Force
and the Long Range Desert Group were established institutions,
L Detachment knew itself to be very much on trial.

*   *   *

The interlude was a period of strain for David and his three
officers. Not only were they trying to put into practice a new
method of night raiding, but they lived in fear lest someone

in Middle East Headquarters, or even 8th Army Headquarters, might discover their whereabouts and suddenly order them back to Kabrit. They asked both Reid and Steele to avoid mentioning them in any signals, and requested that not even junior officers be told of their plans. Security against the enemy was essential, but security against the British General Staff was vital.

Thus, for the next week, they lived the life of ' men on the run.' With their beards and explosives they looked the part; only their gentle manners disturbed the picture. David put forward his frightening proposals in such a soft voice it was hard to hear him. Jock Lewis had a strictly intellectual approach and tried to make a logical sequence out of David's enthusiasm. Bill Fraser listened in complete silence, and Paddy yawned and went to bed.

David's plans were forthright. He and Paddy and ten other ranks would leave with a Long Range patrol in two days' time for Sirte aerodrome which lay on the coast about three hundred and fifty miles away. It was said to be one of the largest and most important of the enemy's fields. Jock Lewis with another group would start out two days later for Agheila field, also on the coast, but only one hundred and sixty miles distant. Both these raids would take place on the night of the 14-15th. Bill Fraser would have to wait in Jalo for ten days, when he would start for Agedabia to carry out the promise given to Reid to deliver a raid on the 21st.

*   *   *

Gus Holliman, a short stocky fair-haired Englishman, who had once been in the Tank Corps and was now in charge of the Rhodesian Patrol of the Long Range Desert Group, was detailed to escort David and Paddy to their target. They moved off shortly after dawn on the 8th of December in seven thirty hundred-weight trucks. There were just over thirty men in all, twelve in David's party and twenty in Holliman's. The trucks were painted rose and green which seemed a startling colour scheme in Jalo, but apparently blended in nicely with the desert landscape. The vehicles were piled high with petrol, guns, spare tyres, water, blankets, camouflage nets, food, ammunition and other necessities.

Mike Sadler, the Rhodesian navigator, rode in the leading truck with Gus Holliman. David and Paddy followed, and the men had to find places wherever they could, straddling supplies on top of the vehicles. Although it was bitterly cold at night, the sun was still strong in the middle of the day, and at eleven in the morning the inevitable striptease act began with the men peeling off sweaters and jackets.

The trucks stopped at high noon to enable the navigator to take his midday check on a sextant. This served as the break for lunch which boasted far more appetising rations than the regular army enjoyed. The Long Range Patrol was noted for its good food, particularly its Irish stews and its New Zealand tinned steaks.

As soon as it got dark the trucks pulled up for the night. Mike Sadler again checked his position, this time by the stars. Then the evening work began. The mechanics serviced the vehicles, while the men cleaned their weapons and mended tyres—there were always punctures. The wireless operator tuned in to L.R.D.G. Headquarters to get the daily signal which had to be decoded. On this particular evening there was no important intelligence, and the war news was static. Rommel was at Gazala and the 8th Army was pausing before its next push.

David and Paddy sat over the camp fire studying their maps. Although fires and lights were strictly forbidden in the forward area, there was no need for caution far out in the desert. If enemy aircraft spotted them they would think they were nomad Arabs; indeed the patrols often saw Arab fires in the distance.

Yet in the daytime David was surprised at how little came across their line of vision. The brooding solitude was like being on the high seas. It seemed strange to think that a life and death struggle was going on along the coast while here in the great desert waste was an atmosphere of infinite peace. For the first three days there was not a sign of life, not even a faraway caravan, only an endless vista of sand and rock and gully, with an occasional escarpment streaking across the horizon. They had no mishaps, except for the inevitable tyre trouble, until the third day when the steering in one of the trucks broke. This took several hours to mend. Nevertheless, the patrol had maintained such a good average that when it halted that night Mike Sadler told the men that they were seventy miles south of Sirte.

The next day their luck changed. The ground suddenly became rocky and broken and they covered only twenty miles in three hours. At twelve o'clock they were looking for cover, so that they could check their position and have lunch, when an Italian reconnaissance plane flew into sight. It came toward them, and Holliman recognised it as a Gibli. All L.R.D.G. trucks were equipped with Lewis guns on air mountings and as soon as the plane was close enough Holliman ordered his black-bearded gunner, Kruger, to open fire. The other trucks followed suit and a cascade of bullets rent the air. They did not damage the plane and it dropped two bombs— but both fell far wide of the mark. Then it flew away.

" We must head for cover as quickly as possible," said Holliman. " More planes will be co ning back. That's what usually happens once they've spotted us. I think we ought to make for that large patch of scrub two miles back. There doesn't seem to be much in front of us."

The trucks turned and went rattling and bumping across the desert as fast as possible. The scrub offered indifferent cover. The bushes were barely two feet high. The men threw camouflage nets over the vehicles then moved a safe distance away from them.

While they lay there, waiting for the enemy's next move, Holliman explained the procedure to David. The Gibli was the enemy's scouting aircraft. It was slow and manœuvrable and could turn on a sixpence. " You should see them following the tracks," he said. " They look like little Cairn terriers on the scent of a rabbit." The Gibli had only one machine-gun, could carry no more than two bombs, and was without armour. Therefore the patrols usually engaged it in the hope of putting it out of action before it wirelessed back to base. But with ordinary fighter or bomber planes it was essential to take cover, or if that was impossible, to fling oneself on the ground and remain motionless. Firing back was rarely effective and only told the pilots exactly where their quarry lay.

They heard the hum of engines and saw three bombers approaching. The planes were flying low and scouring the ground. They flew over the scrubs, which stretched out for nearly half a mile, and Holliman thought that perhaps the group had not been detected. Then the machines turned and one by one came down with a whine that changed into a roar. The pilots did not know exactly where their targets were so they combed the scrub, bombing and strafing for fifteen minutes. To the men on the ground, bullets seemed to splatter all around; and as they watched the bombs spilling out of the racks and hurtling towards them it seemed impossible that they would fail to take a heavy toll. Yet when the planes flew away the soldiers found that no one was hurt, and not a single truck damaged. This experience was frequently repeated, and it never failed to strike the groundsmen as something of a miracle.

Holliman suggested they stay where they were and eat their lunch. It was not until two o'clock that they started moving again. The going improved and at half-past four Sadler told them that they were forty miles from Sirte. It was not the usual practice of the L.R.D.G. to drive closer than this to the enemy coastline in the daylight. However, dusk was falling, it would be dark in an hour, and Holliman decided to continue. He would take the raiders to a ridge which lay about three miles from the coast road and three miles from the airfield. From here they could observe their target the following day.

Suddenly there was a shout. Another Gibli was in sight. This time it did not attack them, and flew high to avoid being fired at. It circled once or twice and disappeared into the gloaming. "It's too late for them to send aircraft after us," said Holliman. "But they'll report our presence all right."

"I wonder what they'll think we're up to," said David.

"Probably the vanguard of the 8th Army," chipped in Sadler.

" If they're Eyeties," said Holliman, " they'll be in an awful flap."

The patrol continued on its way. Soon it was totally dark. They were twenty miles from their destination and they had to do the rest of the trip without lights. Two hours later, at nine o'clock, Sadler announced that they were four miles from the coast road and a mile from their destination. " Ten minutes and we'll be there."

Just then there was a signal from the truck in the rear. It was stuck in soft sand. The other trucks pulled up and turned off their engines. As they did so they were amazed to hear the sound of voices in the distance; then the sound of a motor revving up, excited shouts, the noise of an engine gathering speed, and more shouts.

" The coast road," said Sadler. " We must be almost on it. It obviously curves inland from the sea here. Damn these maps. Why can't they ever get it right."

" Sounds as though they're patrolling the road," said Holliman. " They've had the Gibli report and now they've heard us and they don't know what to make of it."

David had to act in a hurry. " We can't afford to bog up this operation," he said to Paddy and Gus. " Everything depends on it. But since we've got a reception committee lined up, I don't think it's wise to keep all our eggs in one basket. We must change our plans a little and divide up. I'll take one of the sergeants and have a go here. You take the rest of the men and head for Tamit field where you still have the advantage of surprise. If one of us fails the other may be lucky."

Tamit was a coastal town, thirty miles west of Sirte, and was known to have a new airfield. The men nodded in agreement and David outlined the rest of his plan. He and the sergeant would walk two miles beyond the aerodrome and try to find a ridge on the other side where they could get a good view of the field in the morning. They would raid at eleven o'clock at night, at the same moment that Paddy's party was attacking Tamit. Three of Holliman's trucks would pick up David, and three more would pick up Paddy when the raids were over.

The two parties would travel independently to an agreed meeting place eighty miles out in the desert.

David made a date with the L.R.D.G. to meet him as soon as his raid was over, at quarter to one in the morning. " What recognition sign shall I give, Gus ? " " Leave a bush in the middle of the coast road on the Tamit side of the airfield, about two miles away," said Holliman. " We'll be there on the dot."

David chose Sergeant Brough to accompany him. The truck that was stuck in the sand was set free with the aid of sand mats, and the party was ready to start. David asked Holliman to make as much noise as possible moving off, in order to fool the enemy into thinking everyone had left. He did not want footsteps to give his presence away, so Brough and he jumped on the running board of one of the vehicles and rode fifty yards until it reached hard ground.

They felt very much alone as the sound of the trucks died away. According to their calculations the field was three miles distant, and they would have to walk another two miles to reach the high ground on the far side of it. They kept their eyes strained for wire and sentry posts, but found themselves on the edge of the field without warning. One minute they were in the desert, the next a shadowy plane loomed up in front of them.

" Let's do a cautious recce," said David. " Just to get the feel of it."

" Look over there, sir," said Brough. " There's masses of them."

They walked toward a long row of planes. It looked as though the job were going to be too easy. David was tempted to put on his bombs then and there, but decided it would not be fair to the others. Tamit was close enough for any fires to be seen that broke out at Sirte, and a preliminary attack might lose Paddy the surprise he was counting on for the following night.

The two men continued their way round the edge of the field. Suddenly David stumbled over something. A terrified shriek pierced the air. Two men wrapped in blankets were sleeping in a shallow hollow. Their cry was taken up, and one of the guards fired a rifle in the dark. David and Brough hurried off the field and made for the open desert. By this time more guns were going off and the whole airfield was resounding to excited shouts; they even heard an Italian voice calling on the saints for protection. Then an anti-aircraft gun opened up towards the sea. David realised that the enemy had jumped to the conclusion that commandos were landing on the beach in support of an attack from the landward side.[1]

The two men headed for the ridge. They could hear firing going on for at least half an hour. " It is comforting to think that the enemy seems even windier than we are," David laughed.

After an hour they reached the long shallow rise they had pinpointed on their maps. The scrub offered good cover, and they were soon asleep. They awoke early to find that they had a fine view of the sand dunes which stretched along the coast two miles away. On their right, some five miles distant, they could see Sirte village with its white-washed houses shining in the sun, and in the foreground lay the aerodrome.

Everything seemed peaceful again, and during the morning planes were frequently taking off and landing as if nothing had happened. They calculated that there were about thirty aircraft, mostly Italian Caprioni bombers. They made a mental map of all the main features, then with nothing to do but wait, settled down for another sleep. About midday David awoke to hear the sound of a woman talking. He lay still wondering what was happening and where he was. Then he heard laughter and Arabic words. He peered out of the bushes and recalled the business on hand. Not more than ten yards away two Arab women were tending a patch of land. Considering the miles of waste land in the desert, he kicked himself that he should have been so idiotic as to pick a hiding place next to what seemed the only cultivated spot in Libya. He did not know enough about Arabs to risk being seen. Brough awoke and he cautioned him to keep quiet. For three

[1] That night Middle East Headquarters in Cairo intercepted a puzzling enemy message; it was a call for help from the Mayor of Sirte declaring that the town was being invested.

hours the two men lay there, not moving a muscle for fear of being discovered. The ground grew harder each hour. At last the women picked up their things, put their baskets on their heads, and glided away.

They began observing the airfield again. After an hour Brough noticed that the aircraft were taking off in twos and threes and none seemed to be returning. The two men watched with growing dismay. There was no doubt about it, the landing ground was being evacuated. By dusk it was empty. David bitterly regretted his recce of the night before. He should never have risked giving away his presence when the enemy was already on the alert. Now there was nothing to do but kill time until the rendezvous with Gus Holliman.

The coast road was only two miles away. They arrived on it at half-past ten. There was no traffic. At eleven they began looking to the west for signs of Paddy's raid. Half-past eleven came, and finally midnight, and the tranquillity of the night remained unbroken. No doubt his attack had misfired as well.

David began to imagine the worst. After all the weeks of effort the unit was facing total failure. They were not likely to be given any more chances. He could visualise the satisfaction on the face of Major Smith when he learned that the S.A.S. had been disbanded. Then suddenly came a sound sweeter than any symphony. First a great flash glowed in the western sky; then a series of explosions in rapid succession. David and Brough nearly danced for joy. "What lovely work," chanted the sergeant. "It almost makes the army worthwhile."

Waiting no longer seemed an ordeal. The sky was beginning to turn pink and they commented extravagantly on its beauty. At midnight Brough cut some scrub and David placed it on the crown of the road. Then he moved it to a more discreet position at one side. He did not want to stop a German convoy, but equally he did not want Holliman to miss it. Headlights beamed some distance away.

"Captain Holliman said he would be here on the dot of 12.45," said Sergeant Brough. "I make it exactly that now, sir."

" In that case here they come," said David. " We'll put these bushes a little more firmly in the centre of the road."

They listened carefully to the sound of the truck. " It's the L.R.D.G. all right," said Brough.

It was. Holliman detected the pile of branches and his three lorries pulled up. He commiserated with David on hearing his news, and together they watched the flickering glow in the sky over Tamit.

" It's like a prime display of Northern Lights," said Holliman admiringly.

Before leaving the road, David decided to mine it. Brough found some suitable potholes in the tarmac surface and after a bit of excavating planted three pressure mines designed to explode under the weight of a wheel.

They were up to time so they waited in case a victim came by. About ten minutes later an Italian transport truck, travelling fast, perhaps frightened by the conflagration behind him at Tamit, approached. There was a loud explosion and a burst of flames as the vehicle crashed off the road.

" Well, boys," said Holliman, " that's our fun for the evening. Now we must get cracking for the desert rendezvous to welcome home our conquering Irish hero."

*　　　*　　　*

They covered the eighty miles they had to travel by 8.30 in the morning. Paddy's party had not yet arrived, and David waited anxiously for it. At eleven o'clock the sentry reported movement on the horizon. The men stopped what they were doing and strained their eyes toward the small specks. Soon they could make out the shape of three trucks, and finally the rose and green markings. " Let's give them a victory salute," said Cooper gaily. Everyone picked up rifles and tommy-guns and began firing into the air.

Twenty-four planes had been destroyed without a single casualty. Paddy gave a laconic account of the affair but Corporal Seekings and Corporal Bennett livened it up with interruptions. They had met no obstacles. They had made their way single file on to the airfield. For a few minutes they walked blindly, seeing nothing, then found themselves nearing a group of buildings which lined one end of the aerodrome. A faint light was showing beneath the door of a Nissen-hut type of structure, and Paddy crept up to it. He could hear people laughing and talking inside. It was obviously the officers' mess. He flung the door open. Some sort of party must have been going on for there were at least thirty people inside. There was a split second of astonished silence, then he sprayed the room with his tommy-gun, and finished by shooting out the lights.

A minute later the survivors began to answer back. Bullets came through the window. He detailed four of his men to carry on the miniature battle while he and five others hurried around the landing ground putting bombs on the planes.

They covered the field in fifteen minutes. When they had finished, they found that they were one bomb short. Paddy jumped into the cockpit of the remaining plane. " At first I thought he had gone mad," wrote Seekings. " Then I saw him rip the instrument panel out with his bare hands. How he did it I shall never know."

The battle at the building had ended. Paddy had told the four men whom he had detailed to ' handle ' it to make their way back to the L.R.D.G. trucks two miles away. His own group now started off the field. " We had not gone fifty yards," continued Seekings, " when the first plane went up. We stopped to look but the second one went up near us and we began to run. After a while we felt fairly safe and stopped to take another glance. What a sight ! Planes exploding all over, and the terrific roar of petrol and bombs going up.

" We got cracking again. The L.R.D.G. were flashing lights at few minute intervals. We packed our compass away. Next thing we knew we were off our course. A light flashed to our right, we turned towards it but it was soon obvious that the enemy were flashing lights as well. We had an alternative signal—blasts on a whistle. We blew it and were answered nearby, much to our relief.

" I was gasping for a drink. We had no water with us and

Paddy had set a cracking pace. Sgt. 'Jacko'[1] gave me a waterbottle—one of the big type the Rhodesians had. I took a long drink from it. As I took it from my lips I could not get my wind. I realised too late it was neat rum. In a matter of minutes I was three-parts in the blind. I staggered to my truck and fell off to sleep in spite of the rough going.

"I awoke to the sound of hammering and cursing—the steering had broken and the fitter was doing his best to put it right. Jacko had got a fire going and a brew on. I think it was Mike Sadler, the navigator, trying to tell him we were only a few miles from Sirte, to which Jacko replied he did not give a hell if we were only a few yards he intended to have a brew.

"It was Mike's first patrol as navigator. We had to rendezvous many miles out into the desert with the other half of the patrol. In spite of the rough going and darkness he made it dead on. A marvellous performance which he was to repeat often.

"In mending the truck we had been forced to dismantle the brakes and therefore couldn't stop. When we sighted the other patrol we had to coast on towards them. They started to fire everything. We almost died of shock, thinking they had mistaken us for the enemy, but luckily they were firing into the air, giving us a royal welcome—they had seen the fires and explosions in the distance."

*　　　　*　　　　*

David and Paddy were the first to arrive back in Jalo. Bill Fraser had set out for Agedabia only that morning, and Jock Lewis had not yet returned from Agheila. He did not come back for three more days. His men tumbled out of the L.R.D.G. trucks, with only one thought in their heads: water. After they had drunk their fill and eaten, everyone began to talk. They had been unlucky as far as the airfield was concerned; Agheila was only a ferrying point and all aircraft were evacuated from the field at night.

But Jock Lewis had another card up his sleeve which he had

[1] Sergeant Jackson of the Rhodesian L.R.D.G. patrol.

discussed with the L.R.D.G. patrol leader, Lt. Morris. He knew from intelligence reports that a roadhouse at Mersa Brega was frequently used as an informal meeting place for important staff officers and generals. He would raid the building. He had brought an Italian Lancia with him, as part of the convoy, which would now be put to a useful purpose.

This vehicle had not been popular with his men. " We damn, nearly carried it all the way across the desert," wrote Sergeant Lilley. " Every few yards it would get bogged down in the sand, and after a lot of heaving, lifting and digging the thing was free again for a few yards, then the same process all over again. We took it in turns to refuel the Lancia. This was done by syphoning the Diesel oil from a fifty-gallon drum into the tank, and whoever had to suck the tube to get it started invariably got a belly full of oil; how we hated that perishing Lancia."

Jock Lewis explained to the men the reason he had insisted on bringing it. They would drive to the coast road and wait until they saw an enemy convoy heading eastwards. The Lancia would join on to it, and the L.R.D.G. trucks would follow suit. When they reached the roadhouse they would break off, raid it, and capture whatever officers were inside.

To some extent things went according to plan. A convoy passed after a wait of only ten minutes and the British vehicles attached themselves. " There we were," wrote Lilley, " sprawled in the back of British lorries, smoking and chatting as if we owned the road, even waving to enemy trucks as they passed. We reached the roadhouse and pulled up in front where half a dozen vehicles were stationed. As Jock Lewis climbed out a driver from one of the cars—another Lancia I believe—came over and asked him for a light. Lewis informed him that he was a British officer and told the man to jump aboard our truck as he was now a prisoner. This seemed to amuse the Italian very much. He thought we were Germans having a joke with him. He was not left in doubt very long and was only too pleased to jump aboard.

" Jock and two or three others went to the door of the roadhouse with the intention of shooting it up. But the men outside must have spotted the British markings on the trucks. Someone gave the alarm and the enemy began to fire everything they had from inside the roadhouse. Jock shouted at us to let loose with the Breda and the Bren. Jim Almonds tried the Breda— nothing happened. I tried—the same thing. It was a cold night and the oil on the guns had thickened up. Bullets were whistling all round. Finally, after going through all the stoppages I managed to get the Bren going."

Since surprise had been lost Lewis was forced to abandon the plan of shanghai-ing generals. He detailed three men to keep firing at the roadhouse while he and two others planted bombs in the transport, a few yards off to the right. The area was packed with lorries and he managed to deposit between thirty and forty bombs in twenty minutes.

It was time to go. The men jumped aboard their trucks, and once again with the Lancia in the lead went racing down the road until they came to the spot where they could turn into the desert.

*   *   *

Four days later Bill Fraser's party returned. They had achieved the most spectacular success of all. They had destroyed thirty-seven aircraft on Agedabia field and had suffered no casualties. They reached the airfield at eight o'clock at night, but had difficulty in getting past the wire and sentry posts strung around the perimeter. More than one guard passed within a few feet of the party.

They could only move a few yards at a time, and had to lie still on one occasion for more than an hour. It wasn't until midnight that they were able to get in among the planes. Once there, it was easy. They worked in two parties, leap-frogging each other from one plane to the next. Within three-quarters of an hour they had laid their charges on thirty-seven planes, mostly C.R.42's. They found to their annoyance that they were two bombs short. However, the first charge was now exploding and there was no time to lose in getting away.

The explosions were soon occurring every minute and the confusion on the field helped them to escape undetected.

They made their way to the rendezvous where the patrol was waiting for them at 4.30 in the morning. They then drove off as fast as possible for the Wadi El Faregh, which they reached as dawn was breaking.

Brigadier Reid's " E " Force was camping in the wadi for the night, before continuing the advance that would link it with Marriott's troops the following day. Reid wrote in his diary, " At first light there was a certain amount of excitement amongst the forward troops, and recognition signals by Very light were fired. I drove forward to see what was the matter and met Fraser of Stirling's ' L Detachment ' whom I eagerly asked how he had got on. He said, ' Very sorry, sir; I had to leave two aircraft on the ground as I ran out of explosive; but we destroyed 37.' This indeed was a wonderful achievement by one officer and three men. Incidentally, we heard later that Rommel had been in Agedabia that night. He must have had a bit of a headache."

CHAPTER FIVE

THE LONG WALK

DAVID'S THEORIES were vindicated. During a single week his little group of twenty-one men had destroyed sixty-one planes and at least thirty vehicles and had not suffered a casualty. On the night of 23rd December, the day that Fraser (the last to come in) returned to Jalo, the four officers had a celebration.

It was both a reunion and a farewell party, for David and Paddy were leaving the following morning to have another crack at Sirte and Tamit, and Jock Lewis was pushing off to raid Nofilia. If Bill was not too tired and would like to go along with Jock, said David, he might raid the Marble Arch field which was in the same area. That was the way David put things. He seldom gave an order. He just suggested that something might be ' fun.' And viewed in this light no one could refuse; they said yes, of course, as though it were perfectly natural to come in from a harrowing adventure one day and start off on another the next. After all, why else had they joined the S.A.S.?

So the dinner on the 23rd was spent in talking shop. Gus Holliman once again would guide Paddy and David to their targets, and Lieutenant Morris would escort Jock and Bill. " With luck we may get a grand slam this time, fifty planes in a night," said David. The experience they had gained, he went on, was worth everything. As far as he was concerned he would never risk forfeiting surprise again by attempting a recce in advance. Paddy chipped in and said he thought it was a mistake to do what he had done and shoot up airfield personnel before placing the bombs. The shooting should

71

come as a parting gesture. And Lewis felt that he had been
too cautious. The Lancia was not worth the trouble and he
was inclined to believe that British trucks could drive along
the coast road undetected. They all agreed that surprise was
everything; it was more potent than any of them had imagined.
" If you've really got surprise," said David, " you can get away
with murder." This was an unintended joke but it made
everyone laugh.

*   *   *

So once again they started off, David and Paddy and the
L.R.D.G. patrol exactly as before. But this time they would
split into two groups by design, not accident; and they would
head for Tamit and drop off Paddy first. Although David was
confident that the enemy would not expect them back so soon,
he felt it wise not to follow precisely the same route.

He studied the map with Gus Holliman and Mike Sadler.
Sadler was a slim, fair-haired Rhodesian who had recently
transferred to the L.R.D.G. from an anti-tank battery. When
he was asked by his commanding officer whether he would
like to train as a navigator he had replied that he knew nothing
about it, but had always been fascinated by charts and angles,
and would be glad to have a try. He revealed an uncanny
flair for his new job. Although he had only been operating
in his new capacity for a few weeks he already had the air of
a veteran. David was impressed by the fact that he was never
assailed by doubts, and soon learned why. He was nearly
always right. The only mistakes he made were due to faulty
maps. His reputation grew rapidly and at the end of a year
he was acknowledged as the best navigator in the western
desert.

Inaccurate maps, however, presented a serious problem. At
the beginning of the war large slices of the Libyan desert were
still uncharted; and the only maps that existed of Libya and
Cyrenaica were those designed by the Italians. They were
extremely unreliable. Depressions and wadis were sometimes
not marked at all, and roads were often indicated many miles
from where they actually were. The British army was drawing

up new maps, based on the Air Force system of line overlap photography, but they were not yet completed.

"Let's hope they've got the Mediterranean in the right place," said David as he studied his route.

Holliman had agreed to take the S.A.S. to a point on the Wadi Tamit five miles short of the coast. The wadi was a huge ravine that started at the town of Tamit and stretched deep into the desert. Its southernmost regions were marked as impassable, and at many places the descent was steep and precipitous. Nearer the coast it became easier to negotiate; and, once in it, a fairly hard surface made the going reasonably good for long stretches at a time. Paddy's group would probably travel up the wadi to approach the airfield.

This time the passage from Jalo was not disturbed by aircraft. The desert wore an air of innocent serenity and for two days the little fleet of six trucks moved across it like buoyant ships on a high sea. When the sun went down it became very cold and it was good to get the fires going and smell the evening stew simmering in the pot—the pot being a four-gallon petrol tin.

The wireless operator tuned into L.R.D.G. headquarters for the signal. The news was good. Rommel was withdrawing his forces from Gazala to Agedabia. Any planes the S.A.S. could knock out would reduce his badly needed cover. He was reported to be reinforcing a position at Agheila where he would make his ultimate stand.

On the first night the men were busy filling up the trucks with petrol and oil and checking the engines. One of the vehicles had been giving trouble and the mechanics could not find out what was wrong. In the end it was two of David's corporals—Cooper and Seekings—who solved the problem.

David had been struck by the efficiency of these two men ever since they joined the unit. Although they had not known each other until they arrived in the Middle East, they had become bosom friends. Seekings had accompanied David on the last raid and ' Johnny ' Cooper had gone with Paddy; this time they asked if they could be together. In looks and temperament they were complete opposites. Cooper was dark and slim and hailed from the city of Leicester; Seekings was fair and thick-set and came from a country district in Cambridgeshire. Cooper was quick-witted and high spirited; Seekings was slow and steady and shrewd. They were perfect complements to each other. If one did not know the answer, the other did. David was impressed by their energy—they were always the first to give a helping hand—and by their general enjoyment of life. They treated the raids as though they were part of a glorious holiday spree. He made a mental note that they were a useful pair to have around.

The party reached its destination at nine o'clock on the evening of the third day. They planned to operate that same night about 1 a.m., which would allow them plenty of time to reach their targets. Paddy was only six miles away from Tamit field, and David twenty-five miles from Sirte. Holliman was again conveying David's party, and suggested driving to the coast road, five miles away, and travelling down it until they neared the field which ran along it. The desert land between Sirte and Tamit was difficult as it contained treacherous drifts of soft sand; but the coast road was smooth and fast; and if it was like the time before, when Holliman had driven along it to pick up Brough and David, practically empty.

It took two hours to service the vehicles and get the weapons ready. Then the two groups split up. David's party found their route broken and rocky, and averaged only a few miles an hour. Sadler finally told them they were within two miles of the coast. They turned out their lights and slowed down to a crawl. Several hundred yards away they began to hear a loud and steady rumble of vehicles; the earth was trembling with the vibration. They crept forward and concealed themselves in some bushes. A German armoured division was moving along the road, heading for the front. Tanks on huge transport carriers passed, then armoured cars, then more tanks, some making a tremendous clatter as they travelled on their own tracks. They obviously were being sent to reinforce the position at Agheila, two hundred miles away, where they had heard that Rommel was planning to dig himself in.

Much to David's annoyance this traffic continued for the next four hours. It flowed in such a steady stream it was impossible to get on to the road. David and Gus had a whispered conference and decided that nothing would be gained by travelling cross-country to Sirte. They would never reach it before first light. All they could do was to wait and hope that the traffic would come to an end.

At two o'clock the armoured vehicles were flowing past as steadily as ever. At two-thirty they saw a pink glow rising in the direction of Tamit. " Paddy's lit another bonfire," whispered Cooper delightedly. " And all we can do is sit here and watch a blooming parade," said Seekings gloomily.

At three o'clock in the morning the traffic began to thin out and at 3.30 the night was still again. The men climbed into the trucks, the drivers turned on their engines, and the three L.R.D.G. vehicles bumped on to the empty highway.

It did not remain empty for long. Another mile, and dark shapes began to loom up. A moment later the British trucks were driving past armoured cars parked a few yards from the road. From then on they passed stationary enemy vehicles and tented encampments almost continuously. The men had their tommy-guns at the ready. Any moment a light might swing out in front of them, and a sentry might issue a challenge. If this happened there would be no alternative but to shoot it out and race for the open desert.

Two miles from the aerodrome the L.R.D.G. trucks pulled up at the side of the road. Not far ahead was a convoy of armoured cars bedded down for the night, and, half a mile behind, two tank carriers. " We'll wait here for you," said Holliman. " But we must settle on a password. If any suspicious characters come up to investigate us, we'll have to shoot." They chose a word, and David and his five men left on foot to walk to the airfield. It was now four o'clock, and they had only an hour of darkness left.

They walked over the rough ground parallel to the road, about half a mile on the desert side. After a mile they heard the crunching sound of footsteps, and a moment later they could see barbed wire silhouetted against the sky and a sentry on the other side of it. The men did a quick reconnaissance and found that the wire stretched as far as they could see, and was being patrolled; no doubt as a result of David's visit a fortnight before.

There was no possibility of getting through the wire quickly and maintaining surprise. In view of the time factor their best chance was to walk on to the highway again; perhaps the side of the field that bordered the road would not be so heavily guarded.

As they approached the macadam thoroughfare they saw a barricade across it. They neared it and a challenge rang out. They stopped in their tracks and waited; then they stealthily withdrew into the darkness. David considered the situation. It was now 4.30 and Gus Holliman had said he could not wait a minute after five o'clock. There was no hope of cutting their way through the wire and destroying the planes within so short a time. He decided that there was nothing to do but abandon the airfield. If they hurried back to the truck perhaps Holliman would agree to drive along the road and do a bit of shooting.

He instructed the men to return to the lorries. He strode ahead and approached the back of the L.R.D.G. truck a little before the others. He was so preoccupied with his thoughts that he forgot to give the password. He did not hear the sudden click that broke the air. He saw the white face of the L.R.D.G. guard, and below it, the muzzle of a rifle pointing at him. " It's me," he said. " No luck." There was a moment of silence; then in a strangely muffled voice the guard replied, " You've had more luck than you know, sir."

David wondered what he meant; later he learned that the man had fired at him. He had pulled the trigger but by a thousand to one oversight there had been no bullet in the breech. " When he told me about it afterwards it made me feel a bit sick," David commented.

Holliman was delighted with David's shooting-up proposal. Strictly speaking, the L.R.D.G. were not supposed to take part in raids. Their role was that of a reconnaissance and a ferry service, and they were instructed not to risk their vehicles or engage in battle unless it was unavoidable. However, once Holliman had listened to Morris's story of accompanying Lewis's Lancia party to the roadhouse and attacking buildings and vehicles, he was determined to have a crack himself.

The sky was showing the first streaks of light and there was no time to lose. They decided to concentrate on ' soft-skinned ' vehicles as opposed to armour, mainly because they could wreck these and only damage the others. They hurried towards Tamit and drove a mile before they came upon their first target—twelve supply trucks. The crew was sleeping in tents fifty yards off the road. The L.R.D.G. lorries pulled up a short distance behind them, and David and three men crept forward and put a Lewis bomb in each vehicle. This took nearly ten minutes and it was now 4.50.

" There's no time to plant bombs," said David. " Let's just drive along and shoot up whatever we see."

Holliman enjoyed himself so much that he stayed on the road until 5.15. For the next twenty-five minutes the three British trucks raced along the highway, past German tanks, lorries and tents, with all guns firing. They must have presented a strangely defiant sight in the grey morning light. The men stood in the back. Some of them fired tommy-guns, others threw grenades, still others were forced to content themselves with rifles. First they opened up on a tented encampment and watched their bullets ripping through the canvas; then on a second line of lorries. As they looked back they saw figures running from the fields toward their vehicles, many of which were in flames. They were sorry they could not stop to admire the full results of their work. They shot at two more encampments and flung grenades at a tank carrier.

" I'm afraid that will have to do," said Holliman apologetically. " It's practically daylight."

For some time they were apprehensive lest the enemy send a patrol of armoured cars after them. The reason the Germans did not do this undoubtedly was that they had orders to proceed to Agheila and no one had the authority to instruct a section to detach itself and scour the desert for three British trucks.

Whatever the explanation, David and his men reached the rendezvous safely.

*   *   *

Paddy, in the meantime, had scored another victory. He and his five men encountered no difficulty in getting on to Tamit airfield, and found twenty-seven planes waiting for their bombs. He learned later that this was part of a brand-new squadron which had arrived from Italy only twenty-four hours earlier. His patrol used half-hour fuses. These fuses were ingenious but not always very reliable. They were called 'time-pencils.' They worked on the principle of acid eating through wire which, when broken, set off the explosion. The time element was determined by the thickness of the wire and was not wholly accurate.

On this particular night the first bomb which was supposed to work on a half-hour fuse went off twenty-two minutes after it had been set. Luckily the raiders had just finished their work. They did not realise that they could be seen against the background of burning planes and suddenly a voice in front of them barked the word ' *Avanti* '. Paddy replied ' Freund,' then took the pin out of a grenade and threw it into the blackness. The S.A.S. ran as fast as they could until they were well away from the field.

They made good time to the rendezvous and reached it at seven o'clock. David was ragged unmercifully about his second failure to destroy aircraft at Sirte. " It's obvious I'll have to pull up my socks," he said cheerfully. " The competition is too hot."

*   *   *

The two officers had to wait several days for news of the other parties. When it arrived, it was bad. Morris of the L.R.D.G. came bumping into Jalo in a damaged truck packed with men; it was all that was left of the convoy of six vehicles.

Morris had picked up Lewis's patrol after the Nofilia raid, and they had set out together for Marble Arch to collect Bill Fraser. On the way they had been spotted and attacked from the air. Five trucks were destroyed and Lewis had been killed. Despite the fact that the remaining truck was in poor order Morris had continued to the Marble Arch rendezvous; but when he arrived he could find no trace of Fraser's patrol.

Jock Lewis's death was a severe blow to David. Not only was he devoted to him, but he was the officer upon whom he relied the most. His logical, incisive mind was the perfect counterfoil to David's brilliant imagination. He could give any scheme a hard, practical basis. David had admired Jock's talents from the first and had hoped that when they returned to base, he would take complete charge of the organisational side of the unit.

Sergeant Lilley, a tall wiry man who had been one of Lewis's party pieced together what had happened. Morris had dropped the patrol thirty miles from Nofilia on Christmas Eve. " At two o'clock on Christmas morning," said Lilley, " we stopped, sat down and each man took a can of beer from his pack. Jock Lewis produced a tin of cold Xmas pudding and this he shared between the five of us. We all wished each other a Merry Xmas, drank the beer, ate the pudding, had a smoke and a yarn and then we were on our way again.

" We reached Nofilia before dawn and found a place to hide up where we could watch the aerodrome. There were not many aircraft in the field and the few that were there were very widely dispersed, but we noted the positions of them. As soon as it was dark we moved on to the landing ground and put a bomb on the first plane, then moved off in search of the next plane. We had just put the bomb on the second plane when the first one went off (we were only using half-hour time pencils then). After that the airfield became alive with troops and we came very near to getting caught as we beat a retreat. It was a big disappointment to all of us that we had only destroyed two planes."

Lilley went on to tell how they had returned to the rendezvous, then started off for Marble Arch. A low-flying Savoya spotted them. " He circled over us and came in with all guns firing. We blazed away at him with everything we had, but our fire didn't seem to affect him. We abandoned the trucks and tried to find some cover. The pilot came gunning for us. He attacked twice. Jock Lewis was hit. We bandaged him with field dressings, but he died about five minutes later and we buried him in a grave about two feet deep.

" It was as bare as a billiard table," continued Lilley, " and we had not been able to find any cover. Two more aircraft appeared on the horizon. There was nothing to do but walk away from the trucks and lie down in the sand."

In a few minutes the fighters had destroyed all the trucks; then they went for the men. When they finally ran out of ammunition, more planes came to take their place. This went on for several hours. "Jim Almonds and I thought we were the only two left alive," finished Lilley, " and we began making plans for the march back. The next minute there were voices calling from all around and on checking up we found that after eight hours' strafing and bombing the enemy had only succeeded in destroying the transport. By swapping pieces on the burnt-out vehicles we managed to get one in going order. We all clambered aboard and held each other on the truck. Then we carried on to the R.V. to let Bill Fraser know that we hadn't forgotten him and tell him that we would send other trucks out for him. There was no sign of him or any of the party, so we decided to make for Jalo as fast as we could."

*   *   *

A second patrol was sent to look for Bill Fraser, but this, too, was unable to find him. Later it was discovered that there had been a mix-up about the meeting place. Fraser and his four men—Sergeants DuVivier and Tait, and Privates Byrne and Phillips—had found the Marble Arch aerodrome deserted and had returned to the rendezvous, marked on their maps, the following day. They waited six days before giving up hope. By this time their water supply was nearly finished. They had only half a pint per man. They were a little better off for food, reckoning that their ' bully sardines,' hard tack, dried fruit and cheese could last another forty-eight hours.

They had two courses before them; either to surrender to

the enemy, only a few hours' walk away, or to try to get back to their own lines. This probably would mean many days in the desert wilderness, stealing water and food to keep alive.

They decided to try it. They would head for Hasselet, a British position about two hundred miles away. Of course it would mean a long detour.

The battle of these five men against thirst, hunger, fatigue and despair takes its place as one of the great adventures of the African campaign. Sergeant DuVivier scribbled down a day by day account in a notebook that he happened to have with him. " We walked all day but found no water. Thirsty as I was, I was determined not to drink my remaining half-pint as it helped my morale just to hear it in the bottle. Sometimes I took a sip to moisten my mouth, but as it got less I spat it back again. Then I started to suck a couple of small, smooth pebbles to keep the saliva from drying up. By sundown we were very exhausted, and wrapping ourselves in our blankets (we carried one apiece) we fell into an uneasy sleep.

" The next morning we woke up stiff, dry and hungry and after a light snack—light because it was becoming increasingly difficult to swallow owing to the lack of moisture—we set off again with the feeling that perhaps to-day would bring us more luck. But alas, the day went by and still no water. Then we spotted what looked like an inland lake some six miles or so to the south-east and with renewed hope we hurried our pace. We reached the water about midday but to our dismay found that it was salt water, so strong that it was impossible to swallow the smallest amount.

" In desperation we decided to try and distil it. With the aid of two aluminium water-bottles (Italian type) and a four-foot length of rubber tubing, using camel scrub for fuel, we set up an improvised distillery. The bottles had a small teat screwed on each. Over one I fitted the tubing after half-filling it with salt water and making it otherwise airtight; the other end of the tube was fitted loosely into the second bottle. I lit a fire around the one containing water and soon it began to boil. After a few minutes we could hear the slow drip-drip as the steam condensed back into water and found its way into the second container.

"This was back-aching work and very slow, taking one hour to produce less than half a pint of fresh water. The process went on until it began to get dark, and we realised that we were losing more water through perspiration than we were producing on this contraption.

"Bob Tait suggested that two of us should carry on with the distilling while the other three made for the road and tried to raid a truck for water and provisions. We drew lots. Lieut. Fraser and I remained and Bob, Phillips and Byrne did the raiding.

"We could not believe our luck when they returned soon after midnight with two jerry-cans filled with crystal clear and cool water which they had got by shooting up a German truck. What a feast we had that night! We made a brew of tea (we were carrying dry tea and condensed milk) and feasted on bully stew, cheese and biscuits and dried dates for dessert. That night we slept well and did not wake up until just before midday."

For the next three days the men plodded on. They found no more water and soon their thoughts again were dominated by thirst. "We had only walked a mile," wrote DuVivier, "before we saw an enemy convoy, probably Italian, crossing about 100 yds. ahead of us. We threw ourselves flat, but much to our dismay, one of the trucks stopped right in front of us and eight helmeted Italian soldiers got out and began to pitch a tent. It was impossible to remain where we were without being discovered. We rose up and made a wide detour of them never daring to look back until we had put a good mile between ourselves and them. They must have seen us but probably thought that we were also Italian soldiers, our uniforms being somewhat similar in colour—the common khaki.

"We were roughly in the centre of the Wadi Faregh. We surveyed the surrounding terrain with our binoculars. Running up both sides of the valley and about one mile on either side of us we saw large numbers of enemy transport, mostly stationary. One truck was standing a little apart from its neighbours. If we ransacked it we might find water. We took a compass bearing on it. Bob Tait led the way, using his illuminated compass. Soon we were near enough to hear voices. These guided us until we could see the silhouette of the lorry against the starry sky.

" When we were close up we realised that there were about four ' Eyeties ' inside, under the canvas, as we could distinguish different voices. We made our plans and now, action. At a given signal Lieut. Fraser made for the driver's cabin, and Byrne and I, armed with Smith Wesston revolvers covered Bob and Phillips whilst they ' downed ' the flap and ' upped ' the canvas. In a matter of seconds we had grabbed the ' bodies ' and pulled them out, a struggling mass in the sand. We literally caught them with their pants down. They did not put up a fight, but screamed for mercy. Obviously they thought we were a band of Arab cut-throats and we had some trouble in quietening them down. In spite of all the din their neighbours did not bother to investigate, luckily for us as it happened.

" Using French as a common language I assured them that we had no intention of killing them and asked them to keep quiet as we did not want company. I spun them a yarn to the effect that we were a patrol, and that their position was surrounded by half the British Army. They believed me and wanted us to take them prisoner. ' Wait until to-morrow,' I said, ' and you will all be prisoners.' While this conversation was going on Lieut. Fraser attempted to drain the radiator for water but found it to be red with rust and quite unpalatable. The others were busy searching the truck for food and water. Bob Tait put a bottle to his lips of what he thought was water but it turned out to be benzine. Unfortunately he swallowed some and was violently sick. There was no water but we found some tins of something which we stuffed into our packs. We also took a small benzine stove which we thought might come in handy later on.

" Without further delay we set off eastwards. This was a strategic move in case we might be followed. That night we crossed a salt marsh which we judged to be about half-way between El Agheila and Mersa-el-Brega. We had been on the move for six days, and were not only desperate for water, but weak and tired. We decided that as soon as it was dark we must try and steal a vehicle so that we could drive the rest of the way.

" We slept until sundown, then walked to the road and hid behind some rocks. After twenty minutes we saw the head-lights of a vehicle coming down the track towards us. It was travelling slowly as the track was very bumpy, and when it was level with us we pounced as one man.

" The element of surprise was on our side and we had no trouble in disarming the two occupants of the car, which was a small Mercedes Benz equipped with a wireless transmitter. There was only seating capacity for three but we were not going to leave the Jerries behind to raise the alarm and besides, not one of our number could drive the car. However, we all packed in somehow and seating myself behind our German chauffeur with my revolver alongside his left ear we set off on the next phase of our journey in the direction of Mersa-Brega.

" We passed several trucks going in the opposite direction. The Jerries behaved perfectly and did not try to give us away. Needless to say they would have been ' dead ducks ' had they behaved otherwise. We lost track of distance but after about forty-five minutes we came to the Casa-Ristora (Rest-House) at Mersa-Brega. This was the same rest-house which we had raided two weeks previously, and we almost felt at home. This place was literally seething with activity and we did not feel too happy about it. But we were not challenged and kept on moving for another ten kilos along the road where we struck off the road in a southerly direction into the desert.

" Our intention was to follow the same route as we had used to get away after the first raid but unfortunately we misjudged and finished up ' bogged down' in a salt marsh some ten to fifteen miles off the road.

" Here we were able to take a closer look at our prisoners, both soldiers. One was about twenty and the other, I should say, in his forties. Again using French as a common language I learned from the younger one that he was a student and conscripted much against his will—definitely not a Nazi. The older one was a ' regular ' and did not think too highly of Hitler either. They were rather worried, at first, that we were going to shoot them, but we put them at their ease by telling them that we were only interested in saving our own ' bacon.'

" Here we parted with our friends, the enemy, and they set off on foot for the road using the North Star as a guide. I often wondered afterwards what sort of a story they had to tell when they got back to their own unit and what sort of a C.O. they had to face."

The car was useless now, but they were within forty miles of their own lines. They covered the distance in the next two days, and finally sighted an armoured car patrol. Was it British or German ? " We hid and watched them as they approached," wrote DuVivier. " Still we could not determine whether or not they were ours. Suddenly I heard an unmistakably Cockney voice and we almost wept with joy and relief as we rushed forward. With our matted hair and beards, faces caked in dirt, torn clothes, they must have thought we were a band of savages. However, we were soon made welcome . . ."

It was Saturday, the tenth of January. The raiders had been on the march eight days and had covered 200 miles.

CHAPTER SIX

AT THE WATERFRONT

In the meantime David had taken his unit back to Kabrit. L Detachment had destroyed ninety aeroplanes in two weeks. With this achievement he felt it was safe to come out of hiding; it was also imperative. With Jock Lewis dead and Bill Fraser missing,[1] the only officers left were Paddy Mayne and himself. It was vital to return to Middle East Headquarters and secure permission to recruit more men and gather more supplies.

Within a few hours of reaching base David drove to Cairo and asked to see General Auchinleck. He was first shown into the office of the Director of Military Operations. The latter knew all about the S.A.S. operations. David's laconic signal had not told him much but he had received reports from both Brigadier Reid and Brigadier Marriott confirming the daring and useful work the handful of men had accomplished. Nevertheless his manner was restrained. He was polite but not warm, and David felt he must belong to the group who frowned on irregular operations and resented 'independent commands.'

"The commander-in-chief will see you at once," said the D.M.O. Then he paused and gave Captain Stirling a searching look. The young man's tropical uniform was immaculate and his buttons were shining, but his jaw was covered by a dark, curling, five-week beard. "I do think, Stirling, you

---

[1] Lieutenant Fraser returned to Kabrit after his harrowing march, the second week in January.

ought to shave before you see the general," he observed coldly.

David suppressed his anger with difficulty. " I don't expect to be in Cairo very long, sir," he said softly, " and I'll take a chance on the general objecting." The brigadier opened his mouth to answer then thought better of it. " All right," he said. " Come this way."

Auchinleck rose from his desk when David entered the room and approached him smiling. " I say, what a splendid beard ! I don't know which deserves the most congratulations; this fine growth or the really useful raids you've carried out. Sit down. What plans have you in mind? "

David was only too pleased to tell him. He began by congratulating Auchinleck on his successful offensive. Now that the enemy had been driven out of Libya, and Benghazi was about to fall into British hands, he felt that his unit should strike harder than ever at the enemy's bases. A modern war depended on machines and supplies. If you could destroy those machines and supplies before they got into action you were automatically lessening the task of the combat troops. David now came to his main point. In the next forty-eight hours Benghazi would be ours; as a result the enemy was already being forced to re-route his supply ships to the port of Bouerat, some three hundred and fifty miles to the west. Soon it might become an important harbour for fuel tankers to supply Rommel's advanced forces. David proposed to enter Bouerat and blow up whatever ships he found there; also to destroy petrol dumps and tankers.

If Auchinleck had expected David to unfold further plans for the destruction of aircraft he showed no sign of it. David's mind did not work in a conventional way. The achievements on airfields were the beginning, not the end of the S.A.S. potentialities. He was convinced that the Long Range Desert Group could transport his men to any given point on a map; and he believed that if surprise could be maintained there was nothing they could not accomplish.

Auchinleck was silent for a moment. " How many men do you need? "

" Not more than a dozen, sir. I thought I might take an officer along from the Special Boat Section."

No doubt the operation sounded suicidal to Auchinleck. However, David's success in December had far outstripped anything the general had envisaged, and perhaps he was right about Bouerat as well. Very well, he said, David could proceed with his plan. He then asked when the raid would take place, and looked surprised when David replied, " About the middle of the month." David explained that his men could only attack in the moonless period; but there was plenty of time as everything was already being laid on. The twinkle in Auchinleck's eye revealed that he registered the fact that the young man had not hesitated to prepare his plans before receiving the general's authority to execute them. Before David departed he secured permission from Auchinleck to recruit another six officers and thirty or forty men. When he took his leave the general walked to the door with him and said brusquely, " By the way, Stirling, from now on you have the rank of major."

*   *   *

David reckoned he would have to be back in Jalo by the 10th of January. That gave him only a week in Cairo to work out the plan of attack for the Bouerat raid, and to rebuild his unit. He also had to re-establish the training base at Kabrit; to appoint an officer to take Jock Lewis's place; to handpick reinforcements; to wangle new supplies and ammunition; to organise transport. All this had to be done over and above the task of working with the intelligence department to familiarise himself with the layout at Bouerat.

David set up his headquarters in his brother Peter's flat in Cairo. This was situated opposite the British Embassy on a broad, fashionable thoroughfare about ten minutes from the main shopping centre. The rooms were high-ceilinged and spacious, and looked after by a fat, jolly Arab named Mo. Mo

---

[1] The Special Boat Section was a unit developed by No. 8 Commando to do reconnaissance of beaches and harbours by canoe. When Layforce was disbanded it continued to operate independently until, in the spring of 1942, it came under Stirling's command.

was one of the characters of Cairo war-time life. He had two
outstanding qualities; an unfailing memory, and an insatiable
curiosity. He knew more about his master's friends than did
his master. And when he liked the friends, he offered them
flawless service.

He regarded David as a fascinating study and did not seem
to mind the fact that he turned the tidy flat into a bear garden
of maps, ash-trays, photographs, papers and drinks; that the
spare bedroom and even the sitting-room often had half a
dozen camp beds and sleeping-bags in them; that tommy-
guns frequently were parked in the hall. The telephone rang
incessantly and there was constant coming and going. But
here Mo asserted himself. He would never open the door more
than a few inches, and if he did not like the face that greeted
him he would say firmly, " Sir not home," and slam it shut
again. He also took a poor view of those who slipped an odd
knife or fork into their pockets to supplement their mess-kit.
Once he suspected a certain officer; and to show him that his
light fingers had not gone unnoticed he made him an apple-pie
bed with three knives at the bottom.

David was quick to appreciate Mo's ability and put him to
work. He was much more successful on the telephone than
the impatient soldiery, and soon found himself acting as
David's P.A. "Just ring up the R.E.M.E. and ask them what's
happened to our thirty-hundredweight truck. Tell them that
we've got to have it by to-morrow. Use your own judgment
about what to say, but get it. It's really urgent."

Mo soon found himself frequently on the telephone to the
' middle brass ' at Headquarters. His soft voice and tact
seemed to have a soothing effect on the irate tempers that
flared up at some of David's demands, and gradually he became
the trusted executor of all kinds of communications. " Tell
Captain Mayne the Bren guns are being delivered to-morrow."
" Tell Major Stirling Air Reconnaissance has the photographs
he wants," " Tell the C.O. Geneifa we can recruit two more
officers." " Tell the head waiter at Shepheard's to keep a table
for four to-morrow night." And Mo could be relied upon to
do as he was bid, flawlessly.

Despite the prestige David had acquired from his raids, the adjutant general's office was still proving difficult. All sorts of obstacles were placed in the way of recruitment. He discovered, however, that a squadron of Free French parachutists had just arrived in Alexandria from Syria, where they had been kicking their heels for some months due to lack of equipment. He finally got permission for these men to join him—about fifty in all—which brought his numbers up to a point where operations at least were feasible.

First, however, the French had to go through the training course. The commander, Bergé, was volatile and witty; while his second-in-command, Augustin Jordan, was quiet and precise. They shared an equally passionate desire to destroy the enemy, and from the start David realised that he had acquired reinforcements of the highest order. They were fascinated by his methods and flung themselves into the explosive course with enthusiasm. David borrowed an officer from the Royal Engineers to train them. One day a jaunty figure drove up in a truck, with his cap on one side and detonators behind his ears, like cigarettes, and introduced himself as Bill Cumper, R.E. Cumper had risen from the ranks and had a superb Cockney accent and an irrepressible sense of humour. The French took to him at once and soon Kabrit resounded to the sound of his endless crashes and thuds.

One more brush with the A.G.'s office occurred on the subject of cap badges. David felt that his unit should have their own badges and wings. The reply had come that since the S.A.S. was simply a detachment, and not a regiment, it would not be proper; the men must wear the insignia of the regiments from which they had come. David tore up the letter. He was determined to give L Detachment its own identity and he promptly had cap badges designed, consisting of a winged dagger and beneath it the words, " Who Dares Wins." He also gave the men who had been on operations white berets, and when he decided they had done well enough, a pair of wings to wear on their chest.

The white berets had to be abandoned. They provoked too much bravado, which resulted in too many fights in the cafés

of Alexandria and Cairo. But the badges were worn proudly.
David even wore them into the adjutant general's office and
displayed them to the officer who had blocked his application
for authority to have them. He was severely ticked off and
told that the matter would be taken to 'the proper quarters.'
A few weeks later, however, on the steps of Shepheard's Hotel,
he ran into General Auchinleck. " Good heavens, Stirling,"
said the general, " what's that you have on?" " Our operational wings, sir," replied Stirling saluting smartly. " Well,
well," observed the general, " and very nice, too . . . very
nice, too! " The insignia of the Special Air Service had
received its official blessing! [1]

* * *

Fitzroy Maclean was one of the few British officers that
David had managed to recruit. Fitzroy had become a member
of Parliament in order to obtain his release from the Foreign
Office, and once in the House of Commons had promptly
joined the army. He had been sent to the Middle East to take
part in an adventurous 'secret' organisation which was
disbanded as soon as he arrived. He was told he was free to
return to regimental duties. Then he ran into an old friend,
Peter Stirling, a former diplomatic colleague, and soon found
himself the recipient of a warm invitation from David Stirling
to join the S.A.S. He accepted. Naturally he would have to
go through the training course; but in his spare time David
would be pleased to have him help with intelligence.

First the two men informed the Air Force that the S.A.S.
would be raiding Bouerat on the night of the 23rd-24th January.
The R.A.F. had a pre-arranged schedule of bombing during
moonless periods and Bouerat was on the list for the 22nd.
The group captain to whom David talked promised to
postpone the attack until after the S.A.S. operation. " But
stick to your date," he said, " because we can't delay more
than a day or so. We'll bomb on the 24th-25th."

Next David made contact with the Air Reconnaissance Unit
which was presided over by Peter Oldfield. Oldfield was an

[1] *The Filibusters:* John Loder.

enthusiastic supporter of the S.A.S.—indeed, eight months later he joined it himself—and he did all he could to help. He showed David pictures of Bouerat which had been taken a fortnight before. The town looked like most Arab seaside ports, with mud houses, some of them white-washed, a few large storehouses, a pier and a wireless station on the outskirts. Two tankers were anchored in the harbour. Oldfield said it was most unlikely that these ships would still be there. They slipped in and out as rapidly as possible, usually within forty-eight hours. Lately a good many petrol carriers had been reported in the vicinity of the town, and he was convinced that it was being used, not only as a refuelling point, but as one of Rommel's chief storage dumps. He would try to get photographs taken and see if he could identify the exact position of the depots.

All this, of course, would take time. Analysing aerial pictures was a slow process. He could not get the information to David before he left for Jalo, and probably not until he was on his way to Bouerat. But he would signal it to the L.R.D.G. patrol which would be conveying him across the desert. He made a note of the fact that the raid was taking place on the 22nd-23rd and could not be delayed because of the R.A.F. " You must get through to us by the 21st at the latest," said David. " Or else we may just walk by the dumps and not know they're there."

David's work was completed in Cairo by the 10th of January. But he had one task which he put off as long as possible. With the death of Jock Lewis there was no experienced officer to train the new recruits at Kabrit. No one except Paddy Mayne.

It was not easy to break the news to Paddy. David was as tactful as possible explaining that he would only be away for a few weeks.

" So you're going to leave me sitting on my backside while you hop off to Jalo and have some fun," said Paddy coldly.

He spoke as though David were about to embark on a yachting trip in the Mediterranean; and David felt as guilty as though he were.

" I'm terribly sorry. But there's no one else I can put in charge of the training. But it won't be for long. Only a few weeks. And when I return I hope to see the camp in apple-pie order and the new recruits broken in—but not broken up."

" I'll do my best, but I didn't join this unit to cool my heels in Kabrit," said Paddy dejectedly.

David succeeded in placating him a little, but not wholly. when he said good-bye he could still see a mournful look on his friend's face.

*   *   *

David left for Jalo by air with a dozen men on the 11th of January. Two days later Captain Duncan and Corporal Barr of the Special Boat Section, equipped with the necessary limpets and explosives to blow up enemy shipping, and a canvas bag containing the pieces of a portable canoe, arrived to join them. With them was an R.A.F. officer and a flight sergeant attached to Intelligence whom David had met in Cairo and casually invited to join him. The name of the officer was Derek Rawnsley and he was to make many trips with the S.A.S. in the future.

On the 17th of January the raiding party set off for Bouerat. They were escorted by a full patrol of the Long Range Desert Group which consisted of a wireless truck and six transport trucks; a patrol leader, Captain Hunter, a navigator, Mike Sadler, and twelve men who acted as drivers, mechanics, gunners and wireless operators.

Bouerat was only sixty miles west of Sirte and thirty miles from Tamit, so for most of the journey the S.A.S. men were travelling over the same terrain that they had crossed twice the previous month. They had to keep fairly far south to avoid detection by the enemy, and for the first four days saw no sign of life at all. The going varied; sometimes they were able to travel at thirty miles an hour, but the inevitable punctures and repairs slowed down their average to around a hundred miles in a long day's drive.

Before David left Jalo he had talked to Peter Oldfield, who

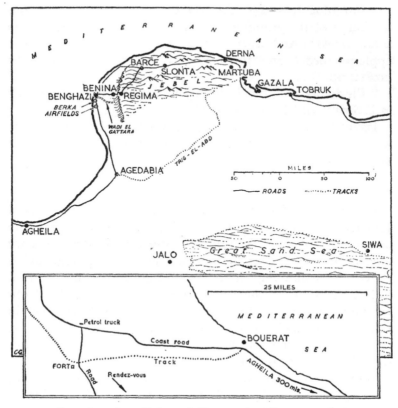

Operations from Jalo and Siwa against Bouerat and the
Benghazi area in the spring of 1942

told him that the air photographs of Bouerat had been taken
and were now in the process of being analysed. Every evening,
when L.R.D.G. Headquarters came on the air and Hunter's
wireless operators took down the messages and decoded them,
David hoped for news from Peter. But the 20th and 21st
passed and still no word.

On the evening of the 22nd the convoy reached the edge of
the Wadi Tamit as the light was fading. Because of the
growing darkness Captain Hunter decided that it would be
better to leave the descent until the morning. The men
pitched camp where they were. That night David waited

anxiously for the Headquarters transmission. At 9.30 the wireless operator picked up a signal from Siwa but after a few garbled words the transmission ended. David felt certain Oldfield must be trying to get through to him; the hours dragged by and there was no further communication.

At midnight he conferred with Captain Hunter. Siwa might be unaware that its signal had not got through; he would like to break wireless silence and radio Oldfield that no message had been received. Normally it was a small risk to take but in this particular area the enemy was known to have radio detection facilities which were constantly on the alert. However, under the circumstances Hunter agreed that it was worth taking a chance and the signal was sent. Within an hour a reply came back that the required information would be sent the following day. It was obvious that Peter had not yet been able to identify the dumps from the photographs.

The next morning, at first light, Hunter decided the party must take cover in the Wadi as rapidly as possible. Since it was likely the enemy now knew their whereabouts there was no time to search for an easy way down. They descended at a precarious point. The trucks were lined up with their bonnets pointing down the Wadi. "We then put tow ropes on the back," wrote Seekings, "so that every man except the driver and the two chaps checking the front wheels could hang on for dear life.

"We had not gone very far when the tail of our vehicle started to swing around and we could not hold it. The driver, instead of baling out, put his foot down hard. It straightened the truck and down he went at a terrifying speed. What nerves he must have had as he kept control and reached the bottom safely."

The descent was made none too soon. "An Italian recce plane came skimming over the edge of the Wadi," continued Seekings. "We sat and prayed it had not seen us but no such luck. It banked steeply and came straight for us. The rocks which I was sitting by suddenly became as small as peas. The driver of our truck jumped behind the wheel. Unfortunately someone had hung his pants over the radiator, and these caught in the fan. So he jumped off again and we scrambled for the nearest shelter."

The plane disappeared in the direction of Sirte and Tamit. The men knew that bombers or fighters would soon be over. They used their short respite to find the best cover they could. The trucks scattered wide, some of them driving four or five miles down the Wadi, until they came to suitable overhangs. Seekings and Cooper found a small cave which they settled in. "In my escape kit," said Seekings, "I had a clean set of underwear, and so as to lighten my load a little in case of a long march I thought I would have a change, forecasting that they would return as soon as I stripped off. Which they did."

There were six bombers and they flew up and down the Wadi bombing and strafing for over an hour. Then there was an hour's relief, three more bombers appeared, and it began all over again. This went on until the middle of the afternoon. At six o'clock Hunter gave the signal to reassemble. The men came out of their hiding-places in twos and threes, each little group looking surprised that the others had survived. None of the trucks was damaged and the party appeared to be wholly intact. Then it was discovered that the wireless truck and the three operators were missing. What happened to them is not known to this day. Whether they were bombed and killed, or whether they drove into the desert and were taken prisoner and later died, has never been established. The L.R.D.G. never saw them again.

The loss of wireless facilities was a serious blow to David. Any hope of last minute information from Peter was gone. Now they would just have to search for the dumps in the dark. The trucks resumed their journey and when they reached a point, three hours later, which was thirty-five miles west of the Wadi Tamit and sixty-five miles from Bouerat, they stopped and Hunter declared that this would serve as their main rendezvous. The ground was undulating and there were a few boulders which would give good shelter.

It was now 8.30 and they would have to hurry. For the next half-hour the men were busy getting their weapons ready and putting the canoe together. Bouerat was likely to be heavily patrolled and it would be impossible to use lights either on the outskirts of the town or at the water's edge. David and Duncan agreed that the best course was to carry the craft fully assembled in the back of the truck.

It was a tight squeeze, for Hunter had decided to take only one vehicle. He would drive the raiding party to within a mile of the port, and he felt that a convoy of two or three trucks might arouse unnecessary suspicion. David's party consisted of sixteen men, added to which were Hunter, Sadler, and two more of the L.R.D.G. Somehow all twenty managed to find a place, with weapons and explosives crammed in the crevices, and the canoe balanced on top of them.

It was eight forty-five when the lone vehicle set off. It had twenty-five miles of rough desert to travel before reaching the hard-surfaced road that led to the Bouerat cross-roads; once on it, they had another fifty miles to the town itself. With luck they might cover the desert drive in an hour and a half. For some time they averaged fifteen miles an hour, which was incredibly fast for night driving. David looked at his watch. It was 10.15 and he reckoned that they were within five miles of the road. " Not bad," he said to Sadler.

The words were scarcely out of his mouth when the truck gave a violent jolt as two wheels struck a sudden cavity. The men in the back were thrown on top of one another and the boat crashed against the side. There was the dreadful sound of breaking wood. A moment later the vehicle was on firm ground again, but the damage was done. The canoe was split in two.

The loss of the wireless truck had been a misfortune; this was a tragedy. The whole operation was foundering. It looked as though the weeks of preparation, the organising, the urging, the thinking, the hoping, were in vain. It is some measure of David Stirling's quality as a leader that when he spoke there was no trace of defeat in his voice. He instructed the men to remove the canoe, dismantle it and pack it up. " We will have to reorganise a little," he said. " There are plenty of targets waiting for us at Bouerat. If we can't get the ships we'll get the harbour installations instead. They're almost as important. If the enemy can't unload his supplies they'll be as useless to him as though we'd sunk them. As for you, Duncan, I think you ought to take a couple of men and go for the wireless station two miles to the other side of the town. It's a splendid target. The idea of passing it up was worrying me, but we didn't have time for both jobs."

The men climbed back in the truck laughing and joking. At least, they said, they had more room without the ' blooming canoe.' Fifteen minutes later they were approaching the road. The driver put out his lights and moved forward slowly. At last he bumped on to the tarmac. There was a sigh of relief. Now they could get up some speed.

They were heading straight for the Bouerat track which crossed their road, twenty-five miles away, and ran at right angles to them. It moved in a parallel line to the coastal highway which was five miles beyond it. They made good time and covered the distance in just over half an hour. They slowed up as they approached the cross-roads. As they did so, David noticed on the left a dark outline against the sky. He saw that it was a large fortress, no doubt built by Italians some time in the thirties. It was so silent it gave the impression of being forsaken. However, they passed it warily and a few yards later came to their turn. Now they had another twenty-seven miles to Bouerat harbour. The driver accelerated and within forty minutes Sadler said, " This is it." The truck pulled ten yards off the road and stopped.

The men could see nothing but flat fields stretching before them. Bouerat, Sadler assured them, was less than a mile away. It was a small village and the houses were clustered within a quarter of a mile of the waterfront. It was now five minutes past twelve. Hunter's deadline was two o'clock, in order to get back to the desert rendezvous before first light. That meant that David's men had exactly one hour and fifty-five minutes to accomplish their work.

Captain Duncan and Corporal Barr, accompanied by Corporal Rose of the S.A.S., started off first. Since the time was so short and they had a three mile walk it was unlikely that they would get back to the rendezvous by two. David arranged to return the next night and pick them up on the track. They arranged to leave stones and twigs at a point eight miles from Bouerat.

David divided the remaining men into two groups of six and seven each. One lot would come with him; the other would go with Sergeant-Major Riley. They would start off within five minutes of each other and approach the harbour from opposite sides. When they had finished their work they would return to the rendezvous. David emphasised the fact that stealth was essential. No one was to use a gun unless absolutely necessary. They were to set all their explosions for 2.30, which would give them plenty of time to get away. This meant starting with two-hour time fuses and shortening them as the minutes passed.

David's group set off first. It was painfully quiet. They began walking across rough desert, which gradually gave way to cultivated fields. They had been keeping fairly close to the road; now they moved away from it, in an arc, to circumvent the village and approach the harbour from the beach. Soon they would make out the shapes of houses. The village was completely dark, and the night so silent the softest footsteps seemed to echo.

The men followed David in single file. They were near the edge of the water now, and he turned along a narrow path with a house on one side and a building on the other. It was obvious that they were close to the quay and he moved cautiously. Any moment they might find themselves coming up against wire and a guard post. He stopped and listened for the sound of pacing steps. He could hear nothing. He led them past the building and to the left. A moment later they were on the pier. They paused to take their bearings. There were quays on either side of the harbour with warehouses stretched along them. First they would walk the length of the jetty and mark out their targets.

David motioned the men to follow him. They kept well into the lee of the buildings. There seemed to be no guards and no defence of any kind. The port appeared completely dead. The only sound was an occasional gentle lap as the water caressed the wooden posts of the jetty. A few fishing-boats were tied alongside, but there was not a sign of a ship on the water.

Peter Oldfield had told David that tankers slipped in and out within a few hours. This was an off-night. David could smell oil, and he had a feeling that a fuel ship had pulled out that very afternoon. It would explain why everyone felt entitled to a good rest. At least it made him feel better about the canoe. Even if it had escaped damage it would have been of little use.

Having finished this reconnaissance, he divided his men into two groups. One lot would stay posted outside the warehouse, while the other lot went inside and deposited the bombs. The first building was unlocked. David and two men walked in to find a large and complicated piece of machinery standing in the middle of the room. From the feel of it they decided it must be some sort of pumping equipment. They placed several bombs on it, and distributed a few more around the room for good measure.

The next building was locked. Fortunately it had a window which was not difficult to open, and they climbed through it. This time David risked flashing his torch. The room was crammed with wooden crates and boxes containing army food rations. Some of the crates went almost to the ceiling. This was a splendid target. The men grinned happily as they walked down the narrow lanes between the boxes leaving their bombs.

They went into three more storehouses. One was empty, another had more machinery, and the third further stores of tinned food. In the last building David discovered a side door and decided to see where it led. It was bolted and he pushed it open. He found himself in a small alleyway running between two buildings. He turned left and headed back to the pier. Another alley ran at right angles and he slipped along it to see if anything lay at the end. He walked stealthily and as he neared the corner he heard a faint rustle. Someone was approaching.

He pulled himself close to the wall and stood perfectly still.

A moment later a figure turned the corner and a body pushed against him.

" What the hell . . ." said a startled voice. It took a few shocked seconds to realise it was none other than Sergeant Riley. " What the blazes are you doing here? You're supposed to be on the other side of the wharf," swore David. Six more men came out of the shadows—the rest of Riley's party.

Riley whispered that they'd finished their work—another food dump, more machinery and a workshop—but that they had suddenly come up against wire and could not find their way out. They were afraid of bumping into a guard post so they had decided to try this side of the harbour.

David told them to wait until his own group got moving. They would make their way back to the rendezvous independently. He went back to the quay, signalled his men and started off. He instructed everyone to keep his eyes strained for anything that looked like a petrol depot, although he felt the chances of discovering an underground dump in the dark were fairly slim. This time he did not lead them in such a wide arc but stayed closer to the main road. When they were less than a quarter of a mile from the rendezvous Corporal Seekings touched his arm and whispered, " Look over there, sir."

At first David thought he must have spotted a dump, but it turned out to be something else. Close to the road, about fifty yards away, were a dozen or more hulking shapes. They looked like a colony of houses but the shapes were too strange for that. The men moved forward to explore, and a minute later found themselves in the middle of an enormous car park. On it were three or four rows of giant petrol carriers. Each had a haulage capacity of twenty tons which meant it would carry four thousand gallons of fuel. And judging from the smell, they were not empty. No doubt they had been filled that very afternoon and were waiting for delivery instructions.

It was too good to be true. This was compensation for the disappointment of not getting Peter's message. Quickly they went to work. The carriers were parked in six rows of three each. They deposited nine bombs in five minutes. They used

one-hour fuses as it was nearly half-past one. David adjusted
the tenth bomb. His men were behind him and he moved
noiselessly across the back of one of the carriers and around it.
He heard a step and before he had time to draw back felt the
impact of a shoulder against him.

For the second time there was a deadly moment of stunned
surprise. And for the second time it was Sergeant-Major Riley.
The situation was so comical David did his best not to laugh
out loud. Riley had come along on the opposite side of the
road, spotted the car park and crossed over. He had been
working one end while David's group had been concentrating
on the other. " I'm glad to see that at least you've learned to
walk quietly," said David acidly. " From now on we'd better
keep together. The rendezvous is only five minutes away."

There was one last bomb to attach before the men returned
to the track. It was 1.45 when they reached it. Hunter
reported absolute quiet; he had seen no movement of any
kind. Riley, on the other hand, had discovered an anti-
aircraft gun emplacement. He had managed to shove a bomb
up the breech although the crew was sleeping in a tent only
a few yards away.

Duncan and his two men had not returned. David peered
in the direction of the wireless station hoping to see their
figures emerging from the darkness. A light flashed half a
mile away. This was followed by another flash and still
another. He wondered whether it was a signal; perhaps
Duncan had run into trouble. There was still fifteen minutes
before Hunter's deadline. He motioned Cooper and Seekings
to follow him. They walked fast and reached the spot in
seven or eight minutes. Once again they found themselves in
a car park. This time there were no petrol carriers, only
supply trucks. David told Seekings and Cooper to stand guard
while he placed the bombs. There were twelve lorries and it
took him less than five minutes to complete his work. The
three men returned to the rendezvous at six minutes past two.

Hunter could not wait any longer. They would have to
return the following night to pick up Duncan. They reached
the cross-roads, and drove past the fort, which was as dark

and silent as ever, at exactly two thirty-five. A few minutes later they heard an explosion, then another and another; by the time they turned off on to the desert the sky was turning a pale grey-pink. " Too bad we can't be there to see it," sighed Seekings.

They were tired but satisfied. The operation which at one moment had seemed doomed to failure had turned into a triumph. Rommel was desperately short of petrol carriers, and they were not easy things to replace. The amount of shipping required to transport them across the sea would add consider-ably to the Axis burden. David felt that he had struck a real blow. The harbour would be unusable for many weeks, and if Duncan succeeded in his task, Bouerat would cease to be one of the chief transmitting centres on the coast for some time to come.

They reached the rendezvous at five o'clock and drank coffee with plenty of brandy in it.

*   *   *

As soon as dawn broke everyone took cover. They knew their work was well done, and that reconnaissance planes soon would be scouring the desert in search of them. Shortly after first light they heard the sound of an engine; from then on until noon there was scarcely a moment without a plane over-head. The L.R.D.G. trucks were draped with nets and were impossible to distinguish from the patches of surrounding scrub.

At lunch time the sky clouded over, and the wind started to rise. It was the beginning of a sandstorm. These storms were the dread of most raiding parties as the sand penetrated the crevices of revolvers and tommy-guns and rendered them useless. However, on this occasion, with the main task accom-plished, the storm was almost welcome. At least it meant there was no more danger of being spotted from the air.

At seven that evening the storm began to die down. David waited until nine o'clock, when it was not much more than a strong, dust-choked wind, before leaving with Hunter to pick up Duncan and his two colleagues, Barr and Rose. He took a handful of men—Riley, Seekings, Cooper and a few others to deal with any opposition that might arise. "Johnny and I had a most unpleasant ride," wrote Seekings. " In case road blocks had been set up it was decided that we two would lie on the wings of the truck with our tommies at the ready. Also it was easy to slide off and use our knives if necessary."

However, these precautions were unnecessary. Once again the truck passed the silent fort, turned abruptly to the right and travelled along the Bouerat track that ran parallel to the coast road. After two miles it came to a halt. A few hundred yards ahead lay a little pile of sticks; the sign that Duncan was in the vicinity. David jumped off the truck and called to him. Twenty yards away three shapes emerged and came running towards them. "Well done!" said David. "Hop aboard. Did you smash up the wireless station?" Duncan nodded.

The driver paused a few seconds so that the men could hear his news. His group had lost its way to the wireless station and had not reached it until after one o'clock. They were just setting about their task when one of them bumped into an empty Jerrycan. A moment later two sentries came out of a nearby building and tried to see where the noise had come from. After a desultory search they stood talking. Finally they went inside. Duncan felt it would not be wise to alert them again so he and his two companions moved with great caution. As a result it took them a long time to place their charges, which amounted to thirty pounds of T.N.T. He set two-hour time fuses and did not finish the job until nearly two. When he reached the rendezvous at 2.30 it was deserted.

Then the quiet was broken by large explosions from the harbour. They were much too close to the port for their liking so began to walk to the second rendezvous (where they were now) which was eight miles away. They kept well away from the road and during the next two hours heard several trucks racing past—no doubt full of soldiers hastening to put out the fires. In the meantime there were more explosions not far from the place they had just abandoned. The blaze was so great the whole sky was lighted up for half an hour. "We couldn't think what you'd been up to," said Duncan. "It

looked as though you'd set fire to a whole fleet of tankers."
" Petrol bowsers," explained David. " The next best thing."
" When we reached this rendezvous," Duncan went on, " we
heard the wireless installations go off. There's no doubt about
it. The enemy had a pretty sticky night."

At first light, continued Duncan, they found a small cave
in the side of a sandy bank where they hid during the day. In
the morning several patrols of armoured cars moved across
country, obviously in search of the raiders. " And now," said
Duncan, " to bring the story up to date the R.A.F. came over
at ten to-night and pasted the harbour for twenty minutes then
flew away. The truth is I don't think there was much left to
bomb."

*   *   *

All this was most satisfactory. Now for the business of the
moment. David told the men that he thought it would be a
shame to move out of the area without leaving a bomb anywhere; so he suggested they cut across to the coast road, turn
left, away from Bouerat, and drive along it until they reached
the right-angle road that led past the fort and the desert. It
was not out of their way and they might find a worthwhile
target.

' Flash ' Gibson was driving with Hunter and David beside
him. The rest of the men were in the back with their guns at
the ready. They bumped over five miles of rough desert before
they reached the coast road. Then they turned left and travelled
away from Bouerat. They drove for eighteen miles without
seeing a single enemy vehicle. It was bitterly cold and there
was still a strong wind blowing. They slowed down as they
approached the point where the desert road joined the coast
road. Gibson was just about to make a turn when he saw a
large shape parked by the side of the road. He pulled up and
David and Hunter hopped out to take a look at it. It was
another giant petrol carrier—the same sort they had destroyed
the night before. It appeared to be abandoned. " It would be
unforgivable to pass this up," said David. " I'm sure the
Long Range Desert Group would like to see a demonstration

of our work. Besides, it's a cold night and you might like to warm your hands."

The truck moved a safe distance away and Seekings climbed out and adjusted a bomb with a ten-second fuse. He placed it on the monster's petrol tank and ran as fast as he could. Nothing happened. " Major Stirling and I went back to the petrol bowser to see what was wrong," wrote Seekings. " As soon as the C.O. picked up the bomb off went the time-pencil. Although we had ten seconds to spare, we dropped the damn' thing and dived across the road to cover. The bomb went off in the road with a terrific bang.

" What happened then was very funny. The door of the cab flew open and out hopped a tiny Italian half-dressed and wearing only one boot. I used a tommy-gun from the shoulder and taking careful aim fired and missed. The Italian then ran direct to us calling on his mother and the saints for mercy. He dropped on his knees, clasping his arms round my legs. He got more terrified when the rest of the patrol came up. I don't think any one of us was under six feet tall, and with our extra clothing and beards it is a wonder we did not frighten him to death."

While this was going on, David placed another bomb with a ten-second fuse on the petrol tank shouting, " Take cover." The Italian driver bolted into the darkness and Seekings and the rest of the patrol ran for their truck. This time the explosion came off as planned and the Lancia seemed to melt away in the huge fire. The men watched their handiwork admiringly then continued their journey.

Probably fifteen minutes had elapsed between the explosion and the moment they approached the fort, which was eight miles away. They saw the dark, silent stronghold, silhouetted against the sky, ahead of them. Suddenly they heard a click and saw a piece of metal spinning in the air. It was a telemine that did not explode. Almost at the same moment shadows loomed up ahead on both sides of the road. They were heading straight into an ambush. David shouted at Gibson, the driver, to swerve off the track, but instead he put his foot on the accelerator. Both Cooper and Seekings were standing in the back of the truck with their tommy-guns poised. They fired point-blank into the enemy. The truck roared through a curtain of machine-gun bullets, running down three or four screaming Italians. Several grenades exploded in mid-air. " As an ambush it should have been a dead-cert, but no one on our side got a scratch," wrote Bennett laconically.[1]

The raiding party continued to career down the road at top speed. When the men had time to collect their thoughts they realised that the fort had never been the deserted bastion they had supposed. No doubt the soldiers and armoured patrols that Duncan had seen the previous night had been supplied by it.

The enemy had probably heard the L.R.D.G. truck pass an hour previously; perhaps a lookout was keeping watch on the road. When the petrol carrier went up on the coast road, eight miles away, the garrison could not have failed to see the fire. This had given it time to establish an ambush.

Even now David's party could scarcely believe its incredible luck in getting away safely. " Not even a ruddy tyre punctured," crowed Seekings in delight. Once again the party arrived at the main rendezvous in time for breakfast.

* * *

The men kept under cover the following day while more recce planes came out and searched for them. At nightfall they started back to Jalo. David took stock of his operation; he still could not understand why the harbour was so deserted. In view of the fact that Rommel had lost the use of Benghazi why were the Bouerat installations not being strengthened?

What he did not know was that Rommel had no intention of being deprived of the use of Benghazi for long. Indeed, at that very moment Benghazi was changing hands again. On January the 12th, the date that David had left Cairo and flown to Jalo, Rommel's line was stabilised in the Mersa el Brega-Agheila area, south of Benghazi. On that day Auchinleck had wired Winston Churchill, " Evidence as to enemy weakness and disorganisation is growing daily."

---

[1] Gibson received the Military Medal for his cool action.

For the next nine days Rommel remained motionless; then on January the 21st, the day before David broke wireless silence to ask Oldfield for information about the Bouerat petrol dumps, he launched his counter-attack. He took his opponents completely by surprise; eight days later he not only had regained Benghazi but the greater part of Cyrenaica. The Eighth Army dug in in the neighbourhood of Gazala.

During the five days from January the 26th to the 31st, the time that it took David and his raiding party to return to Jalo from Bouerat, the battle was at its height. Without wireless, the convoy had no idea what was happening. It was not until the 30th, when Hunter managed to get a B.B.C. news relay on his civilian receiving set, that they learned with dismay that the Eighth Army was in rapid retreat. " Perhaps we've lost Jalo," said David. " We must approach it carefully."

*   *   *

David was right to be wary. The Long Range Desert Group had already abandoned Jalo, and it was only a question of hours before the enemy swept in. This withdrawal was particularly galling for the L.R.D.G. leaders, as only a few weeks previously, when Auchinleck's victory seemed secure, they had sent a lavish amount of war material to the oasis. They had managed to evacuate some of it, but large quantities of enemy supplies, which they had captured in November, and were hoping to use, had to be forsaken. All they could do was to delegate Captain Timpson of G.2 patrol to stay behind and destroy the dumps. He was also instructed to keep an eye out for Hunter and Stirling. However, the fact that nothing had been heard from Hunter's wireless for nearly ten days might mean that the raiders had been killed or captured; and Timpson was told not to wait after he had completed his demolition operation.

This took several days. " At last we seemed to have destroyed all that was feasible to disintegrate," he wrote in his diary. " Even the wells not required for the use of the villagers were filled with Italian ammunition, and redundant jars of sulphuric acid were poured over the contents. Crowbars and burning oil finished off the last of the old Italian Lancias; and the last of the bomb dumps, our most difficult subjects, had gone up in a pillar of smoke and dust. So now we could move away from the fort, where we might have been trapped, and take up our watch for Hunter's patrol among some bushes at Es-Sherif, the extreme north-west corner of the oasis. Here, moreover, there was good water, whereas the water in the main village was poor, and the natives here were less demoralised, for they willingly brought us eggs and vegetables in exchange for tinned fish and biscuits. From this hiding-place we patrolled round the oasis, occasionally returning to the Fort and assuring the natives there that our withdrawal was only temporary and entirely offensive in nature.

"Barber, the signaller, played a fair hand at Bridge; Corporal Stocker knew at least the rudiments of Contract. The difficulty was always to find a fourth. Whenever we got down to initiating a novice something unexpected always happened. On this occasion Guardsman Scourey was making good progress; and we had got to the stage of no longer showing everyone our own hands, when the lookout in the crow's nest up a palm tree called, " Truck ahoy! on a bearing of 230°, heading north-east." The truck was all alone, and it was passing rapidly to our south. So, collecting dummy's hand and all dismantled equipment, half of our force of eleven trucks (we had appropriated that which it seemed a pity to destroy) chased off round the edge of the oasis and came up with the solitary truck soon after it had reached the fort. In it were David Stirling, Antony Hunter, Derek Rawnsley, and others; in fact an advance party of the expected patrol, who had taken the precaution of leaving the other trucks some miles away."

*   *   *

Captain Timpson's account of the meeting does not do it full justice. As the S.A.S. truck approached Jalo the atmosphere looked suspicious. David could see no sign of life and wondered if an enemy ambush were awaiting them. " We were feeling trigger happy," wrote Seekings. " On entering the Fort we found that the L.R.D.G. had pulled out. Good for us, they had left supplies and we were busy wolfing them. As we were drinking a tin of milk we heard the sound of a truck. Away went the milk and we made a dash for our truck and our guns. Cooper and I had got behind our tommies when the leading truck (L.R.D.G.) drove around the corner. It was the very last second before we recognised each other. It made us all feel a bit weak around the knees."

Seekings omits to say that bullets were only one of the dangers. Timpson arrived not a moment too soon. He had amused himself during the previous week by placing all kinds of booby traps in the canteen; indeed the can of milk that Seekings drank was one of the few articles that did not have an explosive attached to it.

That night the men set out for Siwa.

CHAPTER SEVEN

BENGHAZI HARBOUR

DAVID RETURNED to the base at Kabrit to find that Paddy
Mayne had built himself a giant bed and retired to it. He had
tried to do as David had instructed and supervise the training
of the new recruits, but every time he thought of the raiding
party, far away from red tape and boring organisation details,
having the supreme pleasure of coming into contact with the
enemy, his resentment rose. He was deeply distressed by the
fact that his friend, McGonigal had not been heard of since
the first disastrous S.A.S. raid,[1] and it made him more frantic
than ever to get into action. The more he thought about
it the more convinced he was that he was being treated
unfairly.

A few days after David's departure he detailed one of the
sergeants to see that the newcomers were put through their
paces properly, and went to bed. First, he constructed the bed.
It was six feet wide with a base made out of barrels and covered
with the large stuffed mats used to break practice parachute
falls. He then settled down with a series of Penguins. Sometimes he would hardly speak for days; at other times he would
emerge and join the sergeants at the bar. He could be
tremendously convivial when he was so inclined, and might
stay up late laughing and talking and drinking. Sergeant
Bennett wrote that " the session would go on until Paddy

---

[1] There was no trace of McGonigal's group until the 8th Army went into
Gazala in January. Then a story gained currency that a British raiding party
had attacked one of the Gazala landing grounds in November and destroyed a
number of planes. Stirling believes this must have been McGonigal's party,
although he has never been able to track down or confirm the report.

would look at his watch and say, ' Call me sir. It is now Reveille.' "

When Paddy heard the wireless reports of Rommel's counter-attack he grew more disgruntled than ever. It seemed incredible that the fruits of Auchinleck's long-planned offensive, which had been so bountiful in December, were now entirely gone. Rommel had regained almost every piece of lost ground including Benghazi.

When David returned to Kabrit he was furious to find that Paddy had thrown in his hand. The two men had angry words; but at the end of the altercation both had a much clearer understanding of the other. Paddy saw that although David was some years his junior his orders were not to be disobeyed; and David saw that it was a prime mistake to try and turn a brilliant combatant into a desk-chair administrator. From this moment on the two men became the best of friends.

David appointed Sergeant-Major Riley to supervise the training. The French squadron was half-way through the course. Despite the fact that they had all been through the parachute school at Ringway they had flung themselves into S.A.S. methods with alacrity. However, they told David that they regretted the departure of Bill Cumper, who had only been assigned to them for two weeks. His Cockney accent and his sharp wit, far from proving unintelligible, had delighted and amused them, and they longed to have him back. David decided that Cumper was the man to take permanent charge of the sabotage course at Kabrit. After much difficulty he tracked him down; he had been sent to supervise the sanitary fittings of a military hospital in Alexandria. A few days later Cumper was a full fledged member of the S.A.S.; and a few months later he was acknowledged by the Royal Engineers as the best explosives officer in the Middle East.

*   *   *

Now for the planning of the raids. The S.A.S. could only operate in the moonless period, so the next assaults would take place early in March. David gathered from Headquarters that Auchinleck was consolidating his position on the Gazala line, and was not going to attempt an offensive until he had built up substantial reserve, which would take some months. This meant that the string of airfields in the Benghazi area would be the most important targets. Soon a schedule was worked out; the raids would take place between the 8th and the 13th of March. Bill Fraser would take a patrol of three or four men to Barce; Lieutenant Dodds, a new officer, would go to Slonta; and Paddy and David would tackle Berka satellite and Benina, two airfields in the immediate vicinity of Benghazi.

David had another plan up his sleeve. He lunched with Brigadier Marriott in Cairo and told him about it. While he was in the Benghazi area he had decided to have a crack at the harbour. Marriott assumed he was thinking of a sea-borne commando raid. " Oh no," said David, " I thought I'd take a couple of chaps from the Special Boat Section and drive in."

Marriott had no first-hand experience of Benghazi, but he knew it well from studying maps. He was in command of the 22nd Guards Brigade which had joined up with Brigadier Reid's ' E ' Force at Agedabia in the hope of cutting off Rommel's forces when they retreated from the Benghazi area.

" What on earth makes you think you can drive in? "

David pointed out that he had had no trouble getting in to Bouerat harbour.

" But Bouerat's an entirely different proposition," Marriott argued. " It's small, and not nearly so important. Benghazi is the prize of the Cyrenaican seaboard. It's a large town with shops and buses and cinemas. That means it's fairly well organised and policed. You can't imagine for one moment that there aren't a good many roadblocks on the way in. What'll you do when you're challenged? "

" I haven't worked it out," said David, " but I think it's worth trying."

" And the harbour," Marriott continued. " That's bound to be patrolled. Not to mention the wire."

Nothing that Marriott could say would dissuade David; indeed it increased his determination. " Who do you think would be a good guide to Benghazi? " David persisted, " I want someone who knows the city well."

Marriott saw that there was no point in trying to argue any further, so once again he gave him sympathetic co-operation. " I was talking to a chap called Alston the other day who, I believe, went into Benghazi as one of our Intelligence officers. Someone told me he was jolly good. I think he's with the Middle East Commandos now. I should think he's just the sort of person you're looking for. Furthermore," continued Marriott, " you ought to study the model of Benghazi that's at Naval Intelligence Headquarters at Alexandria. It's a wooden model, quite an accurate reconstruction. It will give you a pretty good idea of the harbour perimeter and the buildings round the jetty."

*   *   *

David's desire to attack shipping in Benghazi harbour was not merely bravado. He felt that the ' management,' as he put it, was not yet alive to or fully aware of the type of warfare he was trying to establish. They still clung to the old-fashioned principle of massing troops and fighting out a set-piece battle. David believed more strongly than ever that in a highly mechanised war with troops utterly dependent on petrol, machinery repair bases, and ammunition dumps, blows could be delivered to the enemy's supply lines just as telling as fighting whole battles.

If he had been given his way he would have liked to see five hundred specially trained men raiding the enemy's supply lines mercilessly, all along the coast. If the enemy had to guard the whole length of his supply line they would have to cut down drastically on their front line troops; and if his supplies were systematically destroyed it would be difficult for him to fight any battles at all. But since this would mean establishing a permanent base in the desert, supplied by air, David realised that this thinking was far too revolutionary to be adopted wholeheartedly. He had to be content with what he could get. Nevertheless if he could show them that the S.A.S. was able not only to destroy aircraft but to sink shipping, blow up storage depots, establish roadblocks and interfere for days at a time with transport, he would have accomplished something.

This is what made him so determined to go on with his Benghazi scheme. He had no trouble persuading Gordon Alston to come with him. Alston was a young dark-haired soldier with twinkling eyes and a strong sense of adventure. He thought the expedition sounded ' amusing.' Next David tackled the Special Boat Section, who assigned several men to him, among them Lieutenant David Sutherland and Captain Ken Allot. Thirdly, he secured the services of Bob Melot, a Belgian business man who before the war had worked in the cotton business in Alexandria and was now helping the British Intelligence Service. Melot was an expert Arabist and suggested taking two Senussi soldiers to the Benghazi escarpment with him, so that he could send them to reconnoitre the approaches to the town.

An operation in the Benghazi area had certain advantages. In the first place the rear base, Siwa, was an improvement on Jalo. Siwa was a large, attractive oasis on the edge of the Qattara Depression. It had a good many villages, clear bubbling springs, a few European houses, and miles of olive groves and luxurious green date palms—not the scraggly windswept variety that distinguished Jalo. The L.R.D.G. had established their base here which meant that the S.A.S. always had a chance to swim in ' Cleopatra's Pool ' on their way to and from operations.

The expedition set forth in the early hours of 15th March. It was taken to its destination by the second Rhodesian Long Range patrol led by Lieutenant John Olivey. David Stirling, Paddy Mayne and Bob Melot travelled in a Ford utility wagon which David had appropriated in Cairo, and had disguised to resemble a German staff car. The top and sides had been removed, which gave it more speed, and also meant that there were no windows for the sun to glint upon, betraying its presence to enemy aircraft. Four machine-guns were mounted on it, front and back. It was painted dark grey and bore a German recognition signal. Gordon Alston and Lieutenant

David Sutherland followed in the real thing—a captured German staff car.

The distance from Siwa to the Benghazi area was nearly four hundred miles. The going was fairly smooth until the party reached the Trig el Abd. This was an old caravan trail which ran from the coast to the interior. It was a mass of tracks covering a fairly wide area, and in order to make it unusable the enemy had scattered thousands of Thermos mines along it, which lay half-hidden beneath the sand. One of these mines had enough power to damage a car and injure its occupants. Indeed as the convoy passed gingerly over this ground they had a casualty; the German staff car blew up and Lieutenant Sutherland was wounded in the hand. He and Sergeant Moss had to be taken back to Siwa by one of the Long Range trucks.

There was a feature in the Benghazi area which helped the raiders. The Jebel range of mountains lay forty miles south-east of the city. Its foothills rolled some twenty-five miles to an escarpment about five hundred feet high. This escarpment overlooked a plain that stretched another sixteen miles to the Mediterranean—and Benghazi.

The foothills offered an ideal hiding-place. They attracted some rain, which meant that the dull greys and tans of the desert gave way to thick dark scrub, stunted trees and hills with brown and green patches. The region was populated by Bedouin Arabs of the Senussi sect who wandered over the hills tending flocks of sheep. The Senussi were bitter enemies of the Italians and could usually be trusted not to give away the presence of English soldiers. So when the S.A.S. reached the Jebel the men felt that they were on 'home' territory.

They established a rendezvous in a small ravine. Melot sent his two Arab soldiers out to make a reconnaissance. Paddy Mayne, who was not going with David to the harbour, took two men and set forth to carry out a raid on Berka airfield just south of Benghazi. To those left at the rendezvous, life in the Jebel seemed as carefree as a camping expedition. For once there was the shade of trees, and plenty of water from nearby wells. In the afternoon an Arab shepherd appeared in the ravine, and after much bargaining, sold them a sheep which they roasted that night over an open fire.

The Senussi soldiers returned the next day and reported that there was no road block along the main road. This road ran from Benghazi, across the plain and up the escarpment, to the town of Regima. In the afternoon of the following day the party set forth. It consisted of David, Gordon Alston, Ken Allott, two corporals from the Special Boat Section and Corporals Cooper and Seekings of the S.A.S. The six men rode together in David's cut-down staff car. The L.R.D.G. led them as far as the Regima-Benghazi road. Olivey would wait for them at the rendezvous where he hoped to see them before first light in the morning. [1]

The road had a hard surface and David drove down the escarpment with ease. Although it was now dark and the starlit sky was beginning to cloud they passed groups of Arabs coming home from the fields. At last the expedition to Benghazi was on its way.

For a project which was described at Headquarters as ' hare-brained ' and even ' suicidal ' it was one of the most uneventful adventures of David's career. The Arabs were right; there were no road-blocks and the car swept along the smooth macadam road at seventy miles an hour, its lights full on. The occupants had their guns at the ready, but no one seemed in the least interested in their presence. As they reached the outskirts of the city they slowed down. They passed through the narrow streets of the Arab quarters, which gradually gave way to a thoroughfare with European buildings as they approached the waterfront.

The harbour area was wired off and guarded. David's plan was to launch their boat outside the wire. It would make its way around the breakwater and move into the harbour through a breach, made by bombing, in the outside wall. The car pulled up in front of a bombed-out yard about half a mile from the water's edge. David left Cooper and Seekings to park it inconspicuously behind the debris. He and Alston, Allot and his two corporals, walked along the narrow back-

[1] On the way back he laid some charges on the Barce-Benghazi railway line.

street single file. It was fairly cold as a strong wind was
blowing. It was about midnight. Because of repeated attacks
by the R.A.F. Benghazi had a curfew and rigid black-out
regulations. There was no movement and no light. Only the
wind broke the silence.

The men strode along, their ears strained to every sound.
A howl rent the air. A cat, its eyes gleaming like torches, leapt
across their path. Then came a sudden clatter as someone
banged a window over their heads. At the water's edge the
wind seemed almost a gale. The water crashed noisily against
the side of the jetty, and the men could see whitecaps dancing
out to sea. The sergeant put down the bag containing the
unassembled canoe. This time David had taken no chances.
He would not risk damage by putting it together a moment
before it was needed.

When Allot felt the force of the wind and saw the choppy
water, he shook his head dolefully at David. Canoes were not
made for rough water. " Won't get more than a few yards on
a sea like this," he murmured. David could make out the
shapes of several shadowy hulls only a hundred yards away in
the inner harbour. " Assemble it anyway," replied David.
" We've plenty of time. Maybe the wind will drop in the next
hour or so."

David instructed Alston to keep guard while the men were
working. He would take a quick recce around the harbour.
He did not walk close to the wire as he knew there would be
sentry posts, but he cut through a back street which ran
parallel, and walked along it to the other side. Every now and
then he passed yawning craters where the R.A.F. had dropped
bombs wide of the mark. Most of the buildings were workshops and warehouses. Then he turned down one of the streets
approaching the wire perimeter. He had not gone more than
a few yards before he heard footsteps. Because of the curfew
it must be a soldier or a policeman. He stood perfectly still,
drawn up against a wall. The form came nearer and suddenly
lurched past him. As it did so, David smelled the fumes of
alcohol. A few seconds later the man burst into a loud and
passionate Italian love song. Just a reveller who refused to let

the war spoil his fun. Luckily the wind drowned some of the noise and David moved on quickly. There was something reassuring, he felt, about meeting a midnight drunk in Benghazi.

He had no other encounters. His recce took about an hour. He managed to find out that, apart from the main gate leading through the wire, there was a side entrance with a guard post. But the sentry apparently had a section to patrol as no one seemed to be about.

He returned to where he had left the others. Allot was trying to put the boat together. David did not know much about these canoes, but a vital part was damaged and would not fit into another vital part. It was half-assembled but could not be completed. However, it was obvious that even if the men managed to make it serviceable, it was not going to be of much use. Instead of the wind dropping, it seemed to be gathering velocity. The harbour resounded to the noise of rattling windows, the scraping of tin-foil and debris, and the din of empty cans being blown through the night. The water was beating up against the pier furiously; and stray cats seemed to be trying to compete with the confusion by howling more mournfully than ever.

David agreed there was nothing to do but give it up. He would not leave any explosives. There were no worthwhile targets at hand; besides he might want to pay a return visit and it was better not to arouse the enemy's vigilance. He gave a last, longing look at the shapes in the harbour while Allot put the limpets back in his bag and the sergeant packed up the canoe. They trudged despondently back to the car. Seekings was asleep, and Cooper, who was on the watch, was plainly disappointed at the lack of excitement.

" Did you see anyone? " David asked.

" Only one man who leaned out of the window and asked what we were doing, sir," said Cooper in a voice of some disappointment. " We told him to fade, and he disappeared as good as gold. I'm afraid," continued Cooper, " that there's not much night life in Benghazi, sir. Completely dead. Can't say it would be my choice of a place to live."

" Nor mine either," interposed Seekings. " Look sir, what's that? " Flames were leaping up against the sky half a mile away. David was astonished. " It's not our doing," he said. " Obviously," chipped in Cooper, " someone's dropped a match."

The mystery of the burning building was never solved. British aircraft reported it, and Headquarters believed it to be David's work. He denied all knowledge of it.

" Perhaps you're right," he said to Cooper as he climbed into the car. " One's forgotten that fires aren't always intentional."

Soon they were speeding across the plain. Suddenly the vehicle swerved and David jammed on the brakes. " Flat tyre." Cooper and Seekings got out quickly and changed it.

An hour before first light they were back at the rendezvous.

*   *   *

The attempt on the harbour was only part of David's activities that week. He went down to Benina airfield twice, once to find it deserted, another time to find dummy aircraft on it. However he blew up a small dump of aerial torpedoes, and did a reconnaissance which was to prove useful in a few weeks' time. It was heavily guarded and he discovered that it was one of the Germans' chief repair depots.

The others were equally unlucky as far as aircraft was concerned. Dodds was unable to get on to Slonta because of the heavy defences; Alston lost his way to Berka main and never got there; Fraser found only one aircraft and eight repair wagons on Barce which he demolished.

Only Paddy Mayne was wholly successful. He blew up fifteen planes on Berka satellite. On the way back he got lost, and finally took refuge in an Arab camp. He knew that the L.R.D.G. could only wait for a limited time before returning to Siwa, and he and his two companions had visions of a long walk across the desert to British lines.

But he was lucky. This is the letter he wrote to his brother, Douglas Mayne, describing what happened. " At the moment I am about fifteen miles from Benghazi, so I won't be able to post this for some time. We did a raid on the local aerodrome three nights ago and one of the party hasn't returned yet so we are waiting for him.

" It's very pleasant country here, great change after the desert. Some of the people who know the South Downs say that it is very like it—low hills and valleys, lots of wild flowers and long grass. It is like a picnic—only annoying thing is the Jerry planes flying about, but we are well camouflaged.

" Luckily the Italians treat the Senussi very badly and so they will do anything to help us. The day and night after the raid we couldn't find our rendezvous. The maps are awful. We had been walking from 1.30 a.m. to seven o'clock the next night and couldn't find the damned place anywhere. We must have covered about fifty miles, first of all getting to the aerodrome and then coming away.

" It was no good walking round in circles in the dark. I more or less reconciled myself to a two hundred and fifty mile walk to Tobruk and so we (three of us, two corporals and myself) went to the nearest Senussi camp for some water and, if possible, a blanket.

" The Senussi were very suspicious at first but once they were sure that we were ' Englesi ' everything changed and we were ushered into one of the tents, our equipment brought in, blankets put down for a bed.

" There was a fire just outside the door and everyone crowded in. First of all they boiled us some eggs which were damned good and then platters of dates and bowls of water and a huge gourd of goat's milk was brought in. I think that the form with this is that they never wash the gourd and the sourer it gets the better they like it and I think that they must have liked this stuff very well! "

The party went on for some time and finally everyone went to bed. Paddy lay awake wondering how to solve the problem of finding his way back to the S.A.S. meeting-place. " And now listen to this," his letter continues, " and never disbelieve in ' luck ' again or coincidence, or whatever you like to call it. The men who were waiting for us at the rendezvous—and they would have left next morning—had got a chicken which they had bartered for some sugar. They wanted it cooked and they had an English-speaking Arab with them, so they sent him to get it cooked. In that area there must have been thirty or forty different encampments spread over the three odd miles we were from each other and he picked the one that we were lying in to come to—and so we won't have to footslog it across the desert!

"We have been here now for two days and the trucks for three and I imagine that every Arab for miles knows where we are and not one of them would go down and tell the Jerries or Eyeties where we are. . . . All the best, Blair." [1]

*   *   *

David, for his part, was determined to make yet a third attempt to blow up enemy shipping. He had proved that it was possible to reach the harbour without detection. His two previous efforts had been thwarted by broken or unworkable boats. This time he would leave nothing to chance. Fitzroy Maclean had completed his training, and struck David as a highly competent soldier. He would put him in charge of the boat, and take him along to work it. "I don't care what type you choose," said David, "just so long as it works. And of course it mustn't take up too much room."

Fitzroy gave considerable thought to the problem. "First," he wrote, "I borrowed a selection of R.A.F. rubber dinghies from a thoroughly mystified administrative officer at the R.A.F. station next door. But they were oddly shaped and hard to manage in the water. They were also for the most part orange or lemon-yellow in colour, being designed so as to be visible from as far away as possible; which was not what we wanted. They were inflated, too, by means of a small cylinder of compressed air, which, when we tried to use it, went off with a noise like the last trump, setting all the dogs barking for miles around.

"Then I remembered an article of army equipment known as a Boat, reconnaissance (Royal Engineers), and with the help of Bill Cumper procured two of them. They were small

[1] This was Paddy's real name.

and black and handy and you inflated them by means of a small pair of bellows, which emitted a wheezing sound. Each held two men with their equipment." [1]

David insisted on a practice course. For several nights the black boats were carried down to the Great Bitter Lake, inflated, and taken out for trial runs. A sentry was posted with instructions to shout when he heard a noise, which he did too often and too quickly for Fitzroy's liking. David argued that the enemy would not be so alert; indeed the unsuspecting of any nationality probably would not hear a sound. To prove his point he suggested that they take the boats to Suez and see if they could blow up British shipping. They would paddle out and tie on limpets to whatever target was handy—without explosives, of course.

This was the sort of joke—on the model of Heliopolis—that the authorities did not find nearly so amusing as David. But Fitzroy, Cooper and Seekings gladly entered into the spirit of the enterprise. They drove from Kabrit to the outskirts of Suez in an army lorry which they parked in the town. They walked to the docks and found no difficulty in getting past the guard. At the water's edge they pumped up the boat. An anti-aircraft gunner strolled up and asked them what they were doing but they told him to shove off, and he did. David and Cooper embarked in one boat and Fitzroy and Seekings in another. The water was choppy and it was some way out to the nearest tankers; but both boats reached them. They kept themselves in position by holding on to the hawsers and fixed their limpets to the stern. These limpets were half-moons of metal which clung to the side of a ship by a magnetic device. They could be filled with two or three pounds of high explosive, and were detonated by a time pencil, which usually succeeded in blowing a good sized hole in the hull.

When the empty limpets were securely fixed the men paddled back to the harbour, deflated their boats and returned to the truck. The next day David rang up the Port Authorities and asked them to return the limpets. The Air Force, who had smarted under ' the Heliopolis raid ' for some time, was

[1] *Eastern Approaches:* Fitzroy Maclean.

delighted by the story, which quickly gained a wide audience, but the Navy found it difficult to smile.

*   *

In the middle of May the moment came to set off for the real raid. David did not want more than six men all told, as the party would be travelling once again in his cut-down Ford Utility painted to look like an Afrika Korps staff car and bearing German recognition signals. He selected Gordon Alston, of course Cooper and Seekings, Corporal Rose and Fitzroy Maclean, whose first raid it would be. There was another newcomer whom he had no intention of taking: Randolph Churchill, who had come out to the Middle East with No. 8 Commando. However, the latter had a persuasive tongue, and argued that although he had not been through the training course he at least had done a parachute jump which he felt entitled him to accompany the group as far as the rendezvous, if nothing more.

David could not deny the jump. Indeed he had jumped with Randolph to show him how easy it was. He had leapt out of the plane first with Randolph a few seconds behind him. As soon as the parachutes billowed out he looked up and saw an expression of immense relief on his friend's face. " Thank God the bloody thing opened," shouted Randolph happily. David could not resist shouting back, " Yes, but look how fast you're travelling." True enough; by this time Randolph was level with him, a moment later many feet below. Whether it was due to a faulty parachute or excessive weight no one discovered. Randolph was the first to hit the ground and he hit it hard. Although considerably bruised, he was not seriously hurt; furthermore he held no grievance against David for an observation which must have detracted from the serenity of his descent. Although David was strict about not allowing untrained newcomers to take part in raids, in the end, perhaps by way of making amends, he allowed him to come along.

David drove to Siwa in ' the blitz-wagon ' as it was now termed; there he picked up the rest of his group and an

L.R.D.G. patrol led by Robin Gurdon, and continued on to the Jebel. On the 21st of May, the day the operation was scheduled to take place, Corporal Seekings hurt his hand with a detonator, and Randolph was allowed to take his place.

In the late afternoon the six men set out for the raid. David, Fitzroy and Gurdon rode in the front seat, Randolph, Cooper and Rose in the back. The L.R.D.G. patrol once again escorted them to the Regima road which wound its way down the escarpment. It was now eleven p.m. The S.A.S. plan was to drive to the harbour, blow up the shipping and return to the Jebel the same night. They had about six hours of darkness in which to accomplish the task. They said good-bye to the L.R.D.G. and started on their way.

*   *   *

This mission proved no more successful than the other two, but it was distinguished by an unexpected feature: high comedy.

First of all, the moment the car was on the smooth macadam Benghazi road, it began to make a high pitched scream. David drew up and one of the N.C.O.s got out and tinkered with the track rods in the dark. There was nothing he could do. The front wheels were out of line. So they continued on their way, the noise reaching an appalling crescendo and maintaining it steadily.

Ten minutes from Benghazi they saw a red light swinging in front of their path. David pulled up just short of a wooden bar that stretched across the road. An Italian sentry with a tommy-gun approached the car. Fitzroy Maclean spoke fluent Italian and took charge of the situation. When asked his identity he replied, " Staff officers. In a hurry." The Italian was flashing a torch but did not notice the British uniforms. He pointed to the lights and said, " You ought to get those dimmed." Then he walked to the barricade and swung back the bar.

Soon the S.A.S. vehicle was approaching the outskirts of the town. A car with headlights full on passed them. They looked around and found that it had stopped and was turning. Then it was following them. David accelerated, and driving at top speed went screaming into the city. He swung around the first corner he came to, drove into a bombed-out lot, switched off the headlights and listened. The other car flashed past. A minute later the wailing of sirens broke the silence.

The R.A.F. had promised to leave Benghazi alone on this particular night. It looked as though the raiders had been detected and a search was about to begin. The screaming car had become a liability. David ordered the N.C.O.s to blow it up. The best chance of escape would be on foot. Rose and Cooper placed a detonator among the explosives in the back seat and set a thirty-minute fuse to it. Then, taking their emergency packs, the men started off through the night.

They were in the middle of the Arab quarter. There were many bombed buildings and gaping holes. They stepped through a breach in a wall and found themselves face to face with an Italian carabiniere. Fitzroy thought it better to open conversation than to say nothing. He asked the man what the sirens and rockets were about. " Oh just another English air raid," replied the Italian gloomily. Fitzroy asked cautiously if it might not mean a raid by English ground forces. But the man seemed to think this a huge joke. He laughed loudly. With the British Army pushed back to the Egyptian frontier, he said, there was little danger of that.

On the strength of this conversation, David decided that they had been altogether too ' windy,' and would carry out the harbour raid as planned. But first they must rescue the car from annihilation. There were only a few minutes left before the explosion was due. They hurried back, extricated the detonator from the explosive charge and flung it away. A few minutes later they heard it go off with a sharp crack.

David told Randolph and Corporal Rose to stay behind and hide the car. Carrying one of the boats, he and the other three men started for the harbour. They had explosives in a kitbag and were armed with tommy-guns.

The wire perimeter which surrounded the dock area was ten feet high and made of double strength. David led them to the side entrance he had noted on his reconnaissance, and was relieved to find that the guard post was again deserted. They made their way past cranes and trucks until they reached the water's edge. David left Fitzroy and Rose to inflate the boat and went off on a quick tour of the harbour.

Fitzroy began to pump, and the bellows made their usual wheezing noise. Suddenly, a sentry from one of the ships, only a few yards away from the dock, called out a challenge. "*Militari*," answered Fitzroy sternly. The man called out again and asked what he was doing. "Nothing to do with you," said Fitzroy; fortunately there was silence.

The pumping went on for ten or fifteen minutes but nothing happened; the boat remained flat. It was obvious there was a hole in the rubber. There was nothing to do but go back to the car and get the second boat. Fitzroy and Cooper walked down the street where they had left Randolph, and found him and Rose trying to back the car into the garage of a bombed-out house. They collected the boat and once again trundled down to the harbour. Fitzroy operated the wheezing bellows; but the second boat remained flat. He pumped and pumped in anger and desperation but nothing would make it fill with air. It was a sickening disappointment.

At this point the essential thing was to find David. The two men went through the wire and walked slap into him; as a joke he snapped out a challenge in German, but they did not find it amusing. He had come back for them once and missed them because they were away fetching the second boat. There was a hurried council of war. Only half an hour of darkness remained. Should they plant their explosives on whatever targets were at hand, or should they keep their presence a secret for a possible future operation?

They decided on the latter alternative. They went back to the water's edge to pack up the boat and explosives. As they were walking through the opening in the wire Fitzroy found himself staring into a coal black face. It was the sentry who, no doubt, should have been keeping watch there all the time. "It was an Ascari from Italian Somaliland," he wrote. "I did not like the look of him at all. . . . He grunted menacingly and pointed his bayonet at the pit of my stomach.

" Infusing as much irritation into my voice as I could muster, I asked this formidable blackamoor what he wanted; but he only answered, " *Non parlare Italiano.*"

" This gave me an opening. I have always found that in dealing with foreigners whose language one does not speak, it is best to shout. I did so now. ' *Non parlare Italiano!* And you a Corporale!' And I pointed to the stripe on his sleeve.

" This seemed to shake him. He lowered his bayonet and looked at me dubiously. My confidence returned. Trying to give as good a representation as I could of an angry Italian officer, I continued to shout and gesticulate.

" It was too much for the black man. With an expression of injured dignity, he turned and walked slowly away, leaving us to continue our progress down to the water's edge. There we stuffed the boats and explosives back into the kitbags and started on our return journey, a weary and despondent little party.

" It was at this stage that, looking round, I noticed that there were more of us than there should be. Two sentries with rifles and fixed bayonets had appeared from somewhere and fallen in behind.

" These were a most unwelcome addition to the party. There was clearly no hope of shaking them off in the harbour area, and, with such companions, it would be fatal to try and negotiate the hole in the wire. Alternatively to try and shoot it out with them would bring the whole place about our ears. There was only one hope, and that was to try somehow to brazen it out.

" Assuming as pompous a manner as my ten days' beard and shabby appearance permitted, I headed for the main gate of the docks, followed by David and Corporal Cooper and the two Italian sentries. At the gate a sentry was on duty outside the guard tent. Walking straight up to him, I told him that I wished to speak to the Guard Commander. To my relief he disappeared obediently into the tent and came out a minute or two later followed by a sleepy-looking sergeant, hastily pulling on his trousers. For the second time that night I introduced myself as an officer of the General Staff, thereby eliciting a slovenly salute. Next, I reminded him that he was responsible for the security of this part of the harbour. This he admitted sheepishly. How was it, I asked him, that I and my party had been able to wander freely about the whole area for the best part of the night without once being properly challenged or asked to produce our identity cards? He had, I added, warming to my task, been guilty of gross dereliction of duty. Why, for all he knew, we might have been British saboteurs carrying loads of high explosive (at this he tittered incredulously, obviously thinking that I was laying it on a bit thick). Well, I said, I would let him off this time, but he had better not let me catch him napping again. What was more, I added, with a nasty look at the sentry, who winced, he had better do something about smartening up his men's appearance.

" Then I set off at a brisk pace through the gate followed by David and Corporal Cooper, but not by the two Italians who had shuffled off into the shadows as soon as they saw there was trouble brewing. My words had not been without effect. As we passed him, the sentry on the gate made a stupendous effort and presented arms, almost falling over backwards in the process." [1]

*   *   *

During what was left of that night and the next day the six men hid themselves in the upper story of the half-gutted house where Randolph had concealed the car. They had a few tins of bully beef and Gordon had remembered to bring a flask of rum. The morning was something of a shock, as they had believed themselves to be in a deserted section of the town. However, it soon became apparent that the Arabs only left Benghazi at night to avoid R.A.F. attacks. They returned in full flood with the daylight. Soon the city outside was teeming with activity and resounding to an increasing din through which came a babble of Arabic, German and Italian. Not far down the street was the German Gestapo Headquarters and

---

[1] *Eastern Approaches :* Fitzroy Maclean.

Randolph several times reported black-booted officers striding in and out.

David's usual sense of adventure was dimmed by his acute disappointment at the failure of the operation. Three times unworkable boats had frustrated his efforts. On the other occasions the responsibility was that of the Special Boat Section, but this time it rested squarely with the S.A.S. What could have happened? Maclean and Alston had taken infinite precautions; they had inflated the boats the previous afternoon a few hours before the expedition set off, to make sure they were in perfect condition. Had they been exposed too long to the hot sun and had the rubber perished? Or had they brushed against a treacherous blackthorn bush and been punctured? Maclean had wrapped them in heavy canvas before putting them in the car, so they could not have been damaged on the way to Benghazi.

Whatever the explanation, it was heartbreaking for David. He had proved once again that it was possible to reach the harbour; and if he could only find a workable boat he was more convinced than ever that a handful of men could do immense damage.

Of course the truth was that whereas the Navy and the Air Force experimented for months to find the right boats and dinghies for their particular needs, the S.A.S. had no resources and was forced to improvise. The boats they had found simply were not designed either to be carried across precipitous ground or to be inflated in rough wadis. If anyone took enough interest in the unit to equip it properly, thought David bitterly, it could increase its striking power a hundred per cent.

As evening approached David's gloom wore off. It might be worthwhile, he said, to stroll around the streets of Benghazi; and even to pay another visit to the harbour to look for a target. However, he had made up his mind not to disclose the fact that his men had successfully negotiated the road block and were able to wander about at will, unless they found really worthwhile objects to put their bombs on. He was determined to come back again, when he could make a more profitable visit.

Together the five men walked down the main thoroughfare, laughing and whistling; it always astonished David how unobservant people were. Of course it was dark, but even when a door suddenly opened and a shaft of light fell upon them, no one seemed to notice the British uniform.

When they reached the harbour they found two motor torpedo boats tied up to the quayside. They returned hurriedly to the car, drove it out of its hiding-place and retraced their route. But they were too late. Sentries were pacing up and down.

Reluctantly they said good-bye to Benghazi. Ross had not managed to silence the screaming wheels and they made a noisy exit. Again Fitzroy negotiated the road block with the magic words ' Staff Officers,' and at daybreak they were back at the rendezvous in the Jebel.

They reached Siwa uneventfully, but on the way from Alexandria to Cairo they had a bad car crash. David was driving and passed a long convoy of lorries. The last lorry jutted out to the middle of the road. His rear wheel caught it, and sent his staff car somersaulting into the ditch. The *Daily Telegraph* correspondent, Arthur Merton, to whom he had given a lift, was killed. Fitzroy Maclean went to the hospital for three months with a fractured skull, Randolph Churchill crushed a vertebra and was invalided home, and Sergeant Rose had a badly broken arm. David appeared to be unscathed but found he had cracked a bone in his wrist which meant that he could not drive a car for some time. This was not considered a misfortune by his friends. They felt it increased his doubtful prospects of survival.

CHAPTER EIGHT

THE MALTA CONVOY

WHILE DAVID was trying to blow up shipping during the spring of 1942, the two great opposing armies in the Western Desert stood motionless, glowering at each other across a forty-five mile front of rock and sand. They numbered a million and a half men and possessed literally thousands of guns, tanks and aircraft; yet their strength was so evenly divided that neither judged the time right to move.

In contrast to the quiet that prevailed on the front, a verbal battle raged behind the scenes. " During February," wrote Winston Churchill in *The Second World War*, " it became apparent to us that General Auchinleck proposed to make another four months' pause in order to mount a second set-piece battle with Rommel. Neither the chiefs of staff nor I and my colleagues were convinced that another of these costly interludes was necessary. We were all sure that it was lamentable that British and Imperial armies, already numbering over six hundred and thirty thousand men on ration strength, with reinforcements constantly arriving, should stand idle for so long a period at enormous expense while the Russians were fighting desperately and valiantly along their whole vast front. Moreover, it seemed to us that Rommel's strength might well grow quicker than our own. These considerations were fortified by the German renewal of their attacks on Malta and the consequent breakdown of our means of obstructing German and Italian convoys to Tripoli. Finally, Malta itself was threatened with starvation unless a steady monthly flow of supplies could be maintained. The supreme struggle for the life of Malta now began, and grew in intensity during the whole spring and summer."

What in fact was happening behind the scenes? In order to understand the part that David was called upon to play in the month of June, one must examine the interchange of telegrams between the Middle East Commander-in-Chief, General Auchinleck, and the Prime Minister, Winston Churchill, which began the last week in February. It will be remembered that Auchinleck had attacked Rommel in December after a long delay, which had been sharply criticised by Churchill. The British commander had scored a victory, but his triumph was not long lived. Rommel waited scarcely three weeks before launching a counter-attack which won back all that he had lost and more. The line had become stabilised in the area of Gazala the first week in February. At the end of the month Churchill wired Auchinleck, " I have not troubled you in these difficult days, but I must now ask what are your intentions. According to our figures you have substantial superiority in the air, in armour, and in other forces over the enemy. There seems to be some danger that he may gain reinforcements as fast or even faster than you. The supply of Malta is causing us increased anxiety. . . ." [1]

Auchinleck obviously did not agree with Churchill that he had superiority. He wired back politely but firmly that he did not feel he would have ' numerical superiority ' before 1st June, and ignoring the Prime Minister's argument that Rommel might be able to reinforce faster than he could, said that in his opinion an attack before that date would risk a defeat " which could endanger the safety of Egypt."

Churchill saw that his commander-in-chief was digging in his toes. He believed that a long wait was so dangerous that he invited Auchinleck to return to London and discuss the matter. But Auchinleck refused on grounds of pressing business. Patiently Churchill returned to the printed word. On 15th March he wired, " Your appreciation of February 27th continues to cause deepest anxiety here, both to chiefs

[1] *The Second World War:* Winston S. Churchill.

of staff and Defence Committee. I therefore regret extremely your inability to come home for consultation. The delay you have in mind will endanger the safety of Malta. Moreover, there is no certainty that the enemy cannot reinforce faster than you, so that after all your waiting you will find yourself in relatively the same or even a worse position. . . ." [1]

About this time General Nye, the Deputy Chief of the General Staff, left London to join Auchinleck. Churchill had a long talk with Nye who expressed himself in perfect accord with the Prime Minister's views. Churchill now wired to Stafford Cripps, who had stopped in Cairo on his way to India, asking him to talk with Auchinleck, fortified by General Nye, and try and make him understand the feeling of urgency which prevailed in London. Malta was the key to the Mediterranean. If Malta passed into the hands of the enemy Rommel could get all the supplies he needed across the Mediterranean with little interference. Yet unless Auchinleck could advance and seize airfields in Cyrenaica from which fighter planes could operate to protect supply ships to Malta, the island might be forced to capitulate through starvation.

This was Cripps's mission but instead of impressing Auchinleck he fell under the latter's persuasive powers. He wired Churchill cheerfully that he had talked to Auchinleck, General Nye and others, and that he was " very satisfied with the atmosphere at Cairo "; if the Prime Minister would send the general a friendly telegram to show that there was " no more questioning of his desire to take the offensive " all misunderstanding would come to an end. This caused Churchill to rasp out a sharp rebuke, not to Cripps, but to Nye, who had left London assuring Churchill of his support. " I do not wonder everything was so pleasant," he wired, " considering you seem to have accepted everything they said, and all *we* have to accept is the probable loss of Malta and the Army standing idle. . . ."

However, there was no moving Auchinleck. On 20th April Churchill received a signal from General Dobbie, the Governor

[1] *The Second World War:* Winston S. Churchill.

of Malta, saying, " The very worst may happen if we cannot replenish our vital needs, especially flour and ammunition, and that very soon . . . it is a question of survival. . . ."

A copy of the telegram was sent to Auchinleck but he replied that the risks involved in offensive action were too great to warrant an attack at the present moment. Churchill countered with the observation that the loss of Malta, which undoubtedly would be the result of delay would be " a disaster of the first magnitude for the British Empire and probably fatal in the long run to the defence of the Nile Valley."

By this time the Prime Minister was seriously alarmed, and felt that Auchinleck could no longer be relied upon to take aggressive action unless his hand was forced. He secured the full backing of the chief-of-staff, the War Cabinet, and the Defence Committee, and took the unprecedented step of *ordering* Auchinleck to attack. A time limit was set. During the moonless period in June, two convoys of seventeen ships, approaching from east and west simultaneously, would attempt to reach Malta. If Auchinleck was not prepared to attack at the very latest by the middle of June he must hand over his command. Auchinleck agreed to attack.

But he was too late. On 26th May Rommel moved instead. After five days of fierce fighting Auchinleck wired that the enemy had suffered a setback. " Rommel's plans for his initial offensive have gone completely awry and this failure has cost him dear in men and material." This was perfectly true; but within a week Rommel recovered the initiative and within five weeks—before June was out—his army was at Alamein, sixty miles from Alexandria.

However, we are moving ahead of our story. Churchill congratulated Auchinleck on Rommel's immediate setback, and again emphasised the urgency of helping Malta. " There is no need for me to stress the vital importance of the safe arrival of our convoys at Malta," he wired on 2nd June, " and I am sure you will both take all steps to enable the air escorts, and particularly the Beaufighters, to be operated from landing-grounds as far west as possible." The Prime Minister made further suggestions and ended his message, " Other points will no doubt occur to you."

*   *   *

This was the place where David stepped into the picture. Immediately upon his return to Cairo from Benghazi he was summoned to the office of the Director of Military Operations. He was told that a British convoy of merchant ships would run the Mediterranean gauntlet the middle of June to try and relieve Malta. What could the S.A.S. do to reduce enemy attacks from the air?

Twenty-four hours later David was back with a detailed plan. He would send eight patrols to raid eight separate fields on the night of the 13th-14th June. The patrols would operate in four different areas; their targets would be two fields in the Benghazi sector; three more in the vicinity of Derna (a coastal town about one hundred miles west of Tobruk); one at Barce field which lay sixty miles east of Benghazi; and the eighth on Heraklion aerodrome in Crete.

Kabrit bristled with activity for there was no time to lose. The patrols would have to start moving within the next ten days. The French had not taken part in any operations up until now and this would be mainly their show. Commander Bergé would lead the Crete raid; Lieutenant Jordan, his second in command, would take three French patrols to Derna-Martuba; Lieutenant Zirnheld, another French officer, would tackle Barce, and Lieutenant Jaquier would travel with David and Paddy to the Benghazi area where they would launch a triple operation.

Each raiding unit would not number more than five men. Maps, transport, time-tables were studied closely while Headquarters Intelligence kept the planners informed of all last-minute developments. Everything seemed fairly straightforward to David except for Jordan's raids in the Derna-Martuba region. This sector was rough and hilly, and known to be packed with German reinforcements and staging posts. The airfields here were of the utmost importance, but by far the most difficult to reach.

David searched his brain for a scheme that would get Jordan and his fourteen men to their objectives safely. He mentioned the difficulties at Headquarters and one of the staff officers asked if he had heard of the S.I.G. The initials stood for the meaningless words " Special Interrogation Group." It was composed of about a dozen German Jews from Palestine who had volunteered to operate behind enemy lines posing as Afrika Korps soldiers.

David made further inquiries about this strange and incredibly brave little band of men, and learned that they had sprung into being as an organisation a few months previously, on the inspiration of a British soldier by the name of Captain Herbert Buck, M.C. This officer had been serving with a Punjab regiment when he was taken prisoner by the Germans at Gazala. He managed to escape and started out for the British lines. He spoke German fluently and somewhere on his journey picked up an Afrika Korps cap and badge. He began to wear it and was amazed at how easy it was to move through the German military zones unnoticed. He reached his own lines safely, and immediately went to Headquarters with the idea of a sabotage unit composed of anti-Nazi Germans.

He was allowed to recruit a dozen men and one officer. The officer was Lieutenant David Russell of the Scots Guards, who, like Buck, spoke German perfectly. The men were mostly Jewish. Buck told them that their missions would be varied; but that they would have to be prepared to pose as Afrika Korps soldiers. Although the penalty of capture would certainly be torture and death, not a man demurred.

Buck told them that since their lives would depend on being able to carry off their masquerade perfectly, they would have to learn the latest German military slang, and would be drilled every day in German methods. It was better, he said, to have as little contact as possible with British soldiers.

In order to achieve perfection Buck decided that they must recruit a couple of German N.C.O's. Headquarters Intelligence helped him to find them, and he finally selected two German prisoners-of-war who had been in the Foreign Legion before 1939 and had been drafted into the German Army. Although they were not Jews they declared themselves passionate anti-Nazis. After repeated 'screenings' they were passed on to Captain Buck as wholly trustworthy.

Brückner and Esser were their cover names. Brückner was a fair-haired, broad-shouldered man, jovial, aggressive and brash. Esser was quieter, good-natured and generous.

At first the Palestinian Jews were suspicious of the new-comers; they did not like the idea of having *bona fide* Afrika Korps soldiers around. But as the months passed they accepted them. Both were light-hearted companions, and added to the gaiety of leisure hours.

The daily routine of the S.I.G. was almost as strenuous as that which David Stirling imposed on his men. Of course it was done in German fashion. The day began with a blow on the whistle and the barking command of "Kompanie Aufstehen." This was followed by twenty minutes of P.T., then the 'march' to breakfast. Whereas British soldiers just walked down to the mess tent the S.I.G. was ordered to 'fall in' and made to sing lusty German marching songs.

Training went on for most of the day. It included the study of explosives and weapons, map reading, navigation and un-armed combat. A number of captured German vehicles arrived and every member of the unit had to become an expert driver and mechanic.

Great stress was laid on the weapon training, particularly pistol and other close combat weapons, as every S.I.G. man had to be able to fight back without a chance of support or reinforcement if, for instance, he found himself cornered in an enemy barracks or headquarters.

By the middle of May the training was complete. Each S.I.G. man was equipped with a cleverly forged *Sold Buch*, the German equivalent of the British pay book, with photographs of the bearer in German uniform and the usual maze of stamp marks. German typewriters, German army stationery and all types of 'forms' were also delivered to Captain Buck. The S.I.G. was ready to take the field.

*   *   *

The first request for their services came from David Stirling. He signalled Captain Buck and asked if he would meet him in Cairo to discuss an immediate operation. When Buck arrived David put forward the following scheme. Could the S.I.G. produce two or three Afrika Korps vehicles, and drive the French patrols (who would be concealed in the back) on to the airfields in the Derna-Martuba area?

Buck was delighted with the idea. He believed it was an easy mission to perform, and was enthusiastic about leading it himself. If David would send the French S.A.S. to Siwa he and his ' Germans ' would meet them there, and they would work out detailed plans together. They would have to depart from Siwa not later than 8th June if the raids were to take place on the 13th.

Lieutenant Jordan was informed of the scheme and welcomed it enthusiastically. He and fourteen men left for Siwa by air at the end of May. A Long Range Desert Patrol led by Captain Guild was also awaiting them; they would escort the strange convoy for the first hundred miles of the journey; then they would establish a rendezvous and wait for them until they returned.

*　　　*　　　*

Captain Buck arrived the day after the French. He had eight men with him and four vehicles; these consisted of a Knevelwagen (the military version of the Volkswagen) one Opel, one German three-ton lorry, and a ' captured ' British thirty-hundredweight lorry which had had the Afrika Korps Palm tree and Swastika painted on it, as well as German T.A.C. signs on the doors and tailboard.

It took three days to collect supplies, check weapons and extract necessary information from Intelligence. David arrived from 8th Army Headquarters with last-minute aerial photographs. On 6th June the group started off.

The L.R.D.G. led them through barren and deserted country for four days, on the last morning the S.I.G. men took off their British uniforms and changed into German. Everything was now complete, except for one vital factor.

H.Q. Intelligence had not yet supplied Buck's party with the German password for June. The one for May was known—' Fiume '—but that would not be of much use.

The L.R.D.G. sent an urgent wireless signal to Headquarters but the reply came back that the password was still unknown. Usually it was not difficult for Intelligence to extract it from a prisoner of war, but it was still early in the month and so far it had not been revealed. There was nothing to do but proceed without it.

*   *   *

The convoy made its way northward, with the desert gradually giving way to broken, mountainous ground, covered with scrub and vegetation. Captain Buck was dressed as a German private soldier and was driving the leading vehicle. Beside him sat Esser and Brückner, in the uniforms of N.C.O's. The French parachutists were in the back of the vehicle, under the tarpaulin cover, hidden by knapsacks and supplies. On top of the cabin of each truck sat a pseudo-German, following the example of Axis convoys who always posted a look-out man to give warning of enemy planes.

All the S.I.G. men were armed to the teeth. Each carried a Luger Automatic on his belt with a machine-gun slung over, a bayonet which had been sharpened on both sides to use as a dagger, and German ' potato masher ' hand-grenades primed and ready for instant use. On each lorry, concealed under the canopy, were two machine-guns on special mountings with the feeder belt in position. The hidden Frenchmen were dressed in khaki overalls and blue forage caps; each of them had two British Mills grenades in his trouser pockets and a .45 revolver under his shirt.

Throughout the morning the convoy made an uneventful passage, occasionally passing Arabs working in the fields, or long lines of donkeys laden with water and bulging bundles. The first trouble occurred early in the afternoon when the ' captured ' British lorry broke down while winding its way up a steep escarpment. As it was unwise to abandon it, Captain Buck took it on tow.

An hour later the convoy turned a bend in the road and saw a red and white barrier stretched across their path with a sentry post and a guardroom at one side. Buck drove up to it, while the ' N.C.O.' beside him signalled the guard in a peremptory manner to open it. The Italian started to do as he was bid, then thought better of it. He came forward and demanded the password. Brückner told him he did not know it; he had been sent out on urgent business before the password had been issued. He knew the word for May if that was any help. He had his order of mission in his pocket. He flourished the forged document in the Italian's face. See, he had specific instructions to deliver the four vehicles, placed in his charge at Agedabia, to the workshops at Derna as quickly as possible. By this time an Italian major had joined the group. He suggested that the men come into the guard room and discuss the matter over a bottle of wine.

The major explained genially that his position was difficult. He had explicit orders not to let anyone through unless they knew the password. Buck and the two S.I.G. men went inside and drank the wine. Still the major was adamant. Finally Brückner decided to get angry. He became abusive and threatened to ring up his superior officer and tell him that Italian sentries were obstructing the business of war. Finally the major gave way and agreed to lift the barrier. With immense relief the convoy passed through, and continued on its way.

Another disturbing event took place later in the day. As it was growing dark the convoy approached a second road block near an important junction. A huge, portly German corporal came running up to Buck's car, holding up his hand. At first the men thought some crisis had occurred. But the fat corporal had only friendly words of advice. They ought to pull in at the staging camp half a mile further on, he said, and spend the night. It was not safe to drive after dark as British saboteurs frequently penetrated the area and shot up the transport.

Buck thanked him and decided it would arouse less suspicion

if he did as he was told. The staging area was a hive of activity. The German field kitchen was producing lentils and dumplings and the men were lined up, mess tins in hand, to get their evening meal. Others, a mixture of Luftwaffe and Afrika Korps men, were bedding down for the night. There was much noise and barking of orders.

Buck drew up as far as possible from the general turmoil. Several of the S.I.G. remained with the trucks, but others boldly produced their mess tins and joined the queue for dinner. The French could see what was going on through the slits in the sides of the trucks. After an hour Buck decided it was safe to leave, and the convoy moved out of the camp, attracting scarcely a glance from the troops who were still busy eating, drinking, playing cards or getting their bedding ready. The convoy moved seven or eight miles down the road and camped for the night.

The next day was 13th June, the night the raids were scheduled to take place. Buck and Jordan discussed the situation in the early hours of the morning, and agreed that it was imperative to get the password. Buck decided to try a ruse. He typed out a letter addressed to the fat, good-natured German N.C.O. who had warned them against ' British saboteurs ' the previous morning. The letter would request him to furnish the bearer with the current password, explaining the urgency of their mission and why they were not in possession of it. Two Palestinian Germans, Hass and Gottlieb, dressed as Nazi N.C.O's, volunteered to deliver the message.

They drove together in the *Knebel* to the road junction. Their only anxiety was that the same N.C.O. might not be on duty again, but to their relief his hulking figure emerged from the guardroom as they drove up. They saluted him smartly and he told them in a fatherly manner to stand at ease. The following conversation took place.

" *Herr Unter Officier*, here is a message from our *Feldwebel*."

" Oh yes, I remember. You passed here last night. What, you want to know the password? I don't believe I know it myself! " He laughed merrily and Hass and Gottlieb did their best to laugh too. He led them to the guardroom and asked his Italian colleague, who was sitting at a desk smoking a cigarette, if he could tell them what it was. The Italian shook his head. " See if you can find it, there's a good fellow," he beamed. Lackadaisically the Italian began thumbing through an index book, while the German smiled at the two respectful S.I.G. men. Suddenly the Italian's face lit up with success. " *Ecco.* Here it is," he said. " Challenge, SIESTA. Reply, ELDORADO." The S.I.G. men again saluted smartly; and with gratitude that was genuinely heartfelt departed on their way.

Toward noon Buck's party moved on to a point five miles from Derna, which was to serve as the rendezvous. There was one more important task to be completed before evening came; that was to take Lieutenant Jordan and four of his corporals, Bourmont, Vidal, Tourneret and Royer, on a reconnaissance tour of the area. Although the Frenchmen had to remain concealed under the tarpaulin in the back of the lorry, there were so few of them this time that they each had a look-out hole which gave them a good view.

The reconnaissance was completed, not wholly to Jordan's satisfaction, but without interference. Jordan asked to reconnoitre the two fields in the Derna area, and the two near Martuba. At west Derna he took note of a squadron of Messerschmidt 110's, and at east Derna a dozen Stukas. He was disappointed that Buck felt it unwise to attempt a recce on Martuba because it meant driving across the airfields. The party returned to the rendezvous about half-past five.

In the meanwhile the French parachutists had cleaned and checked their weapons and assembled their supplies. They were due to start out on the business of the night in two hours' time. Jordan gave his final orders. Corporal Tourneret, accompanied by four men, would attack one of the Martuba fields. They would travel in a separate lorry with a ' German ' driver and two ' German ' sergeants. Jordan and Corporal Bourmont, also with four men each, would attack the two Derna fields that they had driven around. They would travel together in the same lorry, Jordan's group being dropped off first and Bourmont's second. Brückner would drive the car dressed as a German private; and two Palestinians, Hass and Gottlieb, would ride beside him in the uniforms of N.C.O.'s.

Just before nine o'clock the Jordan-Bourmont patrols left the rendezvous, hidden under the tarpaulin which had blankets and jerrycans on top of it. The journey seemed interminable. On the afternoon reconnaissance trip the vehicle had moved through the countryside at a fair speed, but now it seemed to be only crawling. It took over an hour to do five miles. Brückner stopped several times complaining of engine trouble; once he thought he had a flat tyre, but it proved a false alarm.

At ten p.m. he pulled up again. This time he had stopped two hundred yards from the west Derna aerodrome cinema. The Frenchmen hidden in the back could hear the sound of the projection quite clearly. Brückner got out, saying something about the engine being hot, and that he had lost the key to the tool chest. He would have to go into the guard-room and get another.

While he was gone a German sentry came up to the vehicle and Lieutenant Jordan heard one of the S.I.G. men explaining about the key. A moment later Jordan was aware of the crunching sound of many footsteps. With a flash of apprehension he decided risk to peering over the back of the truck to see what was happening. As he did so two German guards sprang on him and pulled him out. The vehicle was surrounded by soldiers with tommy-guns. "All Frenchmen come out," barked one of them. The unit had been betrayed.

What happened next is confused. One of the Frenchmen stood up and flung a grenade, and another began firing the machine-gun from the back. The German guard scattered in a panic and the grenade exploded in their midst. At this moment Jordan ran free of his captors.

Then the aerodrome defences started sending up flares, and a machine-gun post not far from the guardroom opened fire. Jordan was running as fast as he could, and suddenly heard an appalling explosion. He looked back to see the truck enveloped in a sheet of flame. One of the Palestinian Germans, Hass, had seen that he was hopelessly trapped, and while still in the lorry, had flung a grenade into the pile of ammunition in the back.

Jordan ran for some way without stopping. Then he took stock of his position and headed for the rendezvous. He reached it two hours later. Buck was waiting for him and was stunned by the news. He found it difficult to believe, yet there was no doubt about it; Brückner was a Nazi spy. The slow trip to the field, the interminable halts were now explained; no doubt Brückner had promised to deliver his cargo at a given hour and wished to be on the dot.

Buck and Jordan felt that it was unlikely that any of the men who managed to escape would return to this particular rendezvous. Knowing that they had been betrayed they would probably make for the L.R.D.G. meeting place twenty-five miles distant. Indeed, Buck and Jordan should not stay where they were a minute longer; Brückner was bound to give the Germans information about everything he knew, and a patrol might appear at any moment.

The two officers reached the L.R.D.G. meeting place at Baltel el Zalegh before dawn. They stayed there for nearly a week waiting for stragglers. But none came. It was not for many months that Jordan learned what had happened to the others. Four of the parachutists had been captured at the time of betrayal; a fifth and sixth were picked up the next day; a seventh was wounded and recaptured four days later. This left only two men out of the Jordan-Bourmont group. These last two, one of whom was Bourmont himself, walked through the night and finally found the rendezvous of the patrol which had gone to Martuba field. But this rendezvous was also betrayed. Soon after the sun rose it was surrounded by a German company. Although the Frenchmen numbered only seven, and were without water or food, a hundred miles behind the enemy lines and surrounded by superior numbers, they gave battle. Several were wounded and all were captured.

Out of the fifteen Frenchmen only one had survived. As far as the S.I.G. Germans were concerned, Hass had been killed, and Gottlieb captured. The enemy soon learned the latter's identity and executed him. Only the driver, Brückner, triumphed. He was flown to Berlin, and intelligence reports were received to say that he had been fêted and awarded the Deutsch Kreuze in Gold, which is two grades higher than the Iron Cross, First Class.

CHAPTER NINE

EVENING OUT

DAVID, Paddy and Lieutenant Zirnheld had taken three patrols to the Jebel. On the same night that Jordan attempted his raid, they attacked the three main Benghazi airfields.

David's party consisted only of himself and Corporals Cooper and Seekings. Originally he had intended to drive down to the Benghazi plain in his staff-car or ' blitz-wagon '; but the car had been put out of action by a Thermos mine on the trip from Siwa, so he had decided to do the operation on foot. The three men walked to the edge of the escarpment and spent a day observing the airfield below them. They were not more than a mile distant and they could hear the hum of testing machinery. Benina, they knew, was being used by the Germans as their chief repair base. Air-frames were fitted with new engines, and pilots took the finished product up for tests. At one end of the field stood a number of large hangars and workshops. These were David's targets.

It was a desperately hot June day and two of the men slept fitfully with flies crawling over them, while the third was on watch. During the afternoon three or four planes were taken into the air, put through their paces and brought back again. In the distance the white buildings of Benghazi sparkled in the sun, and beyond it the Mediterranean spread out like a brilliant blue sash. On the plain below groups of Arab women in red, yellow and green skirts and head-dresses worked in the fields. Along the road came a steady trickle of ragged boys and heavily loaded donkeys, and occasionally a Bedouin with flocks of sheep.

147

As soon as it was dark the three men made their way down the escarpment, following the track along the plain until they reached the airfield. There was no wire, and the guards apparently were on the far side near the hangars.

No sooner had they stepped on to ground, however, than they heard the sound of aircraft above them. David wondered if they were coming down to land; they could not be R.A.F. planes, for Middle-East Headquarters knew that the S.A.S. raids were taking place that night and had promised to keep away from the area. As this thought was flashing through his mind the ground shook with the ugly sound of exploding bombs. " What the *hell* do they think they're doing? " stormed David. " The usual Headquarters service," observed Cooper sarcastically above the din. The bombs had dropped wide of their mark and the planes were now flying away. " Not what I'd call very good shooting," said Seekings. " Just enough to put everyone on the alert."

There were only two aircraft parked on the field. It took the men scarcely a minute to place their bombs. They attached one-hour fuses which they reckoned would give them time to complete the rest of their work. Then they stole across to the long line of hangars and workshops. They approached cautiously and stopped as they heard footsteps. Sentries were patrolling. To the right a dim light was coming from one of the hangars, and not far from it another faint glow indicated what might be the guardroom.

When the sentries had passed David motioned the two men to follow as he made his way to the darkened hangar on the left. David, who had the ability to walk as silently as a cat in the dark, was critical of Seekings. " I had a terrific lecture on deerstalking from the major," he wrote. " Apparently I was not moving quietly enough."

They reached the hangar and David fumbled in the blackness for the catch to the large rolling doors. He found it and pulled it just enough to allow them to squeeze through. The noise of the rollers seemed to echo over the field, but apparently the sentries did not hear it.

The hangar was packed with machinery and tools. The

darkness inside was so complete it was difficult to move through the maze of equipment without stumbling over something. Seekings kept watch near the door, and suddenly hissed to the other two to ' freeze.' The sentries were coming past again. David and Cooper stood in their tracks until the footsteps died away.

When they had placed a generous number of bombs, they tackled the next hangar. This was the one with the light in it, and the door was already partly open. In the furthest corner a working-lamp was shining and four men were bending over a piece of machinery. Not far from them stood a half-dismantled JU 52.

David instructed Cooper and Seekings to stay by the door and keep watch while he crept up and put a bomb on it. He stayed close to the shadowy wall. When he reached the plane he was only five yards from where the Germans were sitting. He attached his explosive and looked around for other targets. He had passed two elaborate pieces of machinery. He returned to these and left his bombs.

He rejoined Cooper and Seekings and the three men headed for the third and last hangar. Once again they rolled back the huge door and squeezed through the crack. Two JU 52's —this time both intact—stood in the centre. Lining the walls on either side were large wooden crates. On closer inspection David saw that the crates contained aircraft engines. There were anywhere from thirty to forty of them. He sent Seekings to keep watch by the door and again he and Cooper put bombs on the planes, then turned to the long rows of crates. They worked hard for twenty minutes and were just completing their task when Seekings hissed that the guard was marching up. A heavy tramp of approaching feet could be clearly heard. No one wanted to be caught inside the hangars, for David had begun to use half-hour fuses.

They slipped out and hid behind a further stack of crated engines in front of the buildings. The guard had been changed. The fifteen or twenty men who had just been relieved marched past and went into the guardroom twenty yards away. Seekings was just moving out from behind the crates when he heard a sentry coming from the opposite direction. He immediately took cover again and David nearly crashed into him. " In a voice of thunder (or so it seemed to me)," wrote Seekings, " the C.O. remarked, ʻWhere the hell are you?ʼ I got back my stripes when I pointed the sentry out to him. He took cover until the Jerry passed, then we quickly made our way down the six crates, placing a bomb on each.

" At the end of the line I had a look back. The second sentry was almost on us. I hissed to the C.O. and Cooper to freeze whilst I kept him covered. But the C.O. did not hear me. Luckily the sentry knocked against a box and the C.O. dropped to the ground. Somehow or other the Jerry had not spotted us. He about turned and marched away.

" Next we crept up to the guardroom. Johnny and I covered whilst the C.O. bashed the door, pulled a pin out of a grenade and threw it in. The twenty Germans who had just come off guard were inside. Their officer was sitting at a desk no doubt making out his report. ʻHere catch,ʼ said the C.O. The Jerry at the desk did in fact catch it, and in a voice of horror cried, ʻ Nein, Nein.ʼ ʻ Ja, Ja,ʼ said the C.O. and closed the door. A moment later there was a big explosion. We then ran like hell as the bombs in the hangars had also started to go off. As we got clear we stopped to look. One of the 110ʼs on the field went up and the cannon started to explode with the heat. It was a pretty picture as the JUʼs in the hangars began to burn. We stopped near a gun emplacement. It appeared deserted so we pushed our last bomb up the breech, which was still warm."

ʻ Pretty picture ʼ was something of an understatement. The whole aerodrome was alight. The flames were soon licking the high roofs of the hangars. Finally they broke through in a conflagration that could be seen for miles. The aircraft on the field were also burning merrily. David hoped that Paddy was watching the fires from Berka.

This scene of total destruction gave David great satisfaction. But it was not the raid itself that pleased him most; it was the fact that it had been accomplished by three men with sixty Lewis bombs. He felt it completely proved his theory that a few trained soldiers could often achieve more devastating results by surprise and stealth than could a whole squadron or regiment by the usual methods. He was certain that a bombardment could not have accomplished such complete havoc. Some of the hangars would have been left intact; besides, the guard would not have been dealt with so effectively and might have managed to save machines and engines. More than any other raid, this one convinced him that forces of S.A.S. men, roaming along the enemy's desert flank and darting in to strike at the right moment, could have a serious effect on the course of the war.

*   *   *

David and the two corporals arrived back at the rendezvous by noon the next day without further incident. In the meanwhile Paddy Mayne was finding things awkward. The S.A.S. was now well-known to the enemy, and no doubt Brückner's information had served to alert them still further. All airfields had been instructed to take ' adequate precautions ' against ' night raids.' But this was easier said than done. If the airfield commandant ordered his planes grouped together on the field and put a guard around them, they immediately became vulnerable to total destruction from the air. If, on the other hand the planes were dispersed around the field a sentry had to be assigned to each one. And since one sentry could not be expected to stay awake all night, a second sentry had to be assigned to relieve him every few hours. This meant that perhaps a hundred men would be tied up each night.

Nevertheless, this is what the commander of Berka satellite had been forced to undertake. His field had been raided several times and he was running no more risks. Innocently Paddy Mayne and his party of three—Corporal Lilley, Warburton and Storey—walked into this delicate situation. They had spent the day ' lying up ' just outside Benghazi, " but what with chickens and fleas running all over us we didn't get much sleep," wrote Lilley. " We had no trouble getting to the airfield that night, but no sooner had we arrived than an air raid warning went, and there we were

at the receiving end of the bombs from the R.A.F. We felt
very uncomfortable lying there in the middle of the airfield;
the whole place was lit up with flares and flashes from anti-
aircraft guns and pieces of shrapnel were spattering into the
ground all around us. One of our planes was hit and crashed
about two hundred yards from us.

"When the raid was over Paddy sent me forward to put a
bomb on the nearest plane. I was challenged by a sentry
standing under the wing of the aircraft. I dropped to the
ground as he fired and at the same time Paddy threw a grenade.
There was a flash and the sentry seemed to part in mid-air.
There were other sentries by the plane. They fired and for a
few minutes there was a pitched battle. Then firing broke out
from all sides of the airfield and they were firing at each other.
We decided to crawl away and leave them to their battle.
Several times, as we made our way off the airfield, we were
fired at but before we left we managed to put our bombs on
a large petrol dump."

Once off the airfield trouble really started. The sky was
glowing with David's fires; and two miles away, at Berka
main, a French party under Captain Zirnheld were having a
pitched battle on the field, during which they destroyed eleven
bomber aircraft and killed many of the guards. Forty miles
further east, at Barce, another French detachment under
Jaquier was blowing up petrol and supply dumps.

The moment the Germans realised that these raids were
part of a concentrated effort they ordered a regiment of mobile
troops to move out into the plain and try and track down the
marauders. Soon the night was alive with the lights of motor
patrols, the sound of roaring engines and excited voices.

Paddy's party had started walking toward the Benghazi
escarpment about ten miles distant. But somehow they got
their bearings wrong. After an hour they saw cars approaching. The ground at this particular place was hard and bare
and offered no cover. They dispersed, flung themselves down,
and kept perfectly still. The cars were coming straight for
them. When the headlights seemed almost on them the
vehicles stopped. Forty or fifty soldiers jumped out and

began to spread over the plain. The four trucks remained motionless. The S.A.S. men saw the drivers light cigarettes and heard them talking to their mates. Paddy was tempted to attack the trucks with grenades but since they were equipped with machine-guns, probably two on each, he decided it would be unwise. For nearly two hours the men were pinned to their inadequate hiding-place, not daring to move. It was now getting light, and it seemed as though they were bound to be discovered. Suddenly one of the trucks revved up. The driver must have received a wireless signal for he called to the others and they all moved off.

The S.A.S. men did not realise that they were, in fact, hiding only a mile away from a large German military establishment. As soon as the trucks departed they began walking again, and soon came to the edge of the camp. It was dawn now and they could make out a house, and behind it a garden with a high hedge. It was the first cover they had seen, and they quickly ran for it. Paddy then decided they had better split up. He would move on, taking Storey with him and Warburton would stay with Lilley.

Lilley still had not taken in the fact that he was well inside the camp. The house was obviously the quarters of an officer. " The two of us remained under the hedge hoping that things would die down a bit," he wrote, " but no, the next minute half a dozen vehicles pulled up outside the hedge and once again troops jumped off and went in all directions, poking their rifles about looking for us. Warburton decided to make a break for it and two or three seconds later I heard a burst of fire. We never saw Warburton again. I still lay under the hedge undiscovered. I felt it wouldn't be long before they found me, and with this thought in my head I mercifully fell asleep.

" I was awakened by voices on the other side of the hedge —two soldiers off duty having a smoke and a chat. I looked at my watch—6.10 a.m. and the sun was shining. As the soldiers moved away a young lady with an Alsatian dog came out of a big house at the end of the garden and proceeded to stroll around. She stopped right by me and I was getting a worm's eye view of a beautiful young lady in a summer frock. Even in this situation I couldn't help but admire her. She moved on, then the damn' dog came to have a smell at me. I smacked him as hard as I could on the nose. He gave a yelp and jumped back. At the same time the lady turned and called the dog and away he went.

" I decided it was no good trying to crawl away, so I left all my kit and just stood up and walked. I walked through two miles of encampment. Men were washing and shaving. Some were queueing up for food, others were cleaning their kit. No one bothered about me, but every minute of the journey I was expecting to be pulled up. However, I was wearing khaki shorts and shirt—and so were most of them— so I suppose I didn't look much different. I walked for a couple of miles beyond the encampment until I reached the railway line that crosses the Benghazi plain. It was a deserted spot and the only sign of life were Arabs in the far distance working in the fields. I was near the road which ran parallel to the railway and suddenly I saw an Italian soldier coming along on a pushbike. He slowed up when he saw me, staring at me very hard. Then he got off his bike and came over to me leaving his rifle on the crossbar. He indicated to me that I was his prisoner and that I had to go back with him to Benghazi. This I had no intention of doing, so we got to wrestling. I got my hands round his throat and strangled him.

" I continued walking. About ten miles over the Benghazi plain I stopped at a Senussi camp for a rest. Vehicles were still patrolling the plain looking for us. After about two hours in the tent one of the Senussi told me there were two soldiers coming towards us. I looked out and in the distance I could see Paddy Mayne and Storey. We told each other of our experiences and then Paddy said we had better get moving. We had only covered another two miles. It was getting dusk and there in front of us was an open German staff car. They stopped about fifty yards from us and looked at us. We got down on the ground ready to make a fight of it. They thought better of it and made off towards Benghazi. That night we

climbed the Benghazi escarpment and the following morning
met up with Major Stirling and party."

*   *   *

David and Paddy were a dangerous combination. They
aroused the competitive instinct in each other, and took risks
that might easily have ended in disaster. Separately, they
exercised shrewdness and cunning. The reason both of them
had come through so many raids unscathed was partly due to
luck, but also to the fact that they now thoroughly understood
the technique they were trying to operate. They had learned
to hug the element of surprise to the last possible moment.
Their aim was to achieve destruction, not to provoke battles.
They knew when an operation was feasible, and when it was
better to withdraw despite having travelled hundreds of miles
to perform it. They were perfectly at home in the dark and
could gauge quite accurately the sort of odds they might take
on and still have a reasonable chance. Above all, they never
lost their heads. They agreed that from a psychological point
it was always good to make their presence known to the enemy
by opening fire once their bombs had ended the period of
surprise; yet they had the control to resist the temptation if
it were apt to bring out too great numbers and make escape
impossible. In fact, after six months of raiding they were
artists at their craft, and drew the same comfort and confidence
from the night as master burglars.

Together, however, it was a different story. They managed
to goad each other into foolhardy risks, which came under the
heading of ' a bit of fun.' On this particular occasion David
was pleased that for once he had accomplished more than
Paddy. " It's a bit of a change to see my fires lighting up the
sky instead of yours."

" How many hangars did you get? " asked Paddy.

" The lot," said David with satisfaction. " They ought to
be still burning. JU 52's make first rate kindling. You
wouldn't like to take a look at the debris? "

Paddy's eyes glinted. " Why not? If we got hold of a car
we could drive right into Benghazi and shoot up some stuff

along the road. I don't like the idea of leaving this place with your aerodrome burning and nothing to show for my own efforts. . . . Anyway," said Paddy provocatively, " I want to make sure you're not exaggerating."

First they had to organise transport. Since David's ' blitz-wagon ' had been damaged, they had to rely on the L.R.D.G. The latter, however, were not supposed to use their trucks for ' offensive action.' L.R.D.G. vehicles were regarded as unex-pendable; they were supposed to convey passengers back and forth between the base and agreed rendezvous, and not to be flaunted in the face of the enemy.

However, on this occasion, the patrol leader was Robin Gurdon, who did not stick too closely to protocol. Robin was admired and respected by everyone. He always remained good tempered; and he managed at the most unlikely times to produce luxuries such as Cooper's marmalade. He was a tall, good-looking man in his late thirties. He could easily have found some less strenuous way to spend his war, but nothing but the most daring activity appealed to him. When David asked him if he could borrow a Long Range truck for the evening, Robin laughed, " I suppose you and Paddy are cooking up something." " Nothing very much," said David, " I just want to show him what used to be Benina." " And considering that for the last twenty-four hours the plain has been alive with enemy patrols looking for you," replied Robin, " you don't expect any trouble? Now listen, David. You can have the truck on one condition. That you absolutely swear to bring it back in one piece."

" I swear," said David solemnly.

David and Paddy took five men with them. One was Lilley. " If we thought we were going to get any rest," he wrote mournfully, " we had another think coming." The others were the steadfast Cooper and Seekings, Corporal Storey and a German Jew named Karl Kahane. David had borrowed Karl from the S.I.G. He had spent twenty years in the German army before he had emigrated to Palestine in the late thirties. He was a squat dark-haired man who knew German military slang thoroughly. He was silent and morose and frequently asked the British soldiers what they found to laugh about. After the May raid on Benghazi David had decided it was a good thing to have a German-speaking soldier in the car to bluff the guards in case they were stopped.

Paddy drove the truck; David with a wrist still in plaster from the car crash, sat in front with him; the rest were in the back. They reached the Regima road on top of the escarpment about eight o'clock and were soon travelling along the Benghazi plain. David felt as though he knew every inch of the way. "There are no road blocks," he said authoritatively. "It's clear until a few miles after we pass Benina. Then there's only an Eyetie sentry with a lamp."

They were now less than a mile from the airfield and David was straining his eyes to see if the fires were still smouldering. Suddenly Lilley said, "Look out, sir, trouble ahead." A red light was swinging across the road about a hundred yards ahead of them.

Considering that they were seven British soldiers in British uniform riding in a British truck, within a few yards of the spot where David had killed fifteen or twenty men the night before, one might have expected them to feel apprehensive. However, they were still under the impression that it was only another 'Eyetie check.' Paddy slowed up. Then, through the darkness, they saw that it was something more than a sentry post. It was a fully fledged German road block with barbed wire across half the road. They could make out the shapes of at least a dozen soldiers with automatic weapons at the ready, and Seekings saw that one of them held a grenade. The N.C.O. came over to the truck and flashed his light over it. "We're coming from the front," said Karl in a peremptory voice. "We haven't had a bath for weeks and we're hungry. So cut out the formalities and let us through."

The N.C.O's face tightened with suspicion. "Password," he demanded. Karl acted with great presence of mind. He began to swear at the man in a flood of German. How could they possibly know the password when they had been at the front for six weeks? Then he contemptuously gave the out-of-date password for May. That's the last they had been

given, he said. While all these guards were sitting on their
backsides in Benghazi, he and his comrades had been in the
thick of things. Their car had been destroyed and they were
lucky to capture this British truck and get back at all. But
they didn't have time to sit around arguing with blockheads . . .

The atmosphere was electric. Then Paddy cocked his
revolver. The German could hear the metallic click in the
stillness. Then there was another click and another. The
sentry had a split second to make up his mind. He knew they
were British but if he gave his soldiers the alarm he also knew
that he was a dead man. If he let them through perhaps he
could telephone a warning ahead. These obviously were his
thoughts, for he suddenly shouted to the guard to raise the
barrier. " As we went through," wrote Seekings, " I kept an
eagle eye on the one who had the grenade. We were carrying
plenty of touchy bombs and meant to get him before he could
throw it."

But no one fired, and Paddy drove swiftly towards Benghazi.
Four miles farther on the sentry post the men had been expecting loomed up. " A party of Italians stepped into the road
waving rifles," wrote Seekings. " But this time Paddy scarcely
bothered to slow down. I swung my Vickers shouting
" Tedeschi! Tedeschi! " They jumped back. Once through
we opened fire."

Paddy and David realised from the excited behaviour of the
Italian guards that the German post must have telephoned
ahead. Under the circumstances it would be suicidal to drive
right into Benghazi. They would have to content themselves
with blowing up whatever they could find along the road.
They passed a cluster of buildings, with a transport filling
station and a petrol storage tank at one side. There were no
sentries, and it was easy to plant the charges. Then they
drove farther along to a village which boasted a roadhouse.
There was a car park next to it with heavy lorries and trailers.
While some of the men busied themselves placing bombs with
ten-minute fuses, the others machine-gunned the house. They
found a camp next to it and shot up that as well. They did
not stay to see what happened. A half-hour had passed since

they had gone through the German roadblock, and it was time to head for home. There were already shouts from the camp and a machine-gun was firing into the darkness.

Since they could not go back along the road they decided to cut across the plain to the Wadi Qattara. This wadi started on the outskirts of Benghazi and ran parallel to the road. It was essential to cross it in order to reach the track on the other side, which offered the only alternative route up the escarpment. But the wadi was so rough it could only be crossed at the point marked on the map.

David worked out the direction by compass while Paddy drove. The plain was incredibly bumpy, and the distance that had to be covered was at least five miles. Paddy was driving with his lights off, when suddenly, a couple of miles away, also cutting across the plain and heading for the same point at the wadi, he saw a vehicle with its lights full on. Apparently the Germans were trying to cut them off. Paddy put his lights on and went as fast as the truck would go.

It rattled and thundered over the ground until it seemed as though every spring was broken. The race was going to be touch and go. At one point it looked as though the enemy vehicle was gaining on them. Paddy drove more furiously than ever while his passengers were flung from one side to the other of the shaking, jolting truck. They hung on to the sides with every ounce of strength they had. Within half a mile of the wadi it was obvious that Paddy was narrowly in the lead.

David prayed that his navigation was correct. If he had miscalculated they would be in great difficulty. As Paddy approached the edge of the wadi the enemy truck could not have been more than a quarter of a mile away. The going was too rough for either side to shoot accurately but the S.A.S. guns fired warning bursts of tracer into their lights. Paddy swung along the edge of the ravine searching for the way down. " Look ! Just off to the right," said David. They had hit the crossing-place dead on. As they disappeared over the edge the enemy vehicle pulled up on the lip of the descent. The race was over, and they had won. " Luckily the Jerries dropped

the chase," wrote Seekings, " they were no doubt windy of
being ambushed if they ventured down the narrow defile. We
finally reached the escarpment. Then more trouble faced us
as the primitive track leading up was not made for cars, and
the truck had difficulty taking the steep grades. In the end
we practically carried it up."

Once on top the group felt reasonably safe. The surface
seemed like glass compared with what they had been travelling
over for the last hour. The men in the back began joking
about their battered limbs, and David pulled a flask of whisky
out of his knapsack and gave everyone a nip.

" By the way," said Paddy, " here we are on the way home
and I forgot to look at those fires at Benina. Do you want
to go back? "

David laughed. " I think you'd better take my word
for it."

They had a fairly long drive to the rendezvous and David
dozed off. Suddenly he heard Lilley shout from the back,
" Hop it, quick. A fuse is burning! " The men were leaping
off and Paddy jumped out without bothering to put on the
brakes. David dived after him, and a split second later there
was a deafening explosion. The truck was blown to smith-
ereens. The back had been full of explosives; apparently the
ride across the plain had set off one of the time-pencils attached
to a Lewis bomb. Seekings and Lilley had smelled the burning
fuse just in time.

The men surveyed the ruin. " What was left of it," said
Lilley, " could have been put in a haversack." Then they all
burst out laughing and could not stop. David and Paddy
laughed louder than anyone when they remembered the
solemn promise that had been given to Robin Gurdon to
bring it back ' in one piece.' Karl, the German driver, looked
at them as if they had lost their senses. " You men must be
made of steel to be able to laugh at things like this," he said
to Seekings. " I am too old! " He then went on to confide
that after the German Army he had had a poor opinion of
the British, but since his experiences with the S.A.S. he had
changed his mind and was convinced for the first time that

the Germans would not win the war as they could not laugh in the face of such danger.

The men continued their way on foot. After an hour's walking they came to a friendly Senussi camp consisting of fifteen or twenty tents and a few mud houses. " The headman took us in and gave us a feed of wheatmeal cakes and honey," wrote Seekings. " He was very good to us. He sent his wives out to watch for enemy patrols. He also sent one of his tribe to the L.R.D.G. rendezvous to ask Lieutenant Gurdon to come and fetch us as we were twenty miles away. His son who worked for the Italians in an underground petrol dump asked us to give him a bomb, but we told him it was too dangerous for him and the Senussi had already lost hundreds of people in reprisals.

" As night came we moved into the bush to sleep. In the morning our man came to us and said it was best he moved out. We bought a sheep from him and saw him strike camp. Shortly after he had gone a friend of his came to show us a hiding-place in an old ' bir '—these were ancient underground storehouses.

" Later a woman came with him bringing a large bowl of rice. We all sat round in Arab fashion, while one of the women came round with water to wash our fingers. We then ate with our fingers. I think it was late afternoon when the L.R.D.G. patrol arrived to pick us up."

*   *   *

Zirnheld reached the rendezvous safely after his battle at Berka main, and the three patrols returned to Siwa. On the way David managed to salvage his ' blitz-wagon,' which had been damaged by a mine, and towed it four hundred miles back to the oasis. At Siwa he found Jaquier, who had just returned from Barce, waiting for him; a few days later Lieutenant Jordan arrived and reported the disaster that had befallen his group.

*   *   *

It was too early yet for news of Bergé and the Crete raid.

It was not until David reached Cairo that the telephone rang and George Jellicoe, Bergé's second-in-command, reported himself home.

Jellicoe was the son of the famous British admiral. A stocky young man with a bronzed skin and a mop of black curly hair, he was an amusing and enterprising companion. He put his courage down to benzedrine, which he took liberally. He had only joined the S.A.S. a month previously, in May, having transferred from the Special Boat Section. Although he had not completed his training he was sent with Bergé for two reasons; first he spoke fluent French and second he knew Crete well.

The twenty-three year old Lord Jellicoe got on well with the quick-witted, temperamental Bergé. They planned the operation together and decided to take with them a Greek guide by the name of Costi and three French privates, Mouhot, Sibert, and a boy by the name of Leostic who claimed to be eighteen but later proved to be only fourteen.

The patrol embarked in H.M. submarine *Triton* from Alexandria on 8th June. At the end of four days they were cruising just east of Heraklion airfield which lay near the coast. They made a periscope reconnaissance and selected a suitable beach. That night, about ten o'clock, the submarine surfaced and the S.A.S. party climbed into two captured rubber boats and paddled ashore. One of them leaked badly and the men had to bail it out with their caps. When the group reached shore Jellicoe weighted the boats, swam out and sank them.

The group walked through the mountains all night. Once or twice they encountered Cretan peasants who shook their confidence by greeting them in English. By dawn they had only covered half the distance they had estimated, and were still eight or nine miles from the airfield. They found a cave in which to hide, and the Greek and the French privates at once fell asleep. But George had prevailed upon Bergé to take some benzedrine and the two men sat shivering, wide awake, in the entrance of the cave.

The day wore away slowly. At last the sun began to drop behind the mountains. Each man checked his equipment, slung his sack over his back, and one by one emerged from the hiding-place. All night they walked. The mountain climbing was arduous, and time and again someone fell with a smothered curse. It was not quite three o'clock when they reached the outskirts of the airfield. Bergé decided it was best to attack immediately, lest something upset the element of surprise. As they came nearer they saw the silhouettes of several aircraft against the sky. They could hear the distant hum of voices and had the impression of considerable activity.

They were moving forward slowly when a German sentry who seemed almost on them barked out a challenge. The S.A.S. stopped dead, then scattered. A shot rang out but it did not come near and they continued walking for at least a mile. They had a hurried conference and decided to try another way in. Once again they nearly ran into a sentry, but this one did not hear them. There was little more than an hour of light left now, and Bergé decided that they must postpone the attack until the following night.

The men found a perfect place to hide in the hollow of a cliff. They could observe the airfield below and counted something like sixty-six Junkers on it. This was obviously one of the main German bases for the assault on Malta. All day Bergé and Jellicoe watched the field, making notes of the guardposts and the disposal of aircraft.

At ten o'clock that night they started out again. Suddenly, within a hundred yards of the airfield perimeter, they heard the marching feet of a patrol. They dropped down and hid in the bushes at the side of the road. The patrol passed; all except the last man, who believed that he had seen something and ran back to look. He shone his light first on Bergé, then on Jellicoe and the three privates. One of the Frenchmen, Mouhot, a man from Brittany, had an inspiration. He let out a loud drunken snore.

Apparently drunken snores were not unknown in Crete, for the German seemed satisfied and ran on to join his friends. It was now essential to move fast. The group crept up to the perimeter wire. Quickly they cut a way through and took refuge in a shed which turned out to be a bomb dump. A few minutes later they heard the German patrol return. One of this group, perhaps the inquisitive one who had taken a second look, discovered the hole in the wire. Their voices began to rise in excitement. The British party undoubtedly was saved by a literally heaven-sent intervention. A flight of eight Junker 88's were coming in to land. Behind them came a daring R.A.F. Blenheim, making the correct signals, but instead of landing went roaring across the field dropping a stick of bombs. Sirens began to blow and the guards and sentries ran around in confusion.

This gave the S.A.S. men a chance to escape from the shed. Quickly they made for the aircraft which were grouped at the far end of the field surrounded by sandbags. They placed bombs on fourteen Stukas; then they started toward an even larger group of aircraft on the opposite side of the runway. Unluckily a posse of ground staff was standing about so they cut across, in front of the hangars, where they found six more aircraft to put bombs on. On their way out of the field they passed one more plane, four trucks and a petrol dump, all of which received explosives.

The bombs had two-hour time fuses, and it was not until the S.A.S. were half-way back to their mountain cave that they heard the aircraft start to explode and saw the sky light up with flame. They had a fine view of their handiwork, and hugged themselves with joy at the success of their mission. They reached the rendezvous where Costi was waiting as dawn came.

They hid up all that day. They could hear patrols, and barking dogs in the distance, but they felt reasonably safe fifteen kilometres away. That night they walked to a point within four miles of their beach. Only one more day of hiding, and they would be safely on board their submarine.

During the morning a group of Cretans stumbled on their hiding-place by accident, took one look and ran away as fast as they could. They obviously took them for Germans. An hour or so later a man dressed in civilian clothes appeared from nowhere and presented himself to them. Costi, the Greek guide, knew him well. They had been childhood friends. The man was tall and slender with dancing eyes, and nervous, artistic hands. He appeared to be eager to help the Allied cause and offered to find them food.

In the meantime Jellicoe and Costi left the rendezvous and went to a village three miles distant. They had been told they would find a Cretan shepherd here, who would put them in touch with a British agent who, in turn, would signal the submarine that all was clear.

The friendly Greek did not return, but at eight o'clock Bergé told Mouhot and Sibert and Leostic to get ready for the last move. They were to meet Jellicoe and Costi on the beach in two hours' time. They had not been on their way ten minutes before they saw two separate columns of Germans approaching from east and west. The little group turned south, but met a third column coming across a ravine. It was apparent that, like Jordan, they had been betrayed.

Bergé decided to fight it out despite their small numbers. It was still light, but in another hour it would be dark and they might be able to escape. The Germans began to attack with both grenades and machine-guns. Bergé's men had nothing but tommy-guns, which were not effective at the same range, so they held their fire until the enemy came nearer. Only one German ventured forward and he was killed instantly. This temporarily cooled the ardour of the enemy, who remained silent for fifteen minutes.

Leostic, the boy of fourteen, could not stand the inactivity. Suddenly he leapt up and said to Bergé, " My Commandant, I cannot obey you any more." He ran out to get in a position to fire. As he opened up, he was struck by machine-gun bullets and fell mortally wounded. The fighting went on until the French ran out of ammunition. Sibert was wounded and taken prisoner. Bergé and Mouhot hid in the bushes still hoping to escape but in the end they were captured and taken away.

In the meantime Jellicoe and Costi were at the beach. A rubber boat came silently across the water at ten o'clock and picked them up.

* * *

When the results of the S.A.S. raids in June were tallied up it was found that the destruction amounted to the following:

Bergé's Crete raid: twenty-one planes, four trucks and a petrol dump.

Zirnheld's Berka raid: eleven planes.

Stirling's Benina raid: five planes, thirty aircraft engines, three workshop hangars.

Paddy Mayne and Jaquier had blown up several ammunition dumps. The grand total of the S.A.S. now stood at a hundred and forty-three planes destroyed.

David hoped that they had contributed something to the voyage of the Malta convoy. When the news came, they learned that out of seventeen ships only two had reached port. The rest had been sunk by torpedo or bomb. Nevertheless, those two ships kept Malta going for the next eight weeks; at the end of that time another convoy ran the gauntlet and five ships got through. Malta survived.

CHAPTER TEN

DESERT RENDEZVOUS

THE S.A.S. PARTY arrived back in Siwa from Benghazi on the 21st of June. This was one of the blackest days of the desert war. David knew from his wireless that Rommel was surging forward, and was not surprised to find that Siwa was about to be evacuated. The Long Range Desert Group was moving its Headquarters south to Kufra. However, he was not prepared for the news that came over the air in the late afternoon. Tobruk, the last sure bastion that stood in the way of an invasion of Egypt, had surrendered to Rommel. The strategic loss was serious enough; added to this the enemy had captured a huge store of priceless war materials. " The booty was gigantic," wrote Rommel's chief-of-staff. " It consisted of supplies for 30,000 men for three months and more than 10,000 cubic metres of petrol. . . ." [1]

David left at once for Cairo. He arrived in the capital to find that Rommel was swiftly organising his pursuit, and that German units had already crossed into Egypt. The British Army was falling back some hundred and fifty miles to Alamein where it would make a stand. Fierce rearguard actions were still being fought and the coastal areas thundered with the noise and dust of skirmishing armour.

Although General Auchinleck was confident that Rommel was over-extending his lines of supply, and that the British Army would hold him on the thirty-five mile front between the coastal town of Alamein and the great Qattara Depression in the south, precautions, nevertheless, had to be taken. Smoke

[1] *Heer in Fesseln:* Westphal.

curled up against Cairo's blue sky as official documents were burned; the Navy was pulling out of Alexandria; workshops and depots were being moved back from the Delta; bombers were taking off for bases in Palestine. It was obvious that Rommel would make one final all-out attempt for a decisive victory. Hitler wired Mussolini, " The goddess of battles visits warriors only once. He who does not grasp her at such a moment never reaches her again. . . ." [1] And Winston Churchill telegraphed his Minister of State in Cairo, " Everybody in uniform must fight exactly as they would if Kent or Sussex were invaded. . . . No general evacuation, no playing for safety. Egypt must be held at all costs. . . ." [2]

During this memorable week David rapidly assembled his force, which now numbered about a hundred trained men, to take the offensive. They would strike against the enemy's forward communications to the limit of their strength. He worked with lightning speed. Within forty-eight hours he had laid his hands on 20 three-ton lorries and 15 jeeps which had just arrived from America. The jeep was something new; and David immediately recognised it as the ideal vehicle for desert raiding.

He had several of them fitted with Vickers K guns. These were fighter aircraft machine-guns, originally used in Gloucesters, and which were now obsolete. He had stumbled on them by chance. The army was unable to supply him with the type of machine-guns that could be mounted on a jeep, so he had stopped at an R.A.F. workshop to see what he could pick up there. They had twelve Vickers K guns and told him he could have the lot. He piled them into the back of his staff car and drove to a Royal Engineers maintenance depot. He asked the sappers to remove the guns already on his car and substitute the new ones. They fitted four guns on twin mountings—two in front and two in back. Later he sent three jeeps to be equipped, one with four guns, and two with two each.

David told his men that they would have the opportunity of

---

[1] *Commando Supremo:* Cavallero.
[2] *The Second World War:* Winston S. Churchill.

doing something really big. " Now that we have our own
transport and are wholly mobile we can strike harder than ever
before." His enthusiasm spread, and soon the entire camp was
working feverishly on preparations. " Maps, explosives,
Vickers guns, food and petrol lay in a turmoil around us,"
wrote one of the officers.

The idea was to take as many supplies and as much equipment as possible. They would raid for several weeks without
returning to base; and in the meantime, if Alexandria fell,
they could always head south to the Sudan or west to Kufra
or Lake Chad. But how would they get behind the enemy's
lines? David thought it was fairly simple. He believed
there would be plenty of holes in the thirty-five mile line
between Alamein and the Qattara Depression. " We ought
to be able to infiltrate somewhere. We'll try at the southernmost point."

*   *   *

The unit was ready to move off on the 1st of July. The
Eighth Army was standing firm at Alamein and Rommel was
regrouping for his next attack. David told his men to assemble
at his brother's flat in Cairo. Those who could not be ready
in time were instructed to drive straight to main Army Headquarters, outside Alexandria, where he would pick them up a
day later.

The Stirling flat may strike the reader as a bizarre rendezvous
for this cut-throat expedition, but apparently it was regarded
as normal procedure. " In those days when private wars
could still be waged," wrote Lieut. Carol Mather, one of
David's officers, " it was no strange sight to see an S.A.S.
expedition parked in the shade of the trees in one of Cairo's
quiet residential areas, with jeeps bulging with bedding and
guns and drivers lolling against the trees wondering, rather
wistfully, whether it was, or was not, done to brew up by the
side of the pavement.

" The flat was crowded out. It was a very curious scene.
David stood at the door having a heated argument with Mo,
the Egyptian servant, about an important message he was

supposed to have sent to G.H.Q. Mo was fat and a philosopher, and his word usually went. On the sofa were sitting some girls and some other officers discussing the racing form at Gezira, whilst across all this we talked about bearings and petrol and ammunition, or sat sprawled on the floor over maps of the desert trying to think above the sound of the gramophone. In the meantime the Germans were only forty miles from Alexandria."

*   *   *

David drove to main Army H.Q. in his staff car accompanied by Robin Gurdon of the Long Range Desert Group. Gurdon's job was to take the S.A.S. party to a rendezvous in the desert, about a hundred and fifty miles distant, where Timpson was waiting with another L.R.D.G. patrol. Then Gurdon and Timpson would escort the various parties to their targets.

Army Headquarters was situated in a maze of dug-outs along the Alexandria road. David saw General Auchinleck's chief-of-staff, who briefed him on immediate plans. The Eighth Army was launching a counter-attack within the next few days. They hoped to drive the enemy from Daba, Fuka, Bagush, Matruh, perhaps even from Sollum. If David could destroy aircraft operating in this area and interfere with enemy communications it would be of the utmost help.

David told the brigadier that he would try to deliver a simultaneous attack on five or six airfields on the night of the 7th-8th and also blast the coast road. That was in three days' time. But he begged the brigadier to keep him well posted. Due to Rommel's advance dozens of airfields had fallen to the enemy at which it was possible to strike; and he would like information as to the ones most heavily used. He would also like to be informed about our own offensive, and the position of our troops. The brigadier promised to do all he could.

While this conversation was taking place the S.A.S. was waiting outside. The contingent from Kabrit had arrived and there were about thirty-five vehicles in all. The trucks groaned with supplies for a three-weeks' stay in the desert. The men were anxious to get off and were relieved when David gave them the signal to start at four o'clock.

However, once they struck out across the desert they did not cover more than twenty miles before the heavy lorries began to bog down in the soft sand. After several stops and three hours' delay ' unsticking ' them, David realised there was nothing to do but lighten the load. Nearly a third of the stuff would have to come off, and some of the officers and men would have to return to base.

They spent that night together, bedding down where they were, but feelings were so strained it was a relief to part in the morning. There was a heavy mist as the detachment started off and the men were drenched to the skin. They were making straight for the edge of the Qattara Depression, the great chasm a hundred and forty miles long and a thousand feet deep that was believed to have once been an inland sea. David was certain his convoy could infiltrate through the enemy lines at the extreme end. But first they had to pass through their own lines. All along the way they passed soldiers of the Eighth Army ' digging in.' Minefields were being laid and gun emplacements set up. The S.A.S. boys waved and whistled as they went by and shouted good-natured jokes about ' the poor bloody infantry.' Every now and then they came across burnt-out vehicles and deserted equipment which marked the place where only a few days before fierce battles had been fought.

There was a cloud of dust as a line of tanks and armoured cars came along the track. Perhaps this was the beginning of the Eighth Army offensive, known as ' Exaltation.' As one of the vehicles swept by, David leaned out of his staff car.

" Exaltation? " he shouted.

The driver couldn't hear, and apparently thought he was asking his directions.

" Depression " he replied.

This delighted the occupants of David's car. " 'E's a truthful bloke," commented one of the sergeants.

David tried again. " Exaltation? " he cried as a tank went by. This time the soldier nodded, and the S.A.S. men waved and gave the V-sign.

They drove until nearly midnight; then they bedded down for the night, and set off again just before first light. They were following the ' Palm Leaf' track which led them along the edge of the Qattara Depression. They could not see its bottom; only a descending series of cliffs and rocks until they were lost in a haze of pink.

There was not a sign of life anywhere; yet they were now well behind the enemy lines. They travelled very fast, for the date of their first operation was now only two days away. The vehicles were strung out over several miles. The heat was stifling and most of the men had stripped off their shirts. Some of them had tied bandannas around their heads to keep the thick dust out of their hair and ears. About three o'clock they passed Qattara and then turned north to the coast. An hour later Robin caught sight of a tiny speck through his fieldglasses. " Navigation perfect," he said with satisfaction. " Looks like Timpson."

*　　　*　　　*

He was right. It was Timpson; the same Timpson who in January had waited in Jalo for David to come back from the Bouerat raid. He was viewing the long crocodile of cars with pleasure and amusement. " In the afternoon," he wrote in his diary, " a great cloud of dust could be seen approaching from the east. The country here is full of escarpments and clefts, and one could see the dust and hear the sound of vehicles long before they hove into view. Robin was in the lead, with his patrol. We directed them to a hide-out next to our own. Then came truck after truck of S.A.S., first swarms of jeeps, then three-tonners, and David in his famous staff car, known as his ' blitz-wagon,' Corporal Cooper, his inseparable gunner, beside him and Corporal Seekings behind. Mayne, Fraser, Jellicoe, Mather and Scratchley were all there; Rawnsley was wearing a virgin-blue veil and azure pyjamas. Here was the counterpart of Glubb's Arab Legion (" Glubb's

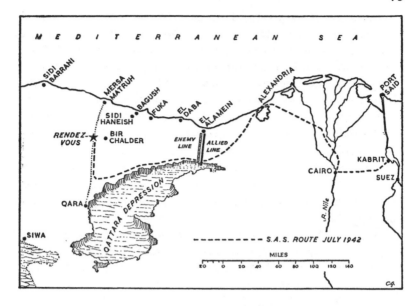

*The route taken by the S.A.S. in July 1942 to establish
a desert rendezvous as a base for continuous raiding
against enemy positions*

Girls ") in the west. Trucks raced to and fro churning up the
powdery ground, until most of them came to roost after a
while in a hollow half a mile away which we had recommended
to them. As aircraft had been flying about we did not quite
approve of all this crowded activity. Yet they had gone
through the Alamein Line undetected; an M.E.110 which
now flew over took no notice; and the reckless cheerfulness
of our companions was at least stimulating.

" Having to rely chiefly on L.R.D.G. wireless communications—and on our navigators—David kept our operators busy
sending and receiving messages for the whole party. We had
a conference that evening and again the next morning, in
which he revealed his plans and gave his orders."

David explained the Eighth Army counter-offensive to the
men—(" Completely abortive, as it turned out," commented
Timpson, " and I doubt if most of those with the main forces

were so much as aware of it. But we, at any rate, took it seriously and with the optimism which fresh hopes for a renewed offensive so easily revived.") Five or six raids, said David, would take place the following night and would be in support of the offensive. They would be co-ordinated, and bombs would be set to explode approximately at 1.0 a.m. The largest group of S.A.S. would be escorted by Robin Gurdon and would head for the Bagush-Fuka area. Here the party would split up into four patrols. Two of them (a mixture of French and British) would do a joint attack on the largest Fuka field; another would raid a neighbouring landing-ground; and David and Paddy would go on together to operate on Bagush.

A fifth S.A.S. party led by Lieut. Schott and Lieut. Warr, and guided by Timpson, would head for Sidi Barrani; and a sixth group, also a Franco-British combination, under Lord Jellicoe and Lieut. Zirnheld, with Hunter escorting them, would raid the El Daba fields.

Immediately after breakfast the convoy left for a forward rendezvous, sixty miles closer to the coast. They completed the journey by lunch time, and hid their vehicles in a large patch of scrub. The afternoon was spent in preparation; guns had to be cleaned, explosives assembled, vehicles checked and rations distributed. Early the next morning jeeps and trucks moved out of their hiding-places and set course for their various targets.

*   *   *

David's group headed for the Qara Matruh track and followed it northward to Bir Chalder. They reckoned to have an eight hours' drive to the Fuka escarpment. They would leave a wireless truck to wait for them there, while others went forward and carried out the raid. In the afternoon they approached the scene of a recent battle. For an hour they drove through a sad wreckage of derelict trucks, burnt-out tanks, and trackless Bren gun carriers. They could see the black marks on the sand where soldiers had stopped to ' brew

up,' and they had to drive carefully to avoid half-dug slit
trenches.

As David's car came over a rise in the ground he spotted
a column of armoured vehicles travelling across his front, not
more than three miles away.

" Jerries! " said one of the drivers. Robin and David
climbed out and examined the column through fieldglasses.
There was a German look about them, the way they bunched
together, but they could see British markings on the vehicles.
" Maybe it's one of our Jock columns," said Robin.

' Jock ' columns were British units, equipped with light
armour and weapons, which were sent occasionally to do rapid,
deep-penetration raids, usually designed to draw away the
enemy's attention from the main attack.

David began to swear. " If those idiots at H.Q. haven't
bothered to let us know. . . . Could they be so stupid? "

" Yes," said Robin, " easily. But of course the column may
be Jerries with captured British material."

[1] " Seems to me they're moving too fast," said David. They'd
be going slower with captured stuff. Well, there's no way to
tell. We'd better get along." But before climbing back in his
car he had a final word with his men. " From now on," he
said, " you must keep your eyes skinned for enemy aircraft
and armoured cars. Remember that we are targets for British
as well as enemy planes, and if we are attacked and get
separated you must all drive on towards the airfields. Remember that! Nobody turns back. If we have to take evasive
action we must still head northwards for our objectives."

He tapped out his pipe on the sole of his boot and then
gave his quick, shy smile. " It will be all right," he added.
" But keep wide awake. Now let's get going."

After half an hour of driving they saw three suspicious-
looking trucks on the horizon, and a short while later the
camouflaged tents of an enemy camp outlined against the
skyline. The column made a long detour and did not

---

[1] The following two paragraphs come from *Born of the Desert* by Malcolm James
(Pleydell).

reach the escarpment until eight o'clock when it was nearly
dark.

*   *   *

David and Paddy left the others and headed in the direction
of Bagush. Their party consisted of nine men besides themselves and three vehicles. David drove his staff car and Paddy
followed in a jeep, both of which were equipped with the
newly-fitted Vickers K machine-guns. A three-ton truck,
filled with bombs, grenades, food, water and spare parts,
brought up the rear.

Bagush aerodrome was about eighteen miles from the Fuka
escarpment. The going was rough and the cars averaged only
three or four miles an hour. They had to stop twice for
punctures, and once because of a leaking radiator. It was
eleven o'clock when they reached the coastal highway. They
had covered eight miles in three and a half hours. They took
their bearings, and reckoned that the aerodrome was another
ten miles farther west. David had been informed by G.H.Q.
Intelligence that a great deal of traffic was moving along this
road. He decided that he would construct a block about
three-quarters of a mile short of the aerodrome, and destroy
any enemy vehicles that passed ; while he was doing this
Paddy would operate on the airfield.

The three vehicles drove along the coast road with their
lights on. On either side the desert stretched out like a black
yawning void. They could smell the sea, which could not have
been more than half a mile away, but there were no lights,
not even Arab fires; only an eerie emptiness.

David put his foot on the accelerator. He was in a hurry to
get off the road and establish his ambush before any enemy
traffic passed him. Usually it did not matter. But if the
column they had seen was really a Jock column, the enemy
might be alerted and he was anxious not to arouse suspicion
before he was ready. Twenty minutes later he slowed up and
bumped off the road. Paddy's jeep followed, with the truck
behind it.

The aerodrome bordered the road and was just over a mile

away. Paddy's group, consisting of five men, apart from himself, would go in by foot and distribute their bombs, then make their way back to the waiting vehicles.

David had three men with him. He gave Paddy half an hour's grace before setting to work. It did not take long to establish a block. Within ten minutes two good-sized boulders had been rolled down a small slope at the far side of the road and placed in the middle of the highway. The men took up positions on both sides, their guns at the ready, and waited.

The minutes passed and nothing happened. After some time Seekings ventured, " Doesn't look as though there's much activity to-night, sir."

" According to army intelligence, ' heavy traffic is now passing along the Bagush-Fuka road,' " replied David ironically.

" Poor things," said Seekings sympathetically. " They're like the weather people. Never get it quite right, do they, sir."

An hour passed while the men strained their ears for sound. David looked at his watch. It was a quarter-past one; fifteen minutes past zero hour and not a single explosion. What had happened to Paddy? Another twenty minutes passed and still silence. At last there was a jet of light and a loud boom. " There they go," said Cooper jubilantly. " Now we can sit back and count."

During the next forty minutes there were twenty-two explosions. The men could see the flames leaping up against the sky. Through the darkness they looked much closer than a mile away; soon the scene resembled a huge camping expedition with a myriad of companionable fires. " Captain Mayne seems to be in good form to-night, sir," observed Seekings. " And he seems to have got away without interference. No machine-gun fire or anything."

He was due back any minute now, but nearly an hour passed before he and his men emerged from the night. David expected to find him in a jubilant mood and was surprised to see a frown on his face. " The bloody bombs wouldn't work," he complained. " Someone put the primers in too soon."

Paddy explained that the aerodrome was packed with planes, at least forty of them. It had taken his men longer than usual to get on, for it was heavily patrolled by sentries. "It's quite obvious," he broke off, "that the column we saw was one of our own Jock columns. Everyone's on the watch."

David nodded. "And it explains why there's no traffic on this blinking road. Wait until I get my hands on Middle East Headquarters."

Paddy continued. The planes were well dispersed in clusters all around the perimeter. He had divided his party into four groups, all of whom had managed to infiltrate between the patrols without alerting anyone. They had placed bombs on forty aircraft, then withdrawn to the desert side of the field and waited, half a mile away, to watch the result.

When the explosions stopped after the twenty-second plane they could not imagine what had happened. The enemy was running about frantically trying to put out the flames. They brought out fire-fighting apparatus but apparently ran out of chemicals, for some of the aircraft continued to burn unhindered.

It was a pleasing spectacle, but too few planes had exploded. Paddy finally solved the mystery by examining one of the bombs in his sergeant's bag. The primer was damp. He made inquiries and found that it had been placed in the plastic twenty-four hours earlier instead of being put in, as it should have been, at the last minute.

There was no point in holding an inquest now and it was difficult to know who was to blame.

"It's enough to break your heart," said Paddy. "Another twenty planes sitting there just asking for it."

David had been silent. "I've got an idea," he said suddenly. "Let's drive on to the field and shoot up the planes from the cars. . . . We've got eight R.A.F. Vickers guns between us. After all, they were designed to shoot up aircraft."

"Not a bad idea," said Paddy admiringly.

"This is the way we'll do it. The truck will head for a point two miles beyond the aerodrome and wait for us. We'll drive the staff car and the jeep straight on to the field. We'll do a quick tour, knocking off as many planes as we can, then make for the truck."

It seemed a simple and sensible plan. David and Paddy selected two men each to serve as front and rear gunners and the rest departed in the truck to set up the rendezvous. After ten or fifteen minutes spent in checking guns and ammunition, the raiding parties were ready.

They approached the field at the farthest point from the road. It was surprisingly quiet. There was no sign of patrolling sentries. It looked as though the enemy had relaxed his watch, operating on the theory that when the horse has bolted there is not much point in locking the stable door.

David stopped and held a whispered conference. " Keep ten yards behind me," he said to Paddy. " I'll sweep right around the perimeter so that both cars can fire from the broadside." Then he turned to the gunners. " Remember to shoot low and aim at the petrol tanks. Right. Off we go."

The operation took no more than five minutes. The planes were in groups of five or six. The guns opened up with a terrifying roar. As soon as the first plane burst into flames it enabled David to see what he was doing. In each cluster there were one or two planes still intact interspersed with burnt-out frames. They traversed three sides of the landing-ground and shot into six concentrations of aircraft. Then David turned on to the main road and headed for the rendezvous.

During this time the enemy seemed completely stunned by what was happening for there was no resistance of any kind. As the raiders left the field, however, anti-aircraft guns opened up and several shells passed close to them. But soon they were engulfed by darkness.

The gunners looked back to see what they had done and counted twelve fires burning. Once again a great expanse of sky was illuminated. Indeed, the glow could be seen eighteen miles away by the S.A.S. on top of Fuka escarpment. Malcolm Pleydell, the doctor, describes the scene in *Born of the Desert*. " Over to the west of us," he wrote, " there was a terrific flash which lit up the skyline like summer lightning. . . .

Now there was a dull red glow over the sky, and through our glasses we could pick out the small pinpoints of fire. 'That's Major Stirling and Captain Mayne,' the men cried excitedly. 'You bet there's some fun over there!'"

David and Paddy found the rendezvous where the truck was waiting. With Paddy's twenty-two and the last twelve, the men reckoned they had destroyed thirty-four planes.[1]

*   *   *

David was delighted with his new technique and would have liked to stop and discuss it with Paddy then and there, but there was no time to lose in moving across the desert. They could not hope to make the desert rendezvous, which was eighty miles away, before the following night, but it was imperative to get as far away from the airfield as possible before dawn.

As Paddy Mayne once put it, desert raiding was like a glorious spree. You paid for your fun the morning after. The trip home was not only wearisome but invariably bedevilled by air attacks.

As the cars travelled over the rough ground, David wondered what sort of landscape first light would reveal. Sometimes morning lifted its curtain on a wadi offering caves and over-hanging ridges; sometimes on a wide expanse which offered no protection of any kind.

That was the case on this particular morning. Not even a patch of scrub or a stray rock revealed itself. The cars drew up together and David and Paddy had a conference. Through fieldglasses it was possible to see a low grey streak that looked like an escarpment. But it was probably fifteen miles away which meant an hour's drive.

There was nothing to do but head for it. They would keep their eyes skinned for aircraft, pull up if one was spotted, and hope for the best. The next miles were anxious going. Every five minutes that passed with no warning seemed a gift from providence. Gradually they were able to pick out the lines

---

[1] An air reconnaissance the following day showed that thirty-seven planes had been destroyed which brought the S.A.S. total to 180.

of an escarpment. It was long and low, and perhaps only five miles distant. Then the truck had a puncture which meant a ten minute stop.

Soon the vehicles were moving again, and David could make out a small conical hill, known in the desert as a 'pimple.' Now the escarpment could only be two miles away. Paddy was well in the lead with his jeep, David was a half mile behind and the truck another mile in the rear.

By the time the aircraft warning came Paddy had almost reached the escarpment and David was still half a mile away. He was a few hundred yards from the 'pimple.' The truck was some distance behind. The planes were flying very low. One was a Gibli and the other two were CR 42's. David and the truck both stopped short and hoped against reason that they would not be spotted. But when they saw the Gibli detach itself they knew what was coming. It dived towards the staff car, its machine-guns firing. The bullets spluttered against the rocky surface of the ground.

The other two planes were concentrating on the truck. The men had scattered from it, as far away as they could get. David watched the Gibli circle, then once again it came toward the staff car and dropped two small bombs which kicked up sand and stone as they hit the ground wide of their mark. Its ammunition was now gone and it headed for home.

The two fighters strafed the truck three times. Finally there was an explosion and the vehicle began to burn. While this was going on David had a few minutes of respite. The pimple could not be more than four hundred yards away. If he could only get the car to it, he might have a chance of saving the vehicle. He shouted to the men to jump in, pressed the starter and roared forward. They reached the base of the conical hill as the two planes circled over it. Then the first one dived to attack. As it came down David moved to the other side of the mound. Then the second one approached from the opposite side. Again he moved around. Four times the two planes dived at different angles, while David kept his eye on them turning around the pimple for shelter.

He knew the planes were bound to get him if he continued

this game much longer and made a dash for the escarpment.
There were two or three boulders near the summit which
formed a sort of semi-circle and might give him cover. To get
to them, however, he had to drive to the top and turn back
into them. He raced up the cliff, the planes coming for the
car and missing it miraculously. He reached the top and saw
that there was no path leading down to the rocks—only a sheer
drop of twenty feet. There was nothing to do but abandon
the car and run for cover. They'll get it now, he thought
to himself; this they did with their last few bursts of ammunition. With a triumphant flourish they turned and flew away.

The men near the burnt-out truck jumped up and walked
towards the escarpment. No one had been hurt, but the only
transport left was Paddy's jeep. He had succeeded in parking
under the lip of a cave. He had done his best to draw the
enemy fire from David by shooting wildly at the planes but
they had refused to be distracted. Now he ran up asking if
anyone would like a lift.

" Let's have breakfast first," laughed David.

" Everything's gone, sir," said one of the sergeants. " The
whole blooming lot, petrol, water, food, spares, went up with
the truck."

" Not everything," said Paddy. " We've got some biscuits
and some chocolate. And here's a bottle of whisky."

They decided to wait at the escarpment until the midday
heat haze made air attacks unlikely. A sentry was posted and
the rest of the men found places in the shade where they could
sleep. At twelve o'clock the hungry, thirsty, unkempt group
started off again. They covered the remaining thirty miles in
three hours. They were the first to reach the rendezvous.

*   *   *

The rendezvous escarpment seemed to offer all the comforts
of home. The soldiers left behind had busied themselves
scooping hollows and even caves out of the soft chalk sides, and
now they had real shelter. The newcomers ate a big meal,
and sat back in the shade of their trucks laughing and talking.
With food, security and good company their fatigue vanished

and they were full of jokes and conversation, telling their stories with classic understatement and humour.

The rest of the parties came in during the next five or six hours, with the exception of Captain Warr and Lieutenant Schott, who had gone with Timpson to the Sidi Barrani area and were not due back for several days. The first to return were the men whom David and Paddy had left on top of the escarpment. They had divided themselves into three sections. Two parties, one English under Bill Fraser, and one Free French under Lt. Jordan, had attacked the main field together; and a third party under Laurie Pike, an R.A.F. officer attached to the S.A.S., had gone for a satellite field. They had all run into trouble. This was due to the fact that the landing-grounds were well defended. The Frenchmen ran slap into a guard post. An Italian sentry challenged them, and Jordan answered in German, pretending to be a friendly patrol. The sentry could not understand what he was saying, but for a few minutes his suspicions were allayed. Hurriedly the men headed to the corner of the aerodrome where a group of Messerschmidt 109 F's were parked. They managed to place bombs with ten-minute fuses on eight planes before the sentry collected his wits and gave the alarm. Flares went up, a Breda gun and several machine-guns opened fire. One of the Frenchmen was wounded by a splinter in his thumb. Nevertheless, they all managed to get off the field and back to the rendezvous safely; and they had the satisfaction of hearing eight explosions on the way.

This sudden outburst, however, spelled disaster for Bill Fraser. At the moment the flares rocketed into the sky and floodlit the field he and his party were crawling under the wire between two guard posts. Instantly pandemonium broke loose. Guns seemed to be firing in every direction. Fraser decided that there was nothing to do but beat a hasty retreat. Arthur Sharpe was also interrupted in his work, for the noise alerted the guards on his own field which was only a mile away. However he managed to plant six bombs before he was forced to withdraw.

While all this was going on Robin Gurdon had decided to

carry out his own operation. He had taken a truck and moved along the coast road until he had come to a canteen and a car park. He had lobbed grenades into the canteen and shot at it by machine-gun fire, then driven into the car park and blown up thirty vehicles.

The party led by Jellicoe and André Zirnheld were the last to return. They had not been able to raid the El Daba airfields, for just before David had started out on his own raid he had received a message to say that Daba was no longer being used. Instead, he had directed them to the Fuka-Galal road—" to strafe " (as Sandy Scratchley put it) " supposedly fleeing enemy transport." George and Sandy had sat by the road for nearly two hours but nothing had passed. Zirnheld was luckier. He and three Frenchmen had walked a few miles farther on, and had come across a stationary lorry, and an aircraft tractor and trailer. They heard voices talking in German and crept up on them. They sprang out, guns poised, demanding their surrender. " *Nein, nein, Tedeschi !* " replied one of the Germans in amusement. He thought the attackers must be crazy, mixed-up Italians; it did not occur to him that an enemy patrol could be so far beyond their own lines.

The Frenchmen soon convinced them that the raid was no joke; they placed bombs on the three vehicles and waited until they exploded. Then they led their prisoners back to the waiting transport. The lorry driver was a sergeant, the other two were eighteen-year-old members of the Luftwaffe ground staff; they had only arrived in Africa a few weeks earlier. They were driven to the escarpment rendezvous, and a few days later sent back to Cairo by truck.

CHAPTER ELEVEN

QATTARA DEPRESSION

AT THREE O'CLOCK in the morning the whole outfit was on the move. This was due to the fact that in the fading light of the previous evening an Italian Macchi had flown over the rendezvous very low. One of the Long Range gunners had lost his head and taken a shot at it. A duel had followed but no damage had been done by either side. However, it meant that the rendezvous was no longer secure. Much to everyone's annoyance it was imperative to seek a new base. About 1.0 a.m. the men were cursing and loading their vehicles and an hour later they moved noisily out of the scrub and headed westward across the desert. They covered about twenty-five miles before dawn. As light broke they saw an escarpment ahead of them, about fifty feet high and several miles long, which looked as though it would provide good cover. This, in fact, became their desert base for the next three weeks.

That night the S.A.S. had a celebration. Someone had brought a couple of bottles of rum from Cairo, and after supper they crowded together into a square formed by three or four trucks and sang and drank under a superb starlit sky. It was a strange scene with the British and French entertaining each other with folk songs, and the German prisoners looking on with puzzled faces. Most of the men had beards and several of them wore bandannas, like eighteenth century pirates. When they ran out of songs someone declared it was time the Germans tried their hand. After some persuasion the prisoners acceded, and, of course, sang much better than anyone else. When they sang "Lili Marlene" there was a thunder of whistling and applause.

They delighted their audience so much that they were given generous helpings of rum; and they found Derek Rawnsley, the air force officer attached to the S.A.S., so warm and friendly they told him their troubles. They also told him that El Daba was Rommel's most important advance airfield; no, they said, it had never been out of use . . .

This information infuriated David. He had enough grievances against Headquarters as it was. The next morning he sent a signal to Cairo from Robin Gurdon's wireless truck. He did not mince his words, and an official report, reviewing the happenings of this period, states that: " Major Stirling in forwarding this intelligence to Army H.Q. emphasised that a good opportunity for crippling the enemy's airpower had been lost owing to an order prohibiting an attack on these landing-grounds. He also pointed out that he had not been warned of the presence of the Jock column which had delayed reconnaissance of the objectives for the night of 7th-8th July; and the lack of detailed information about suitable objectives. He ' never knew how many German aircraft there were or on what aerodromes they were concentrated, and no information as to store dumps or headquarters was forthcoming.' "

Up until now the S.A.S. had made perhaps a dozen raids during the moonless period, returned to their base, gathered new supplies, and started out again the following month. This time David wanted to strike every few days; to keep up a steady series of attacks which would give the enemy no respite. He could only do this if his supplies were replenished regularly, and if he received daily intelligence reports.

*   *   *

David's quarrels with G.H.Q. stemmed not so much from current disagreements as from a totally and fundamentally different conception of the role of the S.A.S. Looked at from a Headquarters point of view the failure to meet his requirements was understandable. The Germans were at Alamein add the thoughts of the General Staff were naturally concentrated on the needs of the Eighth Army. David had to get on as best he could. Intelligence was sent when it was available but it could not be specially gathered for him. After all, the S.A.S. was a sabotage group; brilliantly successful at times, but not indispensable.

It was this attitude that David was fighting. For six months he had tried to make Headquarters understand that his unit could be something bigger than a sabotage group. He felt he had developed a new formula for modern war. If he had sufficient support there was nothing he could not do. He had proved that he could reach enemy harbours; that he could destroy thirty or forty planes a night; that he could disrupt lines of communication. What he wanted was not just enough backing to do these raids once a month but to maintain continuous pressure against the enemy. If he were given personnel and supplies on a large enough scale he felt that he could consistently disrupt the enemy's supply lines. By persistent onslaughts on Headquarters David usually got what he wanted for individual operations; but he had not yet made ' the management ' accept him on a larger scale.

Indeed, his persistence, which was essential if he were to keep going at all, had aroused a certain amount of opposition at Headquarters. It was the same old story; the more conservative elements felt that it was an outrage that he was allowed to operate as an independent unit. His job, they said, was sabotage. Why, then, was he not absorbed by one of the semi-military units, like the S.O.E.[1] for instance?

During the last few months David had heard worrying talk about this outfit. One of the leaders of the S.O.E. had approached him and suggested an amalgamation; and at G.H.Q. more than one officer had hinted that the right step for him was to join this organisation, which had plenty of equipment and held high priorities. David dug in his toes firmly. He did not regard the S.A.S. as either a secret service unit or a sabotage unit. He saw it as a purely military unit operating under military discipline. What he was trying to impress on his superiors was the fact that military tactics must

[1] This was a secret organisation known as Special Operations Executive.

change with the times; with very small lethal weapons, two or three men could now do the job of a whole regiment.

This was the battle between David and his superiors. He was determined to keep his independence until the day came when he could make Headquarters recognise the true potentialities of the S.A.S. and use it properly as a new weapon of war. In order to do this he realised that he must achieve repeated successes in his field. All his energy was bent to this purpose, and he had no shame about badgering Headquarters for what he wanted; the fact that the Germans were at Alamein was all the more reason, he argued, for giving him the equipment and recruits he needed. " By aiming with full energy of purpose at 400 per cent success," wrote Lt. Timpson in his diary, " David would obtain 100 per cent results judged by normal estimates."

*   *   *

These were the battles that went on behind the scenes. To the men of the S.A.S. David always appeared cool and imperturbable. He rarely lost his temper, or even raised his voice. He sat sucking his pipe, bending over maps, discussing plans with his officers, his mind apparently wholly concentrated on the next operation.

His fame had spread widely in the past few weeks. The German radio was mentioning ' the phantom Major ' with increasing regularity; it described him as the leader of a band of British ' desperadoes ' who conducted savage raids behind their lines. Later, when the enemy gathered more information about him, he began to figure in Rommel's diary. Indeed, the general referred to the raids now taking place. " Operations of this kind," he wrote, " were undertaken by the Commandos under the command of Colonel Stirling. These Commandos, working from Kufra and the Qattara Depression, sometimes operated right up into Cyrenaica, where they caused considerable havoc and seriously disquieted the Italians." [1]

However, it was not only the enemy who acknowledged David as a formidable opponent. Although British censorship

[1] *The Rommel Papers:* Edited by B. H. Liddell-Hart.

forbade mention of the S.A.S., tales of his exploits had spread throughout the Eighth Army. " Young, tall, good-looking and dashing," wrote Lt.-Col Peniakoff (Popski),[1] " he had become (much against his naturally modest disposition) the romantic figure of the war in the Middle East. He had raised the first S.A.S. Regiment and trained it, at first for parachute operations, then for land fighting in jeeps. With Mayne and a band of friends they had ravaged the German enemy troops after the battle. With a light heart and cool courage he inspired in his men a passionate devotion and led them to thrilling adventures. Where we plodded, he pranced." [2]

Popski was not the only one who was struck by the rare quality of David's leadership. David Lloyd-Owen, who eventually took command of the L.R.D.G., regarded Stirling as one of the great figures of the war—a man with an indefinable magic that made his followers gladly do what he asked. " He had a power over men which I had not seen before," wrote Lloyd-Owen. " I believe if David had asked his men to jump into the midst of an enemy Armoured Division in broad daylight they would have gone with him without question and in the knowledge that he would find a way to subdue the tanks and bring his men out unscathed and the overwhelming victors." [3]

What were the qualities that made men so eager to follow him? Fitzroy Maclean wrote that he brought to his ventures " what Lawrence called ' the irrational tenth . . . like the kingfisher flashing across the pool '; a never failing audacity, a gift of daring improvisation, which invariably took the enemy by surprise." [4]

This was true, but the audacity was based on an almost uncanny understanding of the psychology of war. The job

---

[1] ' Popski ' was born in Belgium of Russian parents. He took scientific honours at Cambridge during the first World War, trained as an engineer, and in 1924 settled in Egypt, where he became a sugar manufacturer. He spoke many languages including fluent Arabic. His hobby was desert motoring and when the second World War broke out he offered his services to the British Army. He was commissioned and posted to the Libyan Arab Force. He did brilliant work organising and leading the Arabs against the enemy.

[2] *Private Army.*

[3] *The Desert My Dwelling Place:* David Lloyd-Owen.

[4] *Eastern Approaches:* Fitzroy Maclean.

of the S.A.S. was not to engage the enemy, but to outwit them. David knew exactly what advantage he could derive from both the element of surprise and the protection of the dark. He had all the cunning of the country-bred sportsman, and he also knew the moment to withdraw. His insistence was on achievement, not heroics; and as a result the S.A.S. won a reputation for both.

This brings one to the conclusion that the devotion David inspired in his men was based on confidence. This was repeatedly justified by the amazingly small casualties suffered by the unit; and it was further fortified by the fact that David never asked his men to undertake anything he himself would not do.

There can have been few commanding officers in the British Army, responsible for the planning and organisational side of their units, who operated so regularly in the field. David had a cool, almost remote courage. He did not seem to know what fear was. The reason for this was not lack of imagination but utter concentration on the job at hand.

The French regarded him partly as a character out of a story book and partly as an English eccentric. They found his soft voice and perfect manners a startling contrast to his incredible toughness when it came to fighting. One of them commented to Malcolm Pleydell, " Ah, zar Major Stirling, 'e's a fonny one. When we was shooting 'e turns to me and 'e says, ' I like shooting zese Italians, don't you? ' " He shook his head in obvious admiration, and then laughed round at us. " And all ze time 'e looks so gentle and so kind! " [1]

*   *   *

David's renown had brought many new officers and men to his banner. First of all, Mike Sadler had transferred from the L.R.D.G. to the S.A.S. This was a really important acquisition, as the S.A.S. was now getting its own transport and relying on its own navigation. Sadler was not only brilliantly successful at his job, but popular with all the men. Quiet and unassuming, he always created an atmosphere of confidence, because he

[1] *Born of the Desert:* Malcolm James (Pleydell).

himself was so sure. The L.R.D.G. were loath to see him go, but they were on such close terms with the S.A.S. that they gave him their blessing.

Several more old friends had joined David. There was Carol Mather of the Welsh Guards, small, cheerful and bouncy, who had travelled out to the Middle East as a member of Layforce; urbane Steve Hastings, a fellow officer in the Scots Guards; and Sandy Scratchley, whom David had known in London. Sandy bred race horses and was one of the best amateur riders in England; even in the middle of the desert he managed to preserve the raffish look of a horse-coper. There was David Russell, who had transferred from the S.I.G., where he had been helping Captain Buck train his Palestinian German unit, and Chris Bailey who had come from Eighth Army Headquarters.

David welcomed new officers, but none of them lasted long unless they got on with his tried and trusted non-commissioned officers and private soldiers. "Stirling had instituted a thoroughly democratic . . . system," wrote John Loder in *The Filibusters*, "in which the value of officers, in particular, was assessed, not so much by their own protestations and apparent achievements, but by what their men thought of them. After a given operation under a new officer, Stirling would drink a glass of beer with the wretch and then stroll over, Judas-like, towards his sergeant:

" ' Well, Sergeant X, and how did it go? '

" If Stirling found any cause for dissatisfaction, the officers . . . were very rapidly seeking fresh fields for their talents."

*   *   *

Another series of raids took place on the night of the 12th-13th of July. Five parties left for their objectives on the evening of the eleventh. Three of them, led by Jordan, Bill Fraser and Paddy Mayne, would attack three of the Fuka fields; the other two, led by Martin and Jellicoe, would act on the information of the prisoners and raid the El Daba aerodromes.

Only two groups were successful. Paddy Mayne destroyed

15 planes, and Jordan another 7. The rest of the patrols ran into trouble. Jellicoe's party, which included Carol Mather and Steve Hastings, was attacked from the air and two of their three jeeps were destroyed. They arrived back at the rendezvous, nine men in one badly damaged vehicle. They had had to patch up the radiator with plastic from their bombs.

Fraser's party also arrived the worse for wear. He had one of the jeeps fitted with Vickers K guns and had tried to do what David and Paddy had done the week before—attack by car. Unfortunately he had driven into a slit trench and had had much difficulty in extracting himself. The enemy had been alerted, and soon the sky was illuminated by Very lights. Much inaccurate firing took place during which he managed to get away.

Martin's party was the last to come in. Lt. Zirnheld was with him, as well as Robin Gurdon's Long Range patrol. Three miles short of El Daba their vehicles had been spotted and attacked from the air. Robin Gurdon had been killed. He had been unable to resist firing back at one of the fighters; the machine had come down two or three times until it had set his car alight and mortally wounded him.

Robin's death was a tragic loss, for this was scheduled to be his last operation. He had agreed to transfer from the L.R.D.G. and to join the S.A.S. as David's second-in-command. Ever since Jock Lewis's death David had been searching for the right man to take over the organisational and training side of the unit. The responsibility would have to continue to be shouldered by himself for some time to come.

*   *   *

The raiders had been away from their base at Kabrit for over two weeks. Food and ammunition were growing low, and eight vehicles had been put out of action. David decided that the only thing to do was to leave a small holding force at the rendezvous and make a lightning trip back to Cairo with men and trucks to collect fresh supplies. He and George Jellicoe and a few others would go ahead with three jeeps; Paddy

Mayne and Sandy Scratchley, accompanied by a Long Range patrol, would follow with seven or eight trucks. With luck they would all be back at the rendezvous in a week.

George and David left soon after lunch and Sandy and Paddy a few hours later. They knew by the wireless that the route on the edge of the Qattara Depression, which they had taken on the way out, was now closed by the Germans. The only short-cut back was through the Depression itself. This presented certain difficulties. The Depression, which was shaped something like a cutlet, was 150 miles in length and 75 miles across at the widest place. Before the war it had been mapped, but it was considered 'impassable.' This was due to the fact that the bottom consisted of a huge salt bog. It had a cracked crust which was solid enough to take a man's weight. But if a truck went on to it the vehicle would slowly sink out of sight. However, there were one or two narrow tracks across the bog, the best known of which was the 'Kaneitra crossing.' It had a hard surface formed by rock salt, and had been used for years as a caravan route. Slightly south there was a similar track that would also bear considerable weight.

Although these crossings were well-known they were considered too unreliable and treacherous for vehicles to move over them. However, in the past month the Long Range Desert Group had explored both of them. Timpson had made the crossing with six trucks, and so had Gus Holliman, guiding a whole line of vehicles and two hundred and fifty men from the Jaghbub garrison back to Cairo. The track had not stood up well under the heavy weights, and Holliman had signalled " Kaneitra completely wrecked for further crossing."

Under the circumstances Paddy and Sandy decided that once they were at the bottom of the Depression, they would try the other track slightly to the south. But this was not their main problem. The enemy was aware of the fact that the British were crossing the basin and maintained air patrols over both the Depression and the tracks leading to it. It was therefore important to cross the basin either at night or during the midday heat haze. They reckoned the trip over the quicksands was about thirty miles in length and would not take

T.P.M. G

more than three or four hours; and since the track required concentrated driving it was best to go by day.

They left the desert base in mid-afternoon, reckoning that they would reach the Qara track by dusk and get to the bottom of the Depression that night. They would then be ready to move across the marsh the following morning. They kept well up to schedule but as they neared the top of the Depression, they were caught by three enemy aircraft and machine-gunned. No damage was done except for one truck which was set on fire. There was some small arms ammunition in it and Sandy Scratchley remembers the cool action of three men in removing the wheels of the blazing vehicle, because ' we might run short of tyres.'

The convoy spent the night at the bottom of the Depression. In the morning they had twenty-five miles of good going before they hit the bog. Gradually the scene seemed to take on a strange, almost horrific, aspect. In front of them stretched miles of cracked salt. Above them was blue sky and a scorching, concentrated sun. And behind them, to the north, were great cliffs rising a thousand feet in height. These cliffs were made of limestone rocks, and centuries of wind erosion had carved huge and fantastic shapes out of them; it was almost as though a host of giant gargoyles were grinning and jeering at them.

It was high noon and soon every man was wishing that it had been decided to make the journey at night. The sun beat down with pitiless strength and the heat became so stifling that it was an effort to speak. The track was very rough and the vehicles could not average more than a few miles an hour. The fumes from the engine mixed with the terrifying heat-waves in the basin made the exertion of changing a punctured wheel an agonising performance. Some of the men were wearing Arab head-dress and they constantly took them off and dipped them into cans of water on the truck. This, however, was a waste of time for the cloth immediately began to steam.

The truck in front of Sandy Scratchley gave trouble. The petrol did not seem to be running through to the carburettor. The driver discovered that the heat was causing the petrol, which ran through the pipe under the bonnet, to evaporate before it reached the carburettor. He was clever enough to improvise a very successful and Emmet-like feed which kept the vehicle going.

By four o'clock in the afternoon the worst was over. The treacherous salt bog was behind them. " The ground spread out as a flat plain of hard, sandy gravel," wrote Scratchley. " The slow grind was forgotten, thirty miles an hour—or more —raised a breeze and the sun was well over the top. The strain was over. The mind returned from the effort of living. We must have made the best part of two hundred miles from the western edge of the Depression to where we halted to eat and sleep amidst rolling country, spotted with stunted acacia trees. A reconnaissance plane—at a great height—had been sighted during the afternoon. Unidentifiable, it had produced no repercussion. The lookouts relaxed. A wonderful desert sunset, when sometimes the whole horizon seems to be on fire, could be absorbed without another thought.

" Next morning we continued on our way, the colour of the ground changing with the surface. The gravel and sand becoming pebbles and sand until with the undulations continuing so that horizon followed horizon, we topped the final ridge and saw the three triangles of the Mena Pyramids. In the evening light the peculiar technicolour of the scene meant that we were approaching water, civilisation and dirt."

They reached Cairo to find that David, who had had the advantage of travelling in a jeep, had managed to get across the Kaneitra track and arrived the previous afternoon.

CHAPTER TWELVE

THE JEEP ATTACK

IN THE meantime the thirty odd men whom David had left behind led a life of discomfort and anxiety waiting for his return. Their base was only forty to fifty miles from many of the enemy's coastal airfields, and planes frequently passed overhead which meant that there was always the possibility of detection. Consequently no movement was allowed by day. The men lived in the side of the long, fifty-foot high escarpment, like rabbits in a warren. The jeeps and trucks were driven into crevices scooped out of the side, and camouflaged with nets and bushes. From dawn to dusk there was nothing to do but lie under the trucks, or in caves, swearing in the blazing heat, tortured by flies, just waiting.

The men were divided into several groups. The French lived in one cave, and the British in another half a mile away. The Long Range patrol, which Robin Gurdon had commanded, had its own hideout, and two miles to the north was the New Zealand L.R.D.G. patrol which was operating independently and did not come under David's command.

The British contingent consisted of 20 men and 3 officers—Steve Hastings, Carol Mather and Malcolm Pleydell, the doctor. Above their cave a sentry was always on duty. He sat at the top of the blazing escarpment, peering into the interminable dun-coloured wilderness that stretched out on all sides, and was relieved every two hours.

" We were under the continual apprehension that the enemy would discover our hideout by aircraft or by ground patrols," wrote Carol Mather. " There were so many tracks leading from all directions to our escarpment and running along the foot of the cliff itself that we had to take every precaution. Happily there was a broad rocky outcrop immediately to the north over which tracks did not show; but along the cliff itself a white talcum powder dust had been formed by the passing of many wheels, and on this we spent much time in raking out the marks.

" Steve Hastings and I took two hours each day as sentry with the men on the pimple which raised itself from the rocky outcrop. From this point we could get a view of all the surrounding country. And we would search round and round with our glasses over the barren landscape, staring for minutes on end at dust clouds and vehicles which seemed to be making our way, only to disperse in mirages.

" The worst period was the middle of the day, when everything was a shimmer of pink, and the landscape heaved and sank, and at these times bitter thoughts would pass through our minds, when the future held nothing but an endless nomad life in the desert. We soon gave up the alarm whistle which was blown by the sentry for enemy aircraft or for ground patrols. We found it had too shattering an effect on our nerves—instead, the sentry would make his way slowly down to our cave and tell us quietly what he had seen, and we would consider the matter placidly and take whatever steps we considered necessary, which usually consisted of killing a few more flies and telling the sentry not to disturb us again unless he could prove that the camp was being attacked by Germans, or the end of the world had come, or some other major disaster.

" The evening always brought relief. Sometimes we would sit round the embers of the cook-house fire smoking and passing round the big dixie which contained a mixture of rum and lime and water, well calculated to dispel the ugliness of the day and turn the night into something soft and sympathetic.

" Or perhaps we would walk along the escarpment to the New Zealand patrol and lie there lazily on our backs, gazing at the stars, exchanging in a desultory fashion the news of the day. When we visited Jordan and Martin and Zirnheld in the

French cave there would be much singing and much laughter, and talk of Cairo and girls and cinemas. Here we would end our evening for here we slept.

" In the early morning Steve and I would walk down from the French cave, which was not much more than a pile of boulders, to our daytime cave near the cook-house. Here we would spend the remainder of the day. It was a long and low grotto with a floor of soft white sand, at one end a great lip curved over, touching the ground and forming a cool enclosed space, whilst at the extreme end grew a stunted palm. At best it would only contain three men lying down, but there was just room for a mosquito net to be suspended from the eaves which covered us quite easily.

" Once in, it was a question of exterminating the flies that had climbed in with us, and settling down to *The Virginians*, *Seven Pillars of Wisdom*, or *For Whom the Bell Tolls*. The last two were too near home for my liking, and were depressing in their tales of forced journeys in Arabia, and the fate of those who fought behind the lines in Spain. The only alternatives were Thackeray and sleep, both of which made happy partners. Above our heads were embedded a variety of marine fossils and shells and we had the leisure to consider in what strange manner they had arrived there. Which usually began with Steve saying, ' I wonder how those shells got there,' and myself replying that this place must have been under the sea at one time, and ending in silence."

Despite the apprehension of the men left behind, the enemy did not send out patrols to hunt them down. David was always surprised that once the raiding parties had travelled as little as ten or fifteen miles away from the coastal strip, they were safe from ground forces. The enemy tried to track them down by reconnaissance planes and destroy them by bombing and strafing; but up until now, except for the patrols that had searched for David and Paddy on the Benghazi plain the month previously, they had not been pursued by land.

The only explanation is the fact that until the summer of 1942 Rommel did not understand exactly what he was up against. In the beginning he probably regarded the raids as hit and run affairs and did not realise that they were being carried out by a permanent organisation which was gradually increasing its striking power. A few weeks later, as the reader will see, he began to remedy this oversight by organising special units to track them down.

David also found it strange that throughout the whole of the African campaign the enemy never chose to take a leaf from the British book and use the desert flank for their own patrol work. The truth was that both Germans and Italians feared and disliked the uninhabited regions, whereas the British were fascinated by them. Experts have offered theories on the subject, suggesting that it was natural that a great seafaring race should take easily to the huge uncharted wastelands. Sea and desert had much in common. It was necessary to navigate one's way across both; and both offered the same sense of isolation, comradeship, exploration and adventure.

*   *   *

At the end of eight days the food and water situation was serious. In the late afternoon the sentry reported black dots on the horizon. The officers ran out and stood watch with him, wondering anxiously whether it would prove to be friend or foe. The dots grew larger and at last they turned into clearly visible jeeps. David was returning.

Soon twenty brand new jeeps, all of them bristling with Vickers K guns, and a few three-tonners, were threading their way down the escarpment. David walked into the cave laden with tobacco, rum, new pipes, Turkish Delight and a pint jar of Eau de Cologne.

His presence had an electric effect. Not only did he arrive with new supplies and new men but with a startling new idea. As soon as immediate business was attended to—vehicles camouflaged, a Wyndham aerial erected, and ample rations of tea and rum consumed—he spread his maps out in the sand, and explained to the men what he had in mind.

One of the aerodromes in the Fuka area, Sidi Haneish, known as Landing-Ground 12, was serving as Rommel's main staging area for all planes going to or coming from the front.

Reconnaissance reported that it was constantly full of aircraft and contained a large number of JU 52's, transport carriers of which the enemy was reported to be very short. David proposed to destroy every plane on the field by a massed jeep attack in full moonlight. The method was novel enough; and since the Germans would not expect an attack now that the moon was full, the raiders would have most precious of all assets; complete surprise.

Eighteen jeeps would take part. As they approached the perimeter defences of the airfield they would form a line abreast. On a signal from him they would open up with a spectacular display of tracer bullets to silence the defences and give an impression of great strength. Once in the field he would send up a green Very light and they would change to a second formation—two columns with two jeeps connecting them to David's jeep in the lead; a sort of double-lined arrowhead. " Like this," he said, drawing a diagram in the sand.

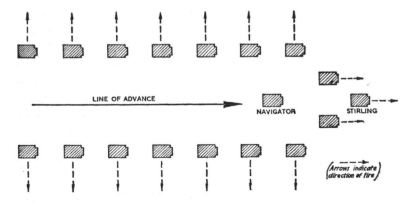

The arrowhead was designed to move between two rows of planes, with the guns of the three leading jeeps firing ahead at the defences and all the other guns firing outwards at the planes. There would be plenty of fire power, David said, for each jeep was equipped with four Vickers K guns which fired at the rate of a thousand rounds a minute; two were mounted into a steel upright in front of the man beside the driver, and two more at the right-hand side in the back. When sixty-eight guns opened up simultaneously, the fire power would be devastating.[1]

David finished by saying that the raid would take place the following night. But practice was necessary; it was like learning a dance routine. So about midnight the strange little party drove into the darkness and staged a weird dress rehearsal. The jeeps formed line abreast and line astern, concentrating on keeping even distance about five yards apart; then David let off his Very light and they made their arrowhead. This drill was not just to achieve perfection; with so many guns firing, a false move could prove fatal. For the drivers it was something of an ordeal, for they not only had to concentrate on their vehicles, but to take care not to get in the way of their own gunners. " Every gun fired outwards," wrote Carol Mather, " and as I was driving and at the end of the left-hand column my front gun fired across my face and my rear gun behind my head, so it was important to sit very still and not to lean forwards or backwards."

*   *   *

It was three o'clock in the morning before the men got to bed, and they were up again at dawn. The jeeps had been put in a long, low cave a mile up the escarpment, and soon the bustle resembled the gold-mining scene from *The Seven Dwarfs*. Men hammered and sang as they fitted new wheels and tyres; others stripped and cleaned the guns; still others sat in a corner making up explosive charges in a litter of black adhesive tape, time pencils, fuses, primer cord and heaps of strong-smelling sticks of 808 and plastic explosive.

During the morning several more three-tonners arrived crammed with water and petrol, explosives and rations. Even a recovery vehicle appeared full of spare parts. The officers checked their petrol and water, and handed out emergency rations and escape kit. George Jellicoe, who was David's assistant on the Q side, sat with a tin of acid drops in front of him trying to work out the impossible problem of how much

---

[1] Sadler, the navigator, would be behind David in the middle of this arrowhead and would not be able to use his guns.

stuff was really necessary; Paddy went to sleep beneath a huge mosquito net with his head against one jeep and his feet under another; and David struggled with wireless signals from Headquarters which were so contradictory and infuriating that he sent back a blasphemous message which at least produced a restful silence.

The party was scheduled to start at sundown. The Sidi Haneish field was forty miles away. The attack was planned for about one in the morning. If all went well this would allow the raiders three hours or more of darkness in which to find reasonable cover before the inevitable aircraft came out to search for them. The timing depended on the accuracy of the navigation. It required great skill to lead a convoy across featureless country in the middle of the night and bring it dead on to its target; but with Mike Sadler in charge everyone was confident the task would be executed perfectly.

*   *   *

Before sundown the vehicles began to assemble. Each jeep had an officer or an N.C.O. driving, and a front and rear gunner. In David's jeep were the faithful Cooper and Seekings. He and Mike Sadler were to lead the party. As the men waited they revved their engines up and down. Finally the signal came to start. " One by one we pulled out," wrote Steve Hastings, " bumping through the soft, churned-up sand at the foot of the escarpment, guns rattling and swinging on their mountings, out on to the firm desert behind.

" It was easy to see at first. We kept no particular formation and the drivers just picked their own way a little to right or left of the man in front and followed his dust; occasionally a jeep would hit a rock or a bad bump and the gun mountings would rattle and the cans and ammo. boxes clash in the back. Mostly we rolled along at a good 20 m.p.h. over flat shingle or sand. Every now and then we would come to small escarpments and then bunch together until we found a way up or down. The dust rose thicker and engines revved as they changed gear. They would pull up one after the other and fan out again on the level."

In three-quarters of an hour it was completely dark and the moon was up. They could see the Siwa track ahead of them. David gave the signal to stop and Mike Sadler climbed out of his jeep, fixed up the tripod of his theodolite and took a shot. He was not taking any chances on this particular night; if he did not bring the convoy dead on to the airfield the whole operation might be spoiled.

The going got tougher as the jeeps proceeded. The rocks and ridges, which were impossible to see until the vehicles were nearly on them, began to take a heavy toll of tyres. There were fifteen punctures in all, and each one took nearly five minutes to fix, during which the whole convoy was obliged to halt.

At one point the vehicles came to a cliff which proved impossible to negotiate. David sent two jeeps out to find a way up. The others sat smoking cigarettes and talking in low voices. Fifteen minutes later the drivers returned and said they had discovered a possible route about a quarter of a mile farther along. " The pass proved to be a wadi running up about twenty feet and very steep," wrote Hastings. " It was pitch dark in the wadi's shadow and the first jeep got about half-way up, hit a rock and slithered sideways to the bottom. There was much grinding of gears as the drivers approached with engines racing and one by one they crashed and bounced up the slope. From my position at the back we could see nothing but the irregular outline of the cliff and the silhouettes of the jeeps as they jolted to the top, paused and then plunged out of sight beyond, engines growling in low gear, like a pack of mechanised wolves."

The men had been driving about three hours now and David gave the signal to stop. He and Sadler climbed out and put a map on the bonnet of the jeep and studied it with the aid of a shaded torch. The men and officers from the other jeeps walked up and gathered round. He told them that according to his reckoning they had covered about thirty miles. The airfield should lie ten miles due north. He wanted everyone to make a last minute check of his guns and ammunition. They would, of course, stop once again when they were close to the field and move into the extended line formation.

They drove for another three-quarters of an hour. They came to the edge of a long ridge and could distinguish what looked like the beginning of the undulating country leading to the coast some twenty miles away. There were clouds in the sky and the moon dipped in and out, casting weird shadows across the ground. Was that a shadow or a vehicle directly across their path? David's car slowed down; then a breeze brought the sour-sweet smell of the recent battle. They were passing burnt-out tanks and trucks, and they could see the shapes of dead bodies sprawling where they had fallen.

For several hundred yards the convoy drove through the desolate scene, then the ground began to get smoother and they knew they were leaving the wilderness and approaching the inhabited coastal belt. Another thirty minutes and David stopped again. Sadler jumped out and said, " By my reckoning we're less than a mile short of the field. It's right in front of us."

It seemed impossible. There was no sign of life; only silence and wilderness. However, David's faith in Sadler's navigation was so complete he accepted his verdict without question. He quietly ordered the men to move into line abreast. " And make sure you keep in it until you get the signal for line astern. Right, we're off."

The jeeps moved into line abreast with the vehicles five yards apart. They were going very slowly now because it was difficult to keep formation on the rough ground. First one and then another would pull slightly in front, then drop back again. All eighteen vehicles showed up clearly under a full moon. The ground was pitted and broken and every now and then a wheel would crash into some unseen cavity. The gunners sat tensely, their thumbs on the catch, their weapons levelled in front of them.

Then came a shock. A half a mile away the landscape lighted up. It was such a surprise that at first the men did not grasp what was happening. There in front of them lay a flood-lit aerodrome. They must have been spotted. This was the first precaution; next the enemy defences would open up on them.

Then, above the noise of the jeeps, they heard the deep-throated noise of an engine. No! A bomber was coming down to land. " It's Brighton Beach! " murmured one of the men in awe.

David did not stop because of the lights. He headed straight for the illuminated runway. He was only a hundred yards away when the plane touched down and bumped along the ground. He opened fire. Sixty-eight guns followed suit. First there was a fantastic slanting cascade of red and white tracer pouring on to the airfield, then the business-like rasp and roar of machine-gun bullets. Instantly the landing lights were switched off.

Two minutes later David sent up a green Very light. His jeep pulled into the lead and the others formed into the two-columned arrowhead behind him. Now they were moving fast. David hit a piece of smooth tarmac and turned in between the rows of planes. Everything seemed to be there; Messerschmidts, Stukas, Heinkels and a large proportion of the important Junker 52's. The jeeps kept perfect formation with their sixty-eight guns making a roaring, deafening cacophony. The planes took longer to catch fire than the men had imagined. It was perhaps thirty seconds before the interior of the aircraft suddenly glowed red, followed by the dull thud of exploding petrol which turned the whole body into a sheet of flame. Some planes did not burn but seemed literally to crumble and disintegrate as the bullets ploughed into them from less than fifty yards.

The blasts of heat were intense, and many men had singed hair and eyebrows. The burning wreckage brilliantly lit up the aerodrome and the raiders could see German soldiers running about in the distance. In the glow David spotted the shadows of other planes parked much farther out on the field. He would go back for them when the circle was completed.

At this point there was a whistle, followed by the familiar thud of a mortar shell. It fell slap between the two jeep lines.

Then a Breda gun began its slow tattoo. " I felt something hot pass beneath my seat," wrote Hastings. " There was a clang, and my face and that of my front gunner were covered in oil. There was a moment of blindness and incomprehension; we wiped the oil out of our eyes and the jeep swerved violently, hit a bump, recovered itself and continued miraculously. ' You O.K.? ' I asked. ' I think so,' he replied."

At the same moment David's jeep was hit by a splinter. No one was hurt but the vehicle was put out of action. The whole movement came to a standstill. He shouted to the gunners to concentrate on the Breda post and signalled one of the jeeps farther down the line to move forward and pick up himself and his crew. Luckily the Breda was firing from much the same position as the mortar and was using tracer which pin-pointed its position. It was soon silenced.

David then gave the order for the drivers to ' switch off ' so they could hear his instructions. There was an uncanny stillness save for the crackle and noise of burning frames. It was a weird setting for a conference but it served its purpose.

First he asked, " Everyone O.K.? "

" Yes."

" How much ammo. have you got left? " " Two drums; one drum; half a drum," came the answers. " God, you've been getting rid of it," said David. " Don't fire unless you're certain of a target. Now listen carefully. We'll finish the circle, then move back and knock off the clump of planes on the perimeter. Then we'll beat it."

The jeeps opened their roaring, belching fire once again as they continued their passage. A small dispersal area marked the completion of their circle, and they fired into tents and a few station buildings. Then they turned and headed for the shapes on the outskirts of the field, which proved to be JU 52's. They quickly shot them up and David gave the signal to leave. As they were moving off they caught sight of one surviving plane silhouetted against the sky. How had they missed that one? Suddenly they saw a man running toward it. He reached up high and placed something on the wing then ran back to his jeep. It was Paddy Mayne, who had put a bomb on it.

A moment later the jeeps were on the rough desert.

Suddenly Steve Hastings's engine seized. The driver tinkered with it a moment but he could not get it going. " I climbed out and signalled the last vehicle which drew up in front of us," wrote Hastings. " We piled in except for my gunner who was busy putting a bomb on the jeep we were leaving behind. We could see him in the dark fiddling with the time fuse. A moment later he came running up and we pulled him in. After a few minutes' haphazard progress we suddenly found ourselves among the others again. They were halted.

" David was talking to the officers. We would split up now, into various parties, and make for the rendezvous independently of each other. The idea was to get as far as we could in two and a half hours, and to ' camouflage down ' before the daylight should betray our whereabouts to an angry and determined enemy in the air. The exact direction of our flight was of little importance, provided that we checked our courses; but we should all try and cross to the west of the big track, with the telegraph poles running along it, which led from Bagush to Qara at the north-western tip of the Depression, and which would certainly be searched by the enemy planes on the following morning. Did we remember the track? Yes, we did.

" We were to lie up the following day and not move until dark. Then to make our own way back to the escarpment. David told us to refill with petrol and get going. It transpired that six jeeps had been hit but were still running and three had been knocked out.

" The group split up.

" David caught sight of my face. ' What on earth are you covered in? '

" ' Oil. I got some through the sump.'

" Sandy Scratchley joined the group. ' You all right? ' asked David.

" ' Yes—but my front gunner got killed.'

" ' God. I'm sorry.'

" We looked at Sandy's jeep which stood close by. A figure was slumped forward in the front seat, the back curiously straight and the head and shoulders resting on the guns.

" ' What happened? '

" ' I don't know. I think it was the first mortar. I was shouting at him to fire at the Breda and nothing happened, so I turned around and he was like that.' "

The group turned back to their jeeps and were soon under way. For a short while they moved close to each other, then they began to split off in twos and threes. It was up to each unit to get back to the rendezvous independently.

CHAPTER THIRTEEN

THE TRIP HOME

DAVID'S PARTY consisted of four jeeps and fourteen men. Two of the jeeps were badly damaged and one contained the body of the dead gunner. The officers with him were George Jellicoe, Sandy Scratchley and Steve Hastings.

It was going to be a race to reach cover before light. The one thing to avoid was being caught near the Qara track, every inch of which was certain to be combed by enemy reconnaissance.

David was in the leading jeep and he drove fast. The ground had a flat rocky surface and the guns swung wildly as the vehicles jolted over it. The second jeep began to slow up and changed into bottom gear. The third jeep passed it, and as the fourth came abreast it stopped altogether. There was no time to stop and inspect the engine. Hurriedly petrol and a spare wheel were transferred. One of the men got out a bomb, pulling the firing pin on a ten-minute delay fuse, and placed it on the tank of the abandoned vehicle. The crew scrambled aboard the waiting machine and off they went again—fourteen men in three jeeps.

During the next two hours they stopped twice while David made a rough check on a prismatic compass. He was looking for a track marked on the map from which he could take a bearing for the rendezvous. But the track never appeared. As dawn approached he estimated that they had covered thirty miles, and must have passed it. The problem now was to find cover. The stony surface did not offer much hope, but mercifully a ground mist had reduced visibility to little over twenty yards. David was going slowly now, carefully following any suspicion of a gulley in case it might develop into a wadi deep enough to give them refuge. But nothing relieved the nakedness. Gradually the fog began to lift, and uneasily the men listened for the dread hum of enemy engines.

" Then the desert became our friend," wrote Steve Hastings. " The fog cleared away and we found ourselves on the edge of a small escarpment dropping about fifteen feet. Before us lay what appeared to be a large bowl-shaped depression about a quarter of a mile broad, the walls of which were cut by fairly deep wadis with thick greenish brown scrub up to three or four feet high. A few minutes before, our position had seemed very grave; now suddenly we had been shown exactly the place we were looking for.

" Our vehicles bumped uncertainly down one of the wadis on to the softer yellower sand below and we made our way along the bottom of the escarpment for some few hundred yards until we reached what appeared to be the thickest patch of scrub. We were in a small dried water course and the sand below the bushes was carved into uneven funnels a foot or so deep. The men needed no orders; they clambered off and swiftly heaved and manœuvred the jeeps into the centre of the water-course among the tallest bush. It was a matter of minutes before enough scrub had been wrenched up and thrown over them, to render them practically indistinguishable, in our sunken position, from as little as fifty yards away.

" Then only did relief set in. Since the vehicles were hidden it would be comparatively easy for each of us to run to cover on the noise of an approaching aircraft. We looked round at each other—we were indeed a ragged-looking bunch. Faces, hair and beards were covered in a thick yellow grey film of dust, eyes were red and strained. Our dirty open-necked battle dress and loose overcoats hung upon us as upon scarecrows and they fitted well into the background of the desert. One officer was trying to scrape large dried and sand-caked bloodstains off his trousers with a stick; the blood of the dead soldier who was lying on his back under a bush with a dirty blanket over the top of his body. Our mouths were dry and

ill-tasting and there was a burning behind the eyes rather
like the symptoms of a hangover—but for the moment we
were safe or at least comparatively so. ' Got any tea, Seekings? '
David said.

" ' Yes, sir '—a large grin spread across the corporal's face.

" ' All right, then, brew up for everyone.'

" Then in a lower voice——

" ' You two—get a spade out and bury him.'

" The officers walked a little distance away, sat down in the
scrub and we each found and lit a cigarette. The relief that
always follows periods of action and strain loosened our
tongues and we talked and laughed over our success. Behind
us the men squatted in a group round the brew. Two charred
tins, one filled with burning petrol, the other with dirty-
looking water, soaked the sand and scrub. A little way away
two figures bent to their work in the scrub, every now and
then came the clink of steel on stone. A certain amount of
mist still hung about; it was 5.30 in the morning.

" Presently the tea was ready. It was passed round in mugs,
black, practically unsugared and brewed in brackish water but
still hot, strong and unbelievably refreshing. The two men
returned with the spade—' We buried 'im, sir.'

" ' Have you got his pay book? '

" ' Yes.'

" There was a silence. What could they do, they had no
Prayer Book, they knew no words to say.

" ' I think we'll just go and stand round the grave a minute,'
said David.

" The officers got up, moved away into the scrub and stood
gathered round the pathetic little heap of sand and stones.
There was no cross, some of the men were trying to make one
from the scrub and a piece of old ration box, but it was not
ready yet. We stood bareheaded, looking at the grave, each
with our own thoughts. Most of us had not even known this
man, who was one of the more recent arrivals; he was just a
name to us or perhaps a cheery red face and a shock of black
hair. It was indeed a curious burial, just a two minutes'
silence with a handful of tired, dirty comrades. Yet for this

short fraction of time, lost in the middle of nowhere, there was dignity."

*   *   *

The men spent the rest of the day here. They had orders to move about as little as possible and to conserve their drinking water. They tried to sleep but the flies were so bad they had nightmarish dreams, and finally just lay in the heat sweating and cursing. At noon three Stukas roared overhead; later they heard the sound of machine-gun strafing and wondered what 'poor bastard' was catching it.

As soon as it was dark they set out again. Since they had no idea where they were David decided to turn back and search for the elusive track. Two of the jeeps were knocking badly, and a third had a slow puncture. They drove slowly, wondering which vehicle would be the next to pack up, but miraculously all kept going. After two hours they found the track. Now they could take a bearing. With luck they would reach the rendezvous before morning.

However, things did not work out so easily. A second puncture developed on the same jeep, and both finally gave way to bursts, leaving the inner tubes in ribbons. There was only one spare left and the vehicle had to bump along on its rims. This cut the speed down still further.

One of the corporals was navigating and rode in the jeep with David. He was certain of his directions, but when dawn came a flat, open expanse spread out before them which was utterly unrecognisable. They were lost again. David discussed the position with his three officers, George and Sandy and Steve, and they agreed to keep on the same bearing for a few miles. All that day they drove, anxiously scanning every inch of the horizon. Several times they discovered tracks that looked like jeep marks but each time they faded away.

About five o'clock in the evening the ground grew rockier and began to rise. It ended in a steep cliff which fell for fifty feet. Below them the desert stretched vaguely into the distance. They could make out a criss-crossing of wadis, but they could see no sign of their rendezvous. And if their rendezvous really was down there, surely they would have recognised the cliff upon which they were now standing. Then a horrible thought struck Hastings. Perhaps the compass had gone wrong. " Do you think it's the coastal escarpment? " he asked. This apparently had occurred to the others too. If so, they had made a circle and moved back to the enemy's threshold; they were at least a hundred miles from where they thought they were, and they certainly did not have a hundred miles of petrol left.

" I think we'll go down the cliff and spend the night," said David quickly. " We'll decide what to do in the morning."

They descended with a shower of stones coming after them, and as soon as they had parked their vehicles flung themselves on the ground and instantly fell asleep.

The next morning they set off at sunrise. They had petrol for fifty miles. David decided that they must continue their bearing despite the fact that the landscape looked so alien and hostile. In less than half an hour they came to a second escarpment. Below them, not more than fifty yards away, they could see a three-ton British lorry and a group of men ' brewing up.' There, in the innocent morning light, was the blessed rendezvous. " Home," as Cooper put it jubilantly, " never looked sweeter."

*   *   *

Most of the other parties had arrived, and the remaining few came in at various times during the morning. There was one tragedy. André Zirnheld, the gay young Frenchman who had amused Steve Hastings and Carol Mather with his songs and stories of Cairo, was dead. Three jeeps with French crews had taken part in the raid. Zirnheld and Martin were driving two of them. They had become detached from the vehicles they were following, due to punctures, and when the fog lifted and light came, they found themselves on the dreaded Matruh-Siwa track, which David had warned them against.

There was no time to search for another place farther afield, and the Frenchmen considered themselves lucky to find a cliff to hide their jeeps beneath. They were undisturbed until noon when three Stukas passed overhead flying very low. They were scouring every inch of the track. At first the Frenchmen thought they had escaped detection, but suddenly the planes wheeled around and dived down, their machine-guns firing. They made nine attacks, and Zirnheld was wounded twice. Undoubtedly they were the same planes that David's group had seen.

The jeeps were riddled with bullets but they were still functioning. Martin made Zirnheld as comfortable as possible and the two vehicles moved off to find new cover. Zirnheld could not stand the motion, however, and they stopped in a small wadi. Martin then set off by himself to bring back the doctor from the rendezvous. When he returned Zirnheld was dead. Martin buried him with full military honours and placed a cross, made out of a packing case, on his grave which was inscribed: " Aspirant André Zirnheld. Died for France on 27th July, 1942."

The French jeeps were the only two to be attacked. Although the sky was alive with planes, and more than one S.A.S. party watched them from their hiding-place, their vehicles were not spotted. Mike Sadler had the luckiest escape. He had been told by David to establish a rendezvous close to the airfield, and to remain there for at least an hour in case any stragglers came in. This he did, and one jeep and three men joined his own vehicle and crew. He had a camera with him and amused himself by taking time-exposures of the burning planes.[1] What astonished him was the rapidity with which the Germans got the field going again. Within a short time all the wrecked planes were cleared away and new planes were coming in to land.

As dawn was breaking his party set off. They were protected by the heavy ground fog, which proved to be a mixed blessing. They were driving along a track when suddenly, with no warning, they came upon a vehicle parked on the road. Another was in front of it and still another. They passed the first one before they realised that the cars were part of a

---

[1] This story had an unlucky sequel. Sadler brought the camera with the film in it back to Cairo. He left it in his car and it was stolen; so the strange record of that historic night ceased to exist.

German motorised infantry unit, no doubt in search of the
S.A.S. raiders. They hastily swerved off the track and were
soon lost in the desert expanse. They remember the bored
expression on the face of one of the German soldiers, who
apparently saw nothing odd in the appearance of the two
jeeps, assuming they must be part of his own force.

The S.A.S. party took cover several miles away in a clump
of bushes between two rises. Sadler was moving to the top
of one of these slight inclines when several Stukas appeared
and flew around the place where his men were hidden. He
thought they must have spotted the jeeps but the planes flew
away without attacking. He returned to where the vehicles
were concealed and was surprised to see Jim Almonds frantically motioning him to take cover. In whispers he was informed
that on the far side of the second rise a German reconstruction
unit was busy dismantling a British lorry. The Germans were
not more than twenty yards away. They worked on for several
hours while the S.A.S. lay under the bushes not daring to
move. Finally they packed up their gear and drove away,
oblivious of the quarry that had eluded them. Sadler's group
left their hide-out at sunset and reached the main rendezvous
that night.

*   *   *

Perhaps even more extraordinary was the experience that
had befallen the group of S.A.S. who, led by Lieutenant Wilder
of the L.R.D.G., had gone to the landing-ground near Bagush
to create a diversion while the massed jeep attack took place.
The men had succeeded in getting on to the airfield and
destroyed fifteen planes. In the morning the Germans had
sent out ground forces in trucks to hunt them down. A short,
sharp battle had taken place with the result that four of the
enemy's trucks were put out of action and the rest took flight.
A short while later the men heard the noise of an aircraft and
took cover. A Feisler Storch approached and circled around
several times. To the amazement of the onlookers, they saw
that it was coming down to land. It bumped along the ground
and stopped about fifty yards from one of the wrecked trucks.

The door opened and out jumped two German officers laughing and talking. Evidently they thought the scene was deserted and had come down to have a look around. As they walked over to the truck the British soldiers opened fire on their aircraft. The Germans halted with a look of astonishment. The L.R.D.G. moved out of their hiding-place and one of the officers pulled a Red Cross armband out of his pocket and cried, " You can't shoot me. I'm a doctor."

Wilder politely explained that they were now prisoners of war and ordered them to climb aboard his jeep. The plane was burning merrily as the little group moved on its way. When they reached the rendezvous the Germans were interrogated. The small dark man, it transpired, was one of Rommel's personal pilots. The taller man, who wore spectacles and spoke English, was a distinguished doctor from Hamburg. His name was Baron von Lutteroti. " I went up for pleasure," he kept repeating, " and it ended unhappily."

*   *   *

After breakfast David discussed future operations with Paddy. Wireless signals were coming in from Headquarters, and David asked for the latest intelligence reports. Later in the morning he called the men together and briefed them. Apparently, he said, the enemy was very angry at the raid and at last were organising armoured car patrols to search for the culprits. Since the ground outside their hide-out was badly churned up by jeeps and trucks, a low-flying aircraft might easily spot it. It was necessary, therefore, to move camp as soon as night fell. They would travel thirty miles westward and establish a new base.

Then he referred to the activities of the night before. It was impossible to say exactly how many planes had been destroyed, but he believed about 25 with at least another 12 damaged. Counting the 15 demolished by the S.A.S. patrol led by the L.R.D.G. party, the night's work amounted to between 40 and 50 in all.[1] " But," he said, " it wasn't nearly good enough. We should have achieved a hundred per cent results. Some of

[1] He claimed only 40 planes which brought the S.A.S. total to 256.

you let off at everything you saw, instead of doing what I told you—shooting low and aiming at targets in your immediate range." He paused a moment. " How many of you ran out of ammunition? " A dozen hands went up. " Well, you shouldn't have done. It's no disgrace to leave an operation with ammunition to spare. If you had aimed more carefully we could have killed every plane on the field, not just wounding some."

The men were too high-spirited to allow David's lecture to depress them. But they recognised the truth in what he said. One of them suggested that they could have done the job as well with half a dozen men on foot. This, David pointed out, was not true. The perimeter defences were too strong, and he did not believe that any group could have penetrated them by stealth; and certainly not in moonlight.

Despite the criticisms he made (partly to prevent them from regarding these raids as ' a piece of cake ') he was satisfied with the outcome. First of all they had destroyed at least fourteen Junker 52's which, due to the difficulty Rommel was having getting his hands on supplies, were worth five ordinary bombers each. But more important still was the outcome of the attack. He had designed it because he wanted to prove that the armed jeep could be substituted effectively for the Lewis bomb when the situation warranted it. Three major advantages had emerged. First, his raiders had become fully mobile which meant that they could attack more than one target on a single night; second, they could overcome almost any type of aerodrome defence; third, and most important, they were no longer confined to dark periods in planning their assaults but could operate on any, or every, night of the month.

*   *   *

In the meantime the German prisoners seemed to have settled down to their strange new surroundings. David offered them parole but they refused it. Consequently they were put under the charge of the British doctor, Malcolm Pleydell, with Sergeant Bennett as guard. They were given cigarettes and beer and sat outside their cave in the shade of a lorry talking and smoking. Once Sandy Scratchley caught them staring quizzically at David's 6 ft. 6 in. figure, and wondered if they knew they were in the presence of the notorious ' Phantom Major ' who lately had received so much publicity on the German radio. Certainly the group of bronzed bearded giants with their vast horde of ammunition must have struck the prisoners as an interesting group, to say the least. Had they ever heard of the S.A.S.? They gave no indication of it and were wise enough not to ask any questions.

However, when invited, Lutteroti gladly engaged in conversation, and had several long talks with Pleydell. He told him that he knew England quite well; in fact he had spent several holidays at Clacton-on-Sea. Then Pleydell asked him if he thought Germany would win the war. " Of course," said Lutteroti in surprise, " don't you? " Pleydell shook his head. Lutteroti was genuinely puzzled. " But in that case you must think you are going to win. How do you think you will do it? " " Well," said Pleydell. " Well . . ." It was a difficult question for him to answer when the Germans were only forty miles from Alexandria. " I became very much aware," he wrote, " that I had not got the faintest notion as to how we could win the war. Of a sudden the situation struck me as being very humorous and I rolled over on to my back and laughed. ' I haven't the faintest idea,' I said, and at that he started laughing too. But I do not really think he understood what I was laughing about, and for the life of me I could not have explained it to anyone." [1]

That night the German prisoners rode with Pleydell in his truck when they made the move to establish a new base. They were model prisoners. They did all they could to help, and the next day Baron von Lutteroti offered to give Pleydell any medical assistance he desired. When George Jellicoe came into the cave where the doctors had set up shop, complaining of a twisted knee, the Baron asked to have a look at it. Pleydell thought it was a cartilage and von Lutteroti thought it was a ligament. (In the end it turned out to be both). They argued about it for some time and in the course of the conversation

[1] *Born of the Desert:* Malcolm James (Pleydell).

the German heard the name 'Jellicoe.' " Not Lord Jellicoe? " he asked. George nodded. " I think you know my wife," said the doctor. It then transpired that George had lunched with the Baroness von Lutteroti in Hamburg before the war.

This story spread among the men and tickled their fancy. They were amused enough by the doctor who had gone up for pleasure and, literally, had been brought down to earth with a rude awakening. They found his solemn references to Clacton-on-Sea comical, and now to think that George Jellicoe was a friend. Already the story was exaggerated, and soon they were telling each other that George had often stayed in the doctor's house in Berlin.

*   *   *

David and Paddy spent the morning checking their store position. Their plan was to remain at the rendezvous for several weeks, carrying out raids every few nights. They were convinced that the way to do real damage was to maintain constant pressure.

Of course the possibility of achieving this depended on their ability to keep themselves supplied with food, petrol and ammunition. David had thrashed out this problem on his lightning visit to Cairo the week before. He had discussed it with Air Vice Marshal Bruce Bennett of the Joint Planning Staff, who had promised to co-operate fully. First Bennett had suggested parachuting supplies to the raiders; then he had decided that it would be better to make use of the unit's old friends, 216 Squadron, and send Bombays in to land. David give him information about a discarded R.A.F. emergency landing-strip which he had reconnoitred several weeks before. It was about sixty miles from Fuka and ten or fifteen miles from the present S.A.S. rendezvous. Bennett said that this would do, and on an S.O.S. from David would send the necessary supplies. The two men had spent considerable time working out signals and flares to ensure the safe landing of the planes.

David now felt that the time had arrived to ask Bennett to fulfil his promise. The raiders were low on water and petrol and would soon need fresh supplies of food. With Paddy's help he concocted a signal and sent it off. Then he turned his attention to working out the details of the next raid.

He called four of his officers together and told them that they would set out on an operation that night. They were Carol Mather, Augustin Jordan, David Russell and Chris Bailey. The plan was this. They would be away about ten days. They would take eight jeeps manned by crews of three each. They would travel in two parties and would launch several attacks against German supply columns and dumps in the built-up area directly behind the Alamein line. The targets ought to be very enticing, said David, as Headquarters reported that a steady stream of supply trucks were moving along the main road, not to mention any number of petrol bowsers. They were to avoid all forms of armour, and only to attack ' soft-skinned ' vehicles. They were to take their time and carry out a thorough reconnaissance before they committed themselves.

While the officers began making preparations, David and Paddy Mayne analysed the intelligence reports coming over the wireless. David felt more sanguine about the future of the S.A.S. than ever before. During the last three weeks the detachment had destroyed over a hundred aircraft, the highest score it had ever achieved in a single month. For once everything appeared to be going without a hitch. Then the blow fell. Instead of the expected message announcing the arrival of supplies a signal came from Headquarters requesting him to bring his party home. A new operation, based on one of David's ideas—(" What idea? " he stormed)—was in the process of being planned and his presence was urgently required.

He read the signal to Paddy, punctuating it with forceful vituperation. What did they mean planning operations behind his back? He was the planner of S.A.S. operations, not some idiot at Headquarters. Besides, if they would only let him alone and keep him supplied he could do real damage in the next few weeks. He sent back a strongly worded protest, pointing out that important targets were within his reach and 'if supported, not thwarted,' he could paralyse Rommel's communications. He added that if the S.A.S. was to come under someone else's planning authority he would refuse to carry out the orders 'under pain of court martial.'

They waited on tenter-hooks for the reply back. It came in an hour. The tone was soothing but stubborn. The projected operation was of vital importance; the S.A.S. were indispensable; of course David would have 'his usual free hand' in the planning of it. Then it got down to business. Three transport planes of 216 Squadron would land on the emergency strip as arranged with Bennett; they would deliver sufficient petrol for the return of all vehicles to Kabrit, and would fly the bulk of the men home. A time schedule was given, and instructions regarding the lighting of flares.

Paddy Mayne received the full blast of David's anger and had difficulty in calming him down. " Usual free hand," he snorted. " If that's what we had, we'd carry out a lightning raid on Middle East Headquarters." There was no use in fussing about it, however. It was obvious that the signals meant business and Headquarters was determined to have its way. The only thing to do was to revise the S.A.S. schedule. The operation on the Alamein line would go ahead as planned, but would have to be drastically curtailed. Instead of being away ten days the raiders would have only four or five days. As for the rest of the unit it would have to return to the rendezvous it had just abandoned so as to be near the landing strip.

That night the jeeps and trucks were loaded again, and the men stood around in the dark waiting for the order to move. The German doctor asked for permission to collect a blanket and moved to the rear of one of the trucks. A few minutes later someone said, " Where is the doctor? " He was gone. There was consternation while the men searched among the lorries; and in that moment the pilot vanished too.

David ordered out search parties, and they hunted for several hours. But they did not find them. " They've only forty miles to walk," said Paddy, " before they make contact with their own side. Cheer up, David. The Jerries will have

a full description of us by noon to-morrow. It's just as well
we're leaving."

David only grunted.

*   *   *

The little posse of jeeps that set out to attack the enemy's
soft-skinned transport (as opposed to anything armoured) did
not meet with success. The reduced time limit of four or five
days was too short to allow them to accomplish their mission.
It was a bold stroke moving into the built-up area behind the
Alamein Line, and they had more than one harrowing experience before they left. Jordan's jeep broke its axle and Chris
Bailey failed to locate his quarry. David Russell on the other
hand achieved some results, and developed a technique all his
own. Russell had transferred to the S.A.S. from the Special
Interrogation Group, where he had served as Captain Buck's
second-in-command. He spoke fluent German and on this
occasion put it to good use. He drew up near the highway
and hailed an Afrika Korps truck as it approached. When it
stopped he asked to borrow a pump. While the driver was
producing it, he slipped a bomb into the back of the vehicle.
He managed to do this eight times.

Carol Mather, the fourth patrol leader, was lucky to escape
capture. He trailed an enemy convoy for some hours in the
dark, thinking it was composed of transport vehicles, but
discovered in the end that it was armoured cars. Since the
Vickers K guns would not penetrate armour he started home.
He was camouflaged down in a ravine trying to get some sleep
when the sergeant on look-out duty suddenly gave a signal of
alarm. " A large column was weaving its way down the
escarpment," wrote Mather, " searching all the inlets. Then
I saw it. A big truck, mounted with a gun, swung into the
middle of the wadi. A German officer with fieldglasses stood
on top of the vehicle staring hard in our direction. He wasn't
more than a couple of hundred yards away, only fifty from the
bush where Down crouched. And then a miracle happened.
He turned away and joined his column. We counted the tanks
as they passed and were just beginning to heave a sigh of relief

when there was a grinding and clanking above the cave where Lambie and I crouched. A tank crossed immediately over our heads. Great chunks of rock came cascading down, and at one moment we thought the roof was going to collapse. It was almost impossible for them to miss us from above, but they did, and continued on their way."

*　　　*　　　*

The patrols arrived back at the rendezvous to find that the main body of the S.A.S. had already been picked up by plane and flown back to Cairo. David had left a watching party, composed mainly of drivers, headed by Sandy Scratchley, to wait for them. They had instructions to return with the transport that had been left behind. They would travel by way of the Qattara Depression.

This time they made the crossing by night, not day; but the treacherous bog, cool in the evening air, managed to take a toll of a different sort. There were twenty-five vehicles in all and thirty men. It took several days' driving to reach the Depression and to negotiate the long and difficult pass leading down it. They began to near the bottom of the great cavity around midnight. "By the starlight we only got a vague impression of the surrounding land," wrote Mather. "Our route descended gradually amongst broken country, and as I was navigating I had to concentrate wholly on the wheel marks I was following. It was very tiring and exacting work. After about fifty miles we swung south-east passing over a flat gravel surface scattered with stunted acacias, giving, in the gentle light, a rather park-like appearance. This scanty vegetation showed us that we were at the bottom of the Depression.

"At about three o'clock the crescent moon began to rise, and we hit the track at exactly the correct mileage. We would have to hurry if we were going to get out of the flat bog by daylight, but we stopped to check our bearings, then drove on for four miles until we lost the track and on turning round we found, to our horror, that we were missing ten vehicles. The drivers were so dead tired they had all gone to sleep at the last halt, and even the cries of ' start up ' and the noise of the engines had not awakened them. After an hour's search we found all ten of them standing motionless in the desert, with drivers slumped over their wheels.

" The situation was getting critical now. There was an hour until daylight, and here we were in the middle of the Depression with no cover within miles. We drove on fast for a few more miles, but after two bad collisions we gave up the attempt and raced back to the escarpment where we would shelter for the day. We turned back and saw in the dim light of dawn the great cliff towering behind us, but it was more than two hours before we plunged into its deep shade.

" Here, lying beneath the 400 ft. cliff we spent our second day. We must have been about twenty miles from the Qattara Spring. It was intensely hot but we felt secure from any enemy planes that might try to attack us. It was pleasing having cheated them so far, for there was no doubt that they had been after our blood for the past three weeks. From where we lay under boulders and wedged between rock clefts, we could see as far as the eye stretched—to the east a firm but broken coast, to the south-east a flat gravel plain, we were unable to see any sign of bog or marsh. However, we thought it would be wiser to retrace our old tracks of the night before until we should come to the main Qara Crossing track. From here we could follow it slowly and carefully until we had passed over the bog.

" That night we made our second attempt to cross the Depression. We followed the beaten track carefully until it became only a few wheel marks. Then we found ourselves following a single wheel track only, very difficult to see by starlight, and so cast left and right to locate the main routes once again. A few miles more and it petered out altogether. Then we found ourselves travelling over a rough rocky surface which continued for about 200 yards. At the end of this distance lay a hard salt crust with a quaking bog beneath. We sent our four jeeps to the four compass points. Three returned and reported bog on all sides, the fourth with all its kit sank beyond recovery, bonnet deep into the bog itself. Again only one hour till daylight. The unfortunate thing was that as the surrounding surface was hard rock we were unable to trace the route we had entered by, and so we seemed to be stranded.

" Then we found an outlet. It was undoubtedly bog beneath, but there seemed to be a fairly stout crust. It might lead us into a further bog—we had no idea what lay beyond, but it was our only chance. For three hundred yards the surface held even our heavy trucks. Then we came to a dyke of soft mud, quite a narrow one only about ten feet across.

" We put tarpaulins, steel sand channels, sand mats and more tarpaulins over this, and each vehicle charged it at top speed. It had to be done very quickly because the stationary vehicles on the near side soon began sinking slowly through the crust, in fact we were too late with our last three-tonner for when its turn came to take the jump it had sunk up to the axles and soon the tailboard began to disappear. We abandoned it and hurried on to the next dyke. This we bridged in a similar manner, and a third, and just when we were beginning to think that to continue was foolhardy and to return was impossible, the ground began to steady. The upper surface became spongy but there seemed to be a firm foundation beneath, and before we knew where we were we had entered a wide flat gravel plain.

" We halted for a few moments to get our direction. Took a bearing on a low constellation of stars, switched on all our headlights and raced at 50 m.p.h. towards the north-east. The dawn was just beginning to break, the billiard table surface lasted, and we covered thirty miles in less than an hour. We raced on until we reached a large grove of acacias under whose friendly shade we finally came to rest." [1]

[1] This description was published in the *Royal Geographical Journal* in April 1944.

CHAPTER FOURTEEN

DISASTER

DAVID ARRIVED back in Cairo in an apprehensive mood. He was not only annoyed at being torn away from his desert rendezvous but suspicious of the new dish stewing on the fire. He was willing to co-operate with anyone in achieving an objective, but it had always been understood that as far as the S.A.S. was concerned, the choice of tactics was his alone. He had little faith in the planning staff; how could officers who had no experience in night raiding know the best way to employ his forces?

When Headquarters unfolded its project he felt that his doubts were justified. It was true that the scheme was based on one of his own ideas. In July he had suggested taking a small party into Benghazi to destroy shipping, on the same lines as his previous three attempts. As an added fillip he had proposed that a small naval unit should accompany him and try to block the mouth of the harbour with a sunken ship. This last suggestion apparently had fired the imagination of the planners and now the scheme had swollen beyond recognition.

The idea was this. Rommel was expected to launch a final thrust towards Alexandria before the month was out. The Eighth Army was confident that it could hold its position on the Alamein line, and did not intend to move into the offensive until the end of October. By that time it would possess an overwhelming superiority in guns and armour and would mount a major attack designed to drive the Africa Korps out of Egypt and Cyrenaica.

In the meantime it was important that Rommel's supply depots should be interfered with as much as possible. His petrol and war materials came across the Mediterranean and were landed at Tobruk and Benghazi. September would be a quiet month. Why not, the planners asked, send 'irregular forces' to launch two large-scale raids against the harbour installations of these vital ports? If the attacks failed little would be lost; if they succeeded the raiders might hold the ports captive for several hours. Some of the planners felt it might even be possible for their men to sail away in enemy vessels. Apparently there was no limit to the possibilities.

In detail, they explained to David that his force would consist of about two hundred and twenty men, forty supply trucks and forty jeeps armed with Vickers K guns. His task would be to drive into Benghazi harbour and destroy everything in sight. In the meantime Colonel Haselden, an Arab expert who for some time had been acting as a British agent behind the enemy lines, would raid Tobruk.

Indeed, Haselden was the prime mover of the scheme. He was the man to whom David had confided his own modest proposal; he had seized upon the idea and inflated it into a full-scale assault. His own operation would be on a larger and even more complicated scale than David's; he would be supported by seaborne commandos and a naval bombardment. Two lesser operations would take place on the same night; the Sudan Defence Force would try and wrest Jalo from Italian hands so that the raiding parties could be assured of a safe route home; and a patrol of the Long Range Desert Group would attack Barce airfield, purely as a diversion.

Initially, David reacted against the plan even more strongly than when he had received the original signal. First of all he had always refused to let anyone take part in S.A.S. operations who had not undergone a period of rigorous training; now he was being asked to swell his ranks with at least a hundred newcomers. Secondly, he felt strongly that the success of the operations of this kind depended on surprise being maintained throughout, and the chances of achieving this with a party of two hundred men and eighty vehicles seemed fairly slim. Thirdly, he did not believe in being tied to a definite time-table. The success of S.A.S. raids often depended on striking when opportunity presented itself, not being forced to adhere to a pre-arranged time schedule. " Indeed, the whole plan," wrote David, " sinned against every principle on which the S.A.S. was founded."

As for the Tobruk raid, that struck David as even more unsound than his own. First of all, Haselden had had no experience of handling men in the field; and secondly, it would be a straightforward commando operation and would make no attempt to maintain surprise after the first hour. He pointed out that in both cases much smaller parties working on S.A.S., rather than commando, tactics would stand far more chance of success.

David was not the only one who was sceptical. Lieut.-Colonel Peniakoff, or ' Popski,' who for many months had been organising Arab resistance behind the enemy lines, was highly critical of the enterprise. " The rooms occupied by M.O.4 in Middle East H.Q. were not lacking in boyish enthusiasm," he wrote. " Very young men developed mad schemes to make an end of Rommel and the Afrika Korps; with a few hundred men, armed, it seemed to me, with little more than pea-shooters, they were going to capture the whole of Cyrenaica from Benghazi to Tobruk and leave the enemy troops on the El Alamein line without a base in their rear—to die of fright, I presume. John Haselden, who was my age and should have known better, showed a more youthful spirit than anyone. His scheme was to drive into Tobruk with eighty men (mainly commandos) pretending to be British prisoners-of-war, carrying tommy-guns hidden under their greatcoats. Their three trucks would be driven by German Jews in German uniforms, pre-tending to be German soldiers escorting the prisoners, who would have no difficulty in getting past unsuspicious road guards. They were to proceed at dusk to the port area and capture the coastal batteries. At dawn the next morning the Royal Navy was to land troops from two destroyers and several M.T.B's, seize and hold the port, liberate four thousand of our prisoners. What was to happen later was obscure.

" Haselden wanted me to join this party; discussing the plan with him I discovered that he relied for ammunition and supplies on what he would find in Tobruk.

" ' Don't be a fool,' he said, ' there will be no difficulty. Tobruk is full of everything.'

" I decided to keep away from Haselden's party and told him I would rather go to Derna, as I knew the country so much better. The projected raid on Derna, which was to be an L.R.D.G. responsibility, was dropped and I got myself transferred to the Barce raid, also with my friends." [1]

Popski was fortunate to be able to pick and choose. David had no such option. He was asked to lead the attack on Benghazi alone. Would he agree? The planners used their full powers of persuasion on him. These raids, they insisted, might prove to be a turning point in the whole African campaign. And if he co-operated with them, they would use their influence to see that his command was expanded. Indeed, if the project came off as they hoped, the forces taking part in the Tobruk, Jalo and Barce operations would come under his command and he would be given the job of systematically destroying all the supply dumps and installations in Cyrenaica. David was a gambler and an optimist and in the end, to his eternal regret, he gave in.

Undoubtedly the following incident helped to influence him as well. The Director of Military Operations called a meeting of important staff officers. Among those present was an Air Vice Marshal. The Air Vice Marshal had no use for the S.A.S. He said he thought they were grossly over-rated and would far rather see regular troops employed in the Benghazi attack than ' colourful individualists.' He recognised the S.A.S. as a ' courageous and enthusiastic outfit ' but would feel happier with a more disciplined unit. As for the experience they claimed to have, he was bound to say quite frankly he believed they had a tendency to ' exaggerate their triumphs.'

David was standing near the D.M.O's desk. He felt himself

[1] *Private Army:* Lt.-Col. Peniakoff.

grow hot with anger. Considering that he had always taken great pains to underestimate his claims, the injustice was unbearable. There was an inkwell on the desk and his hand moved over to it. If the sudden, forbidding eye of the D.M.O. had not suddenly caught his own, he would have thrown it. David was somewhat mollified when an Air Commodore, also present, disassociated himself from his colleague's attack by pointing out that air photographs had more than substantiated the S.A.S. record.

Later, David found an explanation for the Air Vice Marshal's disagreeable onslaught. It seemed that Brigadier Marriott had approached him and suggested that Major David Stirling be given the Distinguished Flying Cross.

" What on earth for? " asked the Air Marshal. " The fellow's not in the Air Force."

" Because he's destroyed two hundred and fifty aircraft. That's more than any squadron of the R.A.F. can boast. I think you ought to consider it."

" How ridiculous," spluttered the Air Marshal. And David caught the brunt of it at the conference.

*   *   *

During the same week in mid-August that the Benghazi-Tobruk-Jalo operation was being discussed, great events were taking place. General Alexander relieved General Auchinleck as Commander-in-Chief of the Middle East; and on August 13th General Montgomery took over command of the Eighth Army formerly held by General Ritchie. These changes had been brought about by Prime Minister Winston Churchill, who, accompanied by his chief-of-staff, General Sir Alan Brooke, and other high officials, had stopped in Cairo for several days to study the situation before proceeding to Russia. Now the Prime Minister's party was due back again for a second stop before returning to England.

Sir Miles Lampson, the British Ambassador to Egypt, gave a dinner party for the distinguished guests and both David Stirling and Fitzroy Maclean were bidden. One of the planning staff warned David strongly against divulging the Benghazi

raid to the Prime Minister. " Why? " he asked. " Because
he's insecure of course; we can't run any risks."

David did not accept this advice. He remembers the long
table, the shining silver, the decorations, the hum of male
voices. He remembers Churchill, pink-faced and beaming in
an ' evening dress siren suit.' And after dinner he remembers
Smuts challenging Churchill to a contest of Shakespearean
quotations. They recited easily for a quarter of an hour, then
Smuts's brow began to furrow and he sat, head in hands,
trying to think of another. Churchill remained unperturbed,
for he gave a huge wink to the guests and started inventing
them. It was some time before Smuts caught on to what was
happening.

When the game came to a close Sir Miles Lampson singled
out David and brought him up to the Prime Minister. He felt
that the young major was a soldier after Winston's heart, and
he proved right. David outlined the Benghazi plan and
Churchill was delighted. He knew about the S.A.S. from his
son Randolph and he pressed David closely about his tactics.
He was amused by the contrast between the young man's
gentle demeanour and his ferocious pursuit of the enemy; and
when David left, he walked over to Field Marshal Smuts and
began recounting some of his deeds. He described Stirling by
giving Smuts a final quotation—not from Shakespeare this
time, but from Lord Byron's *Don Juan*. " He was the mildest
mannered man that ever scuttled ship or cut a throat," said
the Prime Minister triumphantly.

David was asked back to the Embassy the next evening.
Many of the same soldiers and politicians were present;
and again he was invited to talk to the Prime Minister.
He told the latter that his unit was only a detachment and
lived in constant fear of being disbanded. Churchill made
no comment; but later David learned that he had put in a
strongly worded recommendation to General Alexander on
behalf of the S.A.S. This was to bear fruit in a few weeks'
time.

*   *   *

The military code names for the forthcoming operations, scheduled to take place on 13th September, 1942, sounded as light-hearted as a spring day. ' Snowdrop ' meant Benghazi; ' Daffodil,' Tobruk; ' Tulip,' Jalo; and ' Hyacinth ' the L.R.D.G. raid on Barce. The passes through the Qattara Depression were firmly sealed, which meant that the raiding forces had to travel eight hundred miles south to Kufra in order to find a way through the Sand Sea.

The organisational difficulties of a journey of this length were almost insuperable, for the eight hundred miles to Kufra was only half the story; there was still another eight hundred miles to Benghazi. The servicing of the vehicles was a problem in itself; aside from this, twenty new jeeps and twenty new trucks had to be equipped with machine-guns, sun compasses, sand trays and other modifications. Worst of all was the frantic effort to try to teach the hundred new recruits the rudiments of trans-desert driving, and the bare elements of night raiding. Nevertheless David managed to do it, and by September the 7th his large force was assembled at Kufra.

Kufra oasis was something like Siwa with its bright palms and mud huts; and it had two lakes, so salty you could swim sitting bolt upright. Before the thirties only a handful of European explorers had ever penetrated to it. However, in 1931 the Italians had captured it, hailing it as an outpost of their expanding Empire. Ten years later a Free French column under General Leclerc wrested it away; and now it served as a joint allied base.

Kufra was as busy as Euston Station. The other three raiding parties—the Tobruk, Jalo and Barce groups—were also there, and at night their camp fires twinkled in the darkness like a huge constellation. David's force was by far the largest. Besides his newcomers, many of whom were drafted from Middle East Commando, all his regulars were taking part, which gave him a total of over two hundred men. He had 40 jeeps bristling with Vickers K guns and between 35 and 40 three-ton supply lorries which also were heavily armed. The commanders of the various raiding parties kept their own counsel and were responsible for their raids only.

David and Fitzroy Maclean remained in Cairo until
6th September, gathering last-minute intelligence. Fitzroy
had been in the hospital ever since his car accident on the way
home from the Benghazi raid in May. This was to be his
second sortie, and he hoped it would have a more effective
result. However, as he went about his business disquieting
rumours came to his ears. " There were signs," he wrote,
" that too many people knew too much. At Alexandria a
drunken sailor was heard boasting in a canteen that he was
off to Tobruk; a Free French officer picked up some startling
information at Beirut; one of the barmen at the hotel, who
was generally thought to be an enemy agent, seemed much
too well informed. Worse still, there were indications that the
enemy was expecting the raids and was taking counter-
measures." [1]

The talk was only gossip, and it was impossible to alter plans
without firmer evidence; so things proceeded as scheduled.
Fitzroy and David flew to Kufra in a Hudson bomber and a
day or so later the large convoy, which was divided into three
sections, started off. Although the officers had studied the
details of the operation for the past few weeks, for security
reasons the men were not briefed until the day before they
left. They were shown a large scale model of Benghazi and
told that their job was to reach the harbour, take the garrison
by storm, and destroy all the installations they could find.
Two tanks borrowed from the 10th Hussars would lead the
way through the road blocks. Several sailors would accompany
the party in order to take whatever ships were handy and sink
them at the mouth of the harbour.

The trip to Benghazi presented certain difficulties. In the
first place the Sand Sea, an area the size of Ireland, blocked
the way. This sea was composed of soft, glaringly white sand,
which rose and fell in miles of treacherous waves, some of them
several hundred feet high. The L.R.D.G. had proved it
navigable, but the only practical route for a large convoy was
to go to Zighen, a point where the sea narrowed into a bottle-
neck twenty miles wide. Crossing even this short area required

[1] *Eastern Approaches:* Fitzroy Maclean.

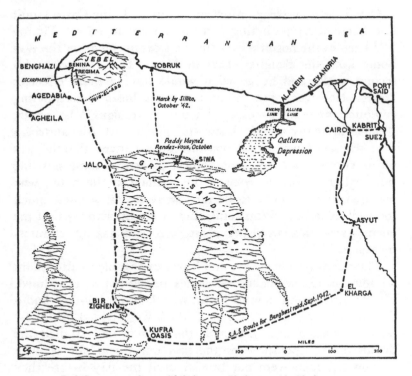

*S.A.S. route from Kabrit to Kufra, and Kufra to
Benghazi for the attack in September 1942. Paddy
Mayne's October rendezvous is also shown*

infinite skill. Indeed the 10th Hussar tanks got hopelessly
bogged and had to be abandoned. The only way to sur-
mount the waves without floundering axle deep in sand was
to rush up them; but sometimes they fell away sharply
and if you rushed too fast you might come somersaulting
down the other side. Even the most experienced drivers
made fatal errors. Several men had been killed, and Lieut.
Timpson of the L.R.D.G. was in the hospital with a cracked
skull.

The convoy was lucky to average a mile an hour across the
Sand Sea. Always one of the vehicles slipped and plunged,
grinding deep into the fine sand. Then out would come spades

and towing ropes and sand mats, and 'unsticking' would
begin.

Besides the arduous driving there was always the danger of
detection from the air. The vehicles in each of the three
sections stretched half a mile across the desert and offered a
delectable target; but the raiders were lucky and all three
groups travelled the whole way to the Jebel without being
spotted, or, for that matter, without even seeing a plane in the
sky. They had to be careful traversing the narrow strip between
the Sand Sea and Jalo, which was still in enemy hands, but
they did the drive at midday when the heat haze obscured
them. They had only one serious mishap; one of the trucks
hit a mine crossing the Trig el Abd track, and two of the
occupants were seriously wounded.

*   *   *

Except for this incident, it was not until the S.A.S. reached
the rough friendly security of the Jebel that their troubles
really began.

The section that Fitzroy Maclean was in was the first to
arrive, and he immediately made contact with Bob Melot,
the British agent who had helped David on his first Benghazi
raid. Melot was hiding up in an Arab cave awaiting the
S.A.S. He had been in the Jebel for several weeks gathering
all the information he could for the operation. What he told
Fitzroy was far from reassuring. The enemy seemed to have
got wind of something and reinforcements were said to have
entered Benghazi in the last few days. He took Fitzroy to call
on two old sheiks, and in a mixture of Italian and Arabic they
confirmed what he had said.

Melot suggested sending a spy into the town to get more
precise information. Fitzroy agreed, but when he saw the
character that Melot was relying upon, his heart sank. A
small, sulky Arab was produced who found it difficult to look
anyone in the eye. He was a deserter from the Italian Army
and had relations in Benghazi. In a gloomy voice Fitzroy
pressed Melot as to the man's reliability, but the latter only
laughed, insisting that the Arab was exceedingly reliable.

The spy had a twenty mile walk into Benghazi. He was told
to remain a day and sound the pulse of the town, then to hurry
back. The hours of waiting were anxious and Fitzroy was
not hopeful of seeing the man again. But on the appointed
day the Arab re-appeared complaining that his feet hurt.
He confirmed the rumours; the enemy was expecting an
attack. Minefields had been prepared, and road blocks
set up.

David had not yet arrived in the Jebel; he appeared that
afternoon with the last convoy and was greeted by Fitzroy's
sombre news. After some consideration he wired Headquarters
asking whether, in view of the leakage, it would be a
good thing to change the time-table of the raid, so that some
element of surprise might be preserved. A signal came back
promptly saying to ignore ' bazaar gossip ' and to proceed as
planned.

From now on everything went wrong. Not far from the
escarpment track, which the convoy would descend to reach
Benghazi plain, stood a small fort with a wireless station. It
was decided that a group must leave slightly in advance of the
main party and knock out the installations. Bob Melot
pleaded to go; he knew the country thoroughly and could
guide the men to the right spot more easily than anyone else.
David had been relying on Melot to navigate the convoy
down the escarpment, but Melot was sure his Arab spy could
do it just as well.

The main attacking force started off as soon as it was dark.
For the first hour or two the countryside was familiar. The
Arab spy was brought forward to guide the vehicles. The
track he selected was rough and difficult. Large boulders
began to block the way, which had to be removed, and the
sumps of the trucks scraped ominously against stray rocks.
Soon it looked as though the path was petering out altogether.
Fitzroy pressed the Arab guide hard; was he certain the way
was feasible? The Arab said it looked as though he had taken
the wrong track.

The process of finding a new way down the escarpment was
long and painful. The R.A.F. raid on Benghazi had been on

for some time and the men could see the flashes in the distance. The column should have reached the plain by now; instead it was trying to find a negotiable track. All this took several hours. By the time the S.A.S. had found the right track and reached the foot of the escarpment it was three o'clock in the morning; only two and a half hours of darkness was left.

The convoy moved forward. At last it hit the tarmac road and gathered speed. Suddenly the first vehicle jammed on its brakes and came to an abrupt halt. A bar stretched across the road. Something seemed to be flapping behind it, and David could make out coils of barbed wire and freshly dug earth, on either side, which looked suspiciously like a minefield.

Bill Cumper, the explosives expert, was in the leading jeep with David and Seekings. He did not usually accompany the S.A.S. on raids, but being an engineer it was his job to climb out and take a look. Yes, they were minefields all right. The vehicles would have to keep strictly to the road. Then he fiddled with the catch on the road block. The bar swung open, and he stepped back saying facetiously: "Let battle commence."

The words were scarcely out of his mouth before pandemonium broke loose. Enemy ambushes were on either side of the road and they answered with everything they had: machine-gun fire, mortar and Breda shells. Cumper managed to get back to Seekings. His only comment was, "If this is the bloody S.A.S. you can keep it, you crazy bastard."

Fortunately, the enemy was excited and began by firing too high which gave David's gunners a chance to spread out and answer back. Sergeant Almonds tried to force his way through the block, but his jeep caught fire and lit up the scene. Soon it was obvious that the Vickers K guns of the S.A.S. were reducing the enemy's enthusiasm. However, several vehicles had been put out of action, surprise was completely gone, and if the Benghazi garrison had not already been informed by wireless what was happening it could be only a matter of

minutes before they were. David had no choice but to give
the order to retire.

*   *   *

It was nearly daybreak. There was no hope of getting to
the top of the escarpment. The men must try to take cover
at the foot of it. The last vehicles had scarcely camouflaged
down before the cold grey morning sky had arrived, and with
it half a dozen angry planes.

It was not long before they spotted one of the trucks. Unfortunately it was filled with ammunition and upon being hit
exploded in a thunderous noise. A large black plume of
smoke arose to mark the spot where more men and vehicles lay
hidden.

All day long planes came in relays, dive bombing and
strafing. There was one spectacular incident when a three-ton
lorry belonging to the French detachment, heavily armed with
Vickers K guns and a Browning 4.5, was spotted by a strafing
plane. The French, who were taking cover some distance
away, suddenly decided to fight it out. They ran up to the
truck, threw aside the camouflage netting and drove it off,
all guns blazing. A duel took place which lasted ten minutes.
It ended in the enemy plane bursting into flame and crashing
to the ground. The French truck had been hit many times
but was still a runner; miraculously there was only one minor
casualty.

That night the party wearily ascended the escarpment, and
found its way back to the rendezvous. It seemed incredible,
considering the amount of ammunition expended, that only
eight or nine vehicles had been destroyed and three or four
men wounded. David learned that Melot's group had been
successful in destroying the wireless station but that he and
two of his companions, Chris Bailey and Corporal Laird, had
been seriously hurt.

The rendezvous was in a deep wadi that offered excellent
cover and the next morning, when enemy planes flew over
again, the men felt reasonably safe. Suddenly they saw a jeep
in the distance heading straight for their hide-out. Clouds of

dust billowed out from behind, and one of the planes circled
overhead several times as though taking note of its destination.
It was an S.A.S. jeep which had become detached from the
rest of the party the night before and now was trying to
rejoin them.

David watched with dismay. This was the price you paid
for green troops. Twenty minutes later a batch of fighters
and bombers came straight for the wadi and began combing
it with machine-gun fire. Twenty-five supply trucks and
eighteen or nineteen jeeps were destroyed during the day, and
others badly damaged.

The situation was serious. There was only enough food and
water left for skeleton rations and so little transport that
twenty men would have to ride in each three-tonner and seven
or eight in each jeep. Worse still, there certainly was not
enough petrol to travel eight hundred miles to Kufra. The
men could only hope to do the four hundred miles to Jalo,
working on the questionable assumption that the oasis was
now in the hands of the Sudanese Defence Force.

After four days of anxious progress the party reached Jalo
outskirts. Fitzroy Maclean and Sandy Scratchley went ahead
cautiously to probe the situation and found that the battle
for the oasis was still going on. For a time they were caught
in the crossfire between the two combatants. When they
finally managed to contact the Sudanese Defence Force they
learned that the latter had occupied Jalo once, but had been
thrown out. Now they had just received a signal from Headquarters to withdraw permanently. The S.A.S. managed to
borrow petrol and food from them, and reached Kufra without
further adventures.

In the meantime David had remained behind in the Jebel
to pick up stragglers. During three days he had rounded up
over a dozen men, then headed for home. A quarter of his
force was killed, wounded or missing; and over three-quarters
of his vehicles were demolished.

*   *   *

The Tobruk raid had ended even more disastrously than

David's. This one failed not because the enemy had prior knowledge but due to a tragic error of judgment; one man was not in the right place at the right time.

Haselden's job of securing a bridgehead on which seaborne commandos could land was successful. He and his eighty men, dressed like prisoners-of-war, were conducted successfully through the town in three lorries, driven by Captain Buck and his ' S.I.G.' men—a handful of Palestinian Jews in German army uniform. They passed several sentry posts, and reached the promontory, which was their objective, dead on time. Then an R.A.F. bombing attack began, planned as a diversion to last the next four critical hours. Haselden's men succeeded in capturing the fort and guns overlooking the beach, and in silencing the wireless station. But here the plan broke down.

The arrangement was this. If the bridgehead was clear, signals would be flashed, beginning at 1.30 in the morning, from both the east and the west side of the bay to guide in the troops waiting on the M.T.B's. The responsibility for this vital operation was given to Lieut. Langton. However, circumstances not under Langton's control contrived to upset it. Major Campbell, Haselden's second-in-command, developed a bad case of dysentery. Haselden was worried about him and instructed Langton to accompany him as far as his first objective in securing certain positions. He was confident Langton would get back to the beach in time to organise the signals.

It was an extraordinary risk to take. Langton arranged for two Royal Engineers to signal from the east side and F/O Scott to signal from the west side if he were delayed. The operation with Campbell took much longer than scheduled, and on the way back Langton had to skirt an enemy camp in a wadi. He did not arrive at the beach until nearly 3.0 a.m. He found Scott signalling from the west side, but from too high a position, so that the light was difficult to see. On the east side there was no one. Langton immediately began flashing a light. Two M.T.B's came in, but soon after the Germans caught on to what was happening and searchlights began to sweep the harbour, followed by heavy gunfire. No more soldiers could be landed.

German troops were quickly assembled to mop up the British raiders, who numbered little over a hundred. " In the early hours of the 14th September," wrote Field Marshal Rommel in his diary, " after relay bombing attacks by a hundred and eighty aircraft on the port and surroundings of Tobruk, the British attempted to land strong forces in the fortress area. According to documents which fell into our hands, their mission was to destroy the dock installations and sink the ships in the harbour.

" The A.A. batteries on the peninsula immediately opened a furious fire on the British. German and Italian assault groups which were quickly formed up succeeded in enveloping the landed enemy troops. Fearing that the British were planning to capture Tobruk, we immediately set a number of motorised units in march for the fortress. But the local forces soon succeeded in restoring the situation. The British suffered considerable losses in killed and prisoners and—according to reports from the A.A. batteries—three destroyers and three landing or escort vessels were sunk. Next day our Air Force caught the British again and reported the sinking of one cruiser, one more destroyer and several escort vessels. A number of British ships were damaged by bombs.

" On the 15th September I flew over to Tobruk myself and expressed my appreciation to the troops of the well-conducted defensive action they had fought. The reports of the British attack had actually caused us no little alarm, for Tobruk was one of our most vulnerable points." [1]

Haselden and many of his men were killed; the rest were taken prisoner. Out of the whole force only six got back to the Allied lines.

*   *   *

' Popski ' had been right to choose the attack on the aero-

[1] *The Rommel Papers:* edited by B. H. Liddell Hart. (The German claims on shipping were exaggerated. Two destroyers and four M.T.B.'s were sunk.)

drome. The only raid that was successful was Jake Eason-Smith's L.R.D.G. assault on Barce airfield. His small party, the manageable size that David had always insited upon, had crossed the full width of the Sand Sea and delivered a smashing, surprise blow, resulting in the destruction of thirty aircraft.

CHAPTER FIFTEEN

THE TIDE TURNS

THE BENGHAZI disaster was the first major failure the S.A.S. had experienced since the initial operation ten months earlier. David kicked himself over and over again for having agreed to a plan which his first instinct had told him was wrong. He arrived back at Middle East Headquarters considerably chagrined, but much to his surprise he was greeted enthusiastically and told his efforts had not been in vain. He had been promoted to the rank of lieutenant-colonel. He found it both ironical and amusing that his one and only debacle since the previous November should have drawn forth this reward.

There was still another piece of good news. On the recommendation of the Middle East Commander-in-Chief, General Alexander (no doubt prodded by Winston Churchill's enthusiastic report), it had been decided to expand the S.A.S. into a full regiment. This was not only an honour, but a tremendous victory. It implied three distinct concessions; first, that the S.A.S. tactics had become an accepted part of modern warfare; second, that the detachment was now a permanent institution; third, that David could recruit sufficient men to bring his strength up to full regimental establishment which would treble or quadruple the number at his disposal.

The fact that a subaltern of twenty-five had managed, in just over one year, to add a new regiment to the British Army was no mean feat. It was the first new regiment to be inspired by an individual since the Lovat Scouts were raised by David's uncle in the Boer War nearly half a century before. Stirling was justifiably proud, and assumed that recognition meant that his unit was now accepted by the Eighth Army as an important instrument in the general strategy. His meeting with General Montgomery, therefore, came as a shock to him.

Here it is necessary to halt a moment. A department known as ' G Raiding Force ' had been set up at Middle East Headquarters, headed by Colonel Shan Hackett. The Director of Military Operations explained to David that the S.A.S. would be serviced by this new branch. Hackett's job was to co-ordinate David's activities with the Eighth Army's forthcoming offensive, and to help him in all his requirements.

David met Hackett at his brother's flat in Cairo. The two men took an immediate liking to each other. Hackett was a stocky, pink-cheeked soldier who had won a great reputation as a commander of the 4th Light Brigade. He had known Peter Stirling for some time, and had heard of David's feats from many sources. He found his quiet manner disarming, and listened sympathetically to his plans for the S.A.S. David was convinced that when the Eighth Army offensive began, the S.A.S. must create havoc in Rommel's rear. It should concentrate on the enemy's lines of communication, making it difficult for Rommel to withdraw in an orderly fashion—in some cases even impossible to withdraw at all.

As far as organisation was concerned, said David, quick action was imperative. In order to carry out raids every night (which was what he had in mind), the S.A.S. would have to strengthen its ranks quickly; and if the raiding parties were to go into action within the next few weeks they would have to be composed of seasoned men. David had made up his mind to try and get Montgomery's permission to handpick his recruits from the best regiments in the army. He had an appointment to see the general at Eighth Army Headquarters.

David knew nothing about Montgomery. He looked upon him merely as another general in a fairly long succession. At that period, it must be remembered, Rommel was regarded by both British and Germans alike as the only brilliant soldier in the Middle East, and it was customary to assess army commanders with a critical eye.

The general's battle Headquarters were only ten miles behind the Alamein line. It consisted of a series of camouflaged tents strung along the coast. David and Shan Hackett met Montgomery in his caravan. To this day the scene and the conversation remain vividly in both their minds. The latter was wearing his familiar black beret, and David was struck by his thin, wiry frame and his piercing blue eyes. He wasted no time on small talk and asked David to state his business.

David outlined the way in which he believed the S.A.S. could assist the main army in their offensive. He told Montgomery that in order to do this, and to bring his regiment up to strength at the same time, he would have to recruit at least a hundred and fifty men, including a high percentage of officers and non-commissioned officers. What he wanted from the general was permission to pick his men from regiments with fighting experience in the desert.

" If I understand you clearly," said Montgomery, " you want to take some of my men from me. Indeed my best men; my most desert-worthy, my most dependable, my most experienced men." As Montgomery spoke David felt himself becoming angry; what did this newcomer mean talking about ' my men '? He had only arrived in the Middle East six weeks previously. " I am proud of my men," continued Montgomery. " Very proud of my men indeed. I expect great things of them." Here he fixed his blue eyes sharply on David. " What makes you think, Colonel Stirling, that you can handle my men to greater advantage that I can handle them myself ? "

David was taken aback. " I don't know what you mean, sir. I need to bring my regiment up to strength, and I need experienced men. Otherwise I won't be able to carry out my immediate plans. It will take too long to train raw recruits."

" But I need experienced men too," said Monty sarcastically. " How long would it take you to train fresh troops? "

" Perhaps a couple of months," said David. " Whereas if I get seasoned men only three or four weeks."

" But I am planning to open my offensive in a fortnight," said Montgomery. " If I keep my experienced men myself I can use them. If I give them to you they won't be ready to play any part in the action."

There was a note of triumph in the general's voice and David felt his irritation mounting. " Perhaps they won't be ready for the next offensive," said David, " but they'll be ready for the one after."

" But I don't intend to have one after! I intend the next offensive to be the last offensive. What's the matter with you, Colonel Stirling. Why are you smiling? "

" Nothing, sir, it's only that we heard the same thing from the last general—and the one before."

Monty gave David a withering look. It was obvious that the young man had got under the Army commander's skin. " I'm sorry, Colonel Stirling, but my answer is no. A flat no. Frankly your request strikes me as slightly arrogant. I am under the impression that you feel you know my business better than I do. You come here after a failure at Benghazi demanding the best I can give. In all honesty, Colonel Stirling, I'm not inclined to associate myself with failure. And now I must be on my way. I'm lunching at Guards Brigade Headquarters. I shall be pleased if you and Colonel Hackett will lunch in the Officers' Mess as my guests, even though I can't be there. I'm sorry to disappoint you, Colonel Stirling, but I prefer to keep my best men for my own use."

Montgomery turned on his heel and clumped out of the caravan. David began to swear. " Failure at Benghazi. . . . What about our successes? " Hackett tried to calm him down, and finally steered him, still fuming, into the Officers' Mess. They sat at a table with three officers they did not know. " This lunch is on the general," said David in a ringing voice. " Let's have a good one." He called the mess waiter and asked what there was to drink. He studied the list carefully and then gave an extensive order; cocktails, wine, kummel, everything that could be procured. " I hear the general is a teetotaller," he observed to his table companions. " I'll put everything we're drinking on his bill," he continued, " and perhaps it will make him look more human at the end of the month."

The wine lifted David's spirits. When luncheon was over

Shan Hackett remembered he had left some papers in the general's caravan and the two men gaily, even hilariously, went back to fetch them. They found that Montgomery had already returned and was working at his desk. His chief-of-staff, Freddy de Guingand, was also there. He was a friend of both Stirling and Hackett. He joined them outside the caravan. David was still light-hearted and began to lash out at the way the war was being conducted. " Your general has plenty of cock-sparrow assurance," he said to de Guingand. " If one could judge by talk the war in Africa is as good as over. Unfortunately we have to judge by results. And frankly, I'm sceptical. Unless you use the S.A.S. my bet is that the only way you'll ever beat Rommel is to have the Americans land in North Africa and smash him on a second front." David was only joking. He enjoyed pulling de Guingand's leg; particularly after Montgomery's patronising manner. But as he mentioned the North African landing he caught a look of consternation in de Guingand's eyes. Instantly he saw he had tumbled on to something. " Well, I'll be blowed! So that's what we're planning, is it? "

" For God's sake," said de Guingand. " Shut up."

David could not resist teasing his friend. " I'm afraid, Freddy, you're going to have to put a little pressure on your general for us. We want men for our regiment. Good men. And he's being awfully stubborn. We expect you to intervene for us. Otherwise we might be forced to let slip about this North African business. Saying, of course, that we'd got our information from Monty's chief-of-staff . . ."

De Guingand couldn't help laughing. " You're incorrigible, David. Of course I'll try to help you. However, for the moment I don't think you'll change my general's mind. He's very determined. But I promise I'll impress him with the S.A.S. record and perhaps after the offensive he'll be more reasonable."

David realised he was beaten. Montgomery was adamant. Nothing would persuade him to part with any of his ' desert-trained ' men. This meant that David would have to recruit from the Infantry Base Depot, composed, for the most part, of troops fresh from England, and from General 'Jumbo' Wilson's 'P.I. Force,'[1] which had not had much battle experience. And it meant that he would not be able to carry out his plan for another two months. Of course he could send 'the old hands' of the S.A.S. to make weekly attacks on a limited sector of the enemy's lines of communication; but that was not what he had in mind. He felt that concentrated raids against eighty or a hundred miles of communications, carried out unceasingly night after night, could have had a profound effect on Rommel's fortunes.

However, he had to make the best of the situation. He formed his experienced operatives into a squadron and put Paddy Mayne in command. He instructed them to leave immediately for Kufra and set up a base on the edge of the Sand Sea. They were to carry out as many raids as possible against the Matruh railway line and the coast road. He, in the meantime, would finish the recruiting and get the training at Kabrit moving as quickly as possible. Perhaps by the end of November the new men would be ready to go into the field.

*   *   *

As the crow flies, the enemy were only forty miles from Alexandria, yet the S.A.S. had to travel well over a thousand miles to reach them. Since the line from Alamein to the Qattara Depression was defended solidly, and the Qattara passes blocked, they had no option but to travel south to the oasis of Kufra, then move up through the Sand Sea and cut across to the coast behind Rommel's lines, just as they had done for the Benghazi raid.

The L.R.D.G. was also using Kufra as a supply depot for their own operations. Paddy took his squadron of seventy or eighty men, plus thirty-five three-tonners and jeeps to this attractive oasis and established a rear base not far from the Long Range Headquarters. Then Mike Sadler, the ace navigator of the S.A.S., led the party through the Sand Sea to set up the forward point.

This base was about a hundred and fifty miles south of the

---

[1] This was the Palestine-Iraq force.

Matruh railway line, and two hundred miles behind the enemy's advanced position at Alamein. Although the raiding parties would have a two or three days' drive to get out of the Sea on to the relatively hard desert that led to the coast it had obvious advantages. The rendezvous was safe from enemy attack, for bombers and fighters did not waste their time flying over the wilderness.

Life was not at all disagreeable. The squadron ' camouflaged down ' in a deep hollow surrounded by a mass of sand dunes. The men had plenty of food and water and although the silence and lifelessness was sometimes oppressive, at least there were no flies to bother them.

Paddy immediately sent out sorties. During the next six weeks his men wrought much havoc on the coast road, blew up considerable lengths of the Matruh railway line and ambushed many trains. One of Paddy's new recruits, a tall fair-haired Irishman by the name of McDermott, had the experience of laying a dud pressure mine on the track. The train came through and swept harmlessly over it. McDermott was so annoyed he decided to capture the station and destroy it. This he did, much to the consternation of the Italian attendants who were rounded up and taken prisoner.

Another newcomer to Paddy's unit, a private soldier by the name of David Sillito, (who later became an officer), made history by incredible courage and endurance. He had taken a small group of men to a point near Tobruk to lay charges on the railway. The enemy spotted and attacked them, and Sillito became separated from his companions. He had three courses open to him; one was to march a few miles north and surrender himself to the enemy; the second was to head towards the coastal belt at Alamein and hide with Arabs until the 8th Army advanced over the territory; the third was to turn toward the hot, empty, blazing desert and try to walk the 180 miles back to Paddy's desert rendezvous. Sillito chose this last course. Not a man in a million would have had the courage to try it with no food and only a small flask of water which could last scarcely twenty-four hours. All he possessed was a compass and a revolver. The march of Du Vivier and his companions had seemed remarkable enough, but Sillito's walk surpassed it, for he was utterly alone. It seems incredible that a human being could survive eight days without food and water and walk nearly 200 miles. However, this is what he did. He reached the rendezvous on the eighth day, almost a skeleton, with sore and bleeding feet. He was sent to Kufra and a fortnight later had recovered completely. So much for the human spirit.

Another man who had an extraordinary experience, of a very different kind, was Lieut. Sandy Scratchley. He could not accomplish the mission on which he was sent, but he had the doubtful experience of being caught in the middle of the Battle of Alamein on the wrong side of the line! Somewhere about the 18th October a message came through to Paddy from Eighth Army Headquarters, asking for a party to proceed to El Daba to join up with a naval landing party which would try to cut ground communications behind the enemy lines.

" I can't remember how many men or jeeps we had, or how many days we drove to reach our objective," wrote Scratchley. " All I do know was that the night of October 23rd was brilliant and clear with a full moon. We figured we were about thirty miles behind the German side of the Alamein line, and twenty miles from Daba. As we jogged along under a wonderful starlit sky, it seemed strange to be so close to the enemy and hear nothing.

" It may have been ten o'clock or midnight when the barrage that started the great battle which was to mark ' the beginning of the end ' of the African campaign broke the stillness.[1] The effect was colossal. Every inch of the distance between El Alamein and the Qattara Depression was lit up by the explosions of bursting twenty-five-pounder shells. From our

[1] " The Battle of Alamein," wrote Winston Churchill in *The Second World War*, " differed from all previous fighting in the Desert. The front was limited, heavily fortified, and held in strength. There was no flank to turn. A break-through must be made by whoever was the stronger and wished to take the offensive. In this way we are led back to the battles of the First World War on the Western Front. We see repeated here in Egypt the same kind of a trial of strength as was presented at Cambrai at the end of 1917, and in many of the battles of 1918, namely short and good communications for the assailants, the use of artillery in its heaviest concentrations, the ' drum-fire barrage,' and the forward inrush of tanks."

distance of twenty miles it struck us more as a magnificent
sight than the horror it actually was."

Scratchley had been told that he would receive a signal *en
route* regarding the position of the naval unit. But it never
arrived, and Paddy ordered him back to base.

A week later a second mission was assigned to him; again
to head for El Daba, this time to blow up the main Afrika
Korps petrol dump. So once again he set out with his three
jeeps. The Alamein battle was still going on and as the little
posse neared the coast they found themselves in the middle of
a strange scene. Instead of the usual wilderness the landscape
was dotted with innumerable cars and tanks swanning about
in all directions.

' The fog of war ' was never more clearly illustrated, for the
raiders felt that no one seemed to be following a logical course.
" It was like a Marx brothers film gone wrong," wrote
Scratchley. " It was quite impossible to understand what was
happening. Once three German tanks stopped a half a mile
away and regarded as silently; another time three British
armoured cars, with pennants flying, passed straight across our
front—and opened fire on us with their machine-guns.
Frantically we waved our headgear up and down, in a vain
effort to persuade them that we were friends. They disappeared
on their way without hitting us. This was probably a troop
of the Royals—commanded by Peter Thin—which had broken
through and was making for the coast road."

As Scratchley's party neared El Daba, around 4th November,
they saw the night bombers of the R.A.F. going full blast
up and down the coast, the flash and noise of their bombs
continually illuminating and shaking the darkness. " Suddenly
an enormous explosion lit the sky in the direction we were
heading. The navigator and I took a bearing on the centre of
the blaze and said together, ' They've hit the petrol dump.' "

After this, Scratchley's party headed for the track along the
edge of the Qattara Depression hoping to cut off retreating
supply lorries, but saw nothing. " It was now only too obvious
that the whole trip had been a complete failure and I turned
my thoughts to getting back," wrote Scratchley. " We had

come this far and the enemy was retreating so there was no point in returning to Paddy. Besides, we hadn't enough petrol and were running short of food. We might as well do the round trip and end up in Cairo.

" We headed north-east. Soon afterwards we came upon a dejected party of Germans walking westwards. They offered no resistance, and told us that they had been left in the lurch by their own armour. We pointed them in the right direction and took the six most important officers with us as prisoners. They told us the battle had been won by us.

" The next morning we got a bit of a shock. So often in the past an apparent victory had been turned into a retreat that we were still on our guard. Before dawn we were relieved to hear the well-known reveille call of the Eighth Army—a Bren gun fired into the air.

" As soon as the light made it possible to pick things out we motored over to a large body of men by which was a Daimler armoured car, flying a pennant as ours all did, and a Ford truck. To our horror, as we neared them, we saw that they were Germans, fully armed, sitting on the ground eating breakfast. I looked across at the driver of one of my jeeps, and his face was a study in frustration. By the time we saw what they were we were too close to do anything about it.

" As they did not pay the slightest attention to us we kept on up to them. The armoured car showed no sign of life so I stopped the jeep, and walked up to it and banged on the side saying ' anybody about.' A damned silly thing to say with about six hundred Germans on the ground nearby, but it had the desired effect. A corporal in the Household Cavalry popped his head out of the turret and said, ' Good morning, sir.' I nearly cried with relief. Apparently the Germans had surrendered with such alacrity no one had bothered to disarm them yet.

" The corporal seemed a bit doubtful of us as we must have looked a scruffy collection but luckily he had heard of the S.A.S. Presently an officer and a sergeant of the Military Police came up and we learnt that the Germans were a battalion of paratroopers. Apparently the battle was going well, though sticking a bit in the north, as far as they knew.

" After a good breakfast they gave us the bearing through the minefields and on to rear Army H.Q. where we met a disbelieving major who would insist that, if we were not Germans, we must be Americans from North Africa.[1] In this way did we learn of the new Anglo-American landing and our audible reaction to this surprising thought soon impressed the major that we were English."

Sandy Scratchley got back to Cairo safely. Shortly after his arrival he developed diphtheria and was sent to hospital. This prevented him from taking any further part in S.A.S. activities in the desert. He learned, however, that on the 6th of November, the day he made contact with the Eighth Army, General Alexander had wired Churchill, " Ring out the bells ? Prisoners now estimated at 20,000, tanks 350, guns 400, motor transport several thousand. Our advanced mobile forces are south of Mersa Matruh. Eighth Army is advancing."

Nevertheless it was not, as Montgomery had predicted, the last offensive. The Eighth Army Commander was forced to halt south of Agheila to regroup before he could take the offensive again. He remained stationary on this line for about a month.

[1] The Anglo-American landings in North Africa, known as ' Torch,' had begun on 8th November.

CHAPTER SIXTEEN

THE ROAD

In the meantime David was at Kabrit organising the new men under his command. He was bitterly disappointed that the S.A.S. Regiment had not been able to play a more important role in the Battle of Alamein. However, Montgomery's refusal to allow him to recruit desert-trained soldiers left him no option but to take on green troops and try to whip them into shape as quickly as possible. Kabrit, which for weeks at a time had been deserted and forlorn, bristled with activity. Once again men were being put through gruelling night tests, marching thirty miles on a bottle of water, jumping from moving platforms, and experimenting with the latest type of explosives. In October David went to hospital with desert sores, but his activities scarcely slackened; the hospital ward became his regimental headquarters and he continued to badger the high command as persistently as ever.

In contrast to the defeat he had suffered at Montgomery's hands, he was scoring striking victories in other fields. Churchill's enthusiasm for the S.A.S. had been communicated to General Alexander and was now bearing fruit. Aside from the recruits David had gathered himself, and the French Squadron which had served with him for the past year, he was given command of the Special Boat Section, of the remnants of the Middle East Commando, and of a group of Greek volunteers known as the Greek Sacred Squadron. The total strength at his disposal was about eight hundred men. And this was not all. His brother Bill had been given permission to raise a second S.A.S. regiment which would leave shortly for North Africa and be brought up to full strength out there. When he confided this news to one of his colleagues the latter replied, " At last I know what ' S.A.S.' stands for. Stirling and Stirling."

By the middle of November it was obvious that Rommel's defeat was only a matter of a few months. Montgomery's next offensive, designed to push the Afrika Korps into Tunisia, would not take place until some time in December. David's mind was racing ahead to the role the S.A.S. could play in other theatres. He decided that Paddy Mayne's squadron should go to the Lebanon shortly and take a course in skiing which would fit it for possible operations in Persia or Turkey should the Germans threaten the Caucasian passes.

At the same time, he had not abandoned the idea that the S.A.S. must play a decisive role in the remaining weeks of the desert war. He sent a paper to Colonel Shan Hackett, who now co-ordinated all raiding forces in the Middle East, outlining his plan. He would send a force of about two hundred and twenty men, equipped with trucks and jeeps, behind the enemy lines. These men would be divided into sixteen sub-sections. They would spread along a four hundred mile stretch of the coast road, from Agheila, where the Germans had dug in, to Tripoli. Each sub-section would attack and mine the road every three days, which would mean four or five raids each night.

David would begin his assault about the same time in December that Montgomery was scheduled to open a new offensive. The S.A.S. aim would be to create sufficient havoc to prevent Rommel from using the coast road at night. Since this highway was the only road suitable for heavy lorries and armour, it ought to make his supply problems so intolerable that he would be forced on to the road by day. This would allow the Royal Air Force to take a heavy toll.

David's plan met with Montgomery's approval and he was

told to proceed with it. He signalled Paddy Mayne to send Mike Sadler up from Kufra to find a suitable rendezvous behind the enemy lines where the S.A.S. forces could join up. A week later a wadi known as Bir Zalten was agreed upon as a meeting-place. It was about one hundred and fifty miles south of Agheila. David then instructed Paddy to take A squadron to this spot; he would join him there with B squadron which was just completing its first month of training.

B Squadron was composed almost entirely of newcomers. Except for Lieut. Carol Mather and Lieut. Martin, the Frenchmen, even the officers were untried in S.A.S. methods. Major Vivian Street and Major Peter Oldfield had both left office desks to join David; Captain Hore-Ruthven had transferred from the Rifle Brigade; Lieut. Hough, Lieut. Maloney and Captain Galloway had come from the Middle East Commando. David had no alternative but to use these men and hoped that their enthusiasm would make up for their lack of field practice. However, because of their inexperience he decided he must accompany them to their zone of operations, which would be in the vicinity of Tripoli, many hundreds of miles behind the enemy lines, and launch them on their mission himself. He felt he could continue instructing them on the journey.

Shan Hackett protested loudly. David had several hundred men in training at Kabrit, there were innumerable decisions to be made, not to mention future plans to be drawn up. But David was adamant that his journey ' was really necessary '; he pointed out that he was leaving George Jellicoe behind as second-in-command, and placated Hackett to some extent by promising to return as soon as the attacks began, and not to get involved in the raids himself.

*   *   *

The squadron left Kabrit on the 20th of November. It numbered about 90 men, 30 jeeps and a dozen lorries. The supply position presented difficulties, for every jeep had to be self-sufficient and capable of operating away from the forward base for at least two weeks at a time. After a certain amount

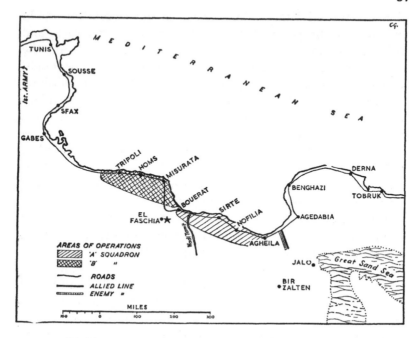

Division of A and B Squadrons for raids November and December 1942

of experimenting it was found that each jeep could carry (roughly) 2 men, 2 Vickers K machine-guns, 12 mines, 1 rifle, 1 Sten gun, 35 gallons of petrol, 40 gallons of water, 20 days' rations, kit, binoculars, compasses, etc.

The convoy travelled to Agedabia by road and then turned south into the desert, outflanking the enemy's front line positions. It reached Bir Zalten on 29th November where Paddy Mayne was waiting for them.

The rendezvous consisted of a series of chalk and sandstone cliffs. Paddy's men had already hollowed out caves as sleeping-quarters and cover for their vehicles. Fires were burning, supper was cooking, mechanics were checking their engines, sappers assembling their explosives, men cleaning weapons and mending punctures.

The officers pored over charts and maps while David

divulged the full details of his scheme. Paddy's squadron would
operate on the sector between Agheila and Bouerat; and
B Squadron, under Vivian Street's command, would take the
stretch from Bouerat to the west of Tripoli. This meant that
B Squadron still had many miles to cover before establishing
a forward base, and their first attack could not take place
before 13th December, while Paddy's operations would begin
at once. After the initial raids targets would be decided by
each section officer and sorties sent out as often as possible.
The raids would continue until the Eighth Army occupied the
territory, which, in the case of Tripoli, David reckoned would
be sometime in the middle of January.

While David was talking to the men a signal was received
from Shan Hackett. It was a message of encouragement,
informing David that General Montgomery regarded the S.A.S.
project as of the utmost importance to the forthcoming
offensive. David was surprised by the message. He had talked
to Montgomery several times since their first encounter, and
had come to have a high regard for him, but the Army
commander, though always a model of civility, was not in the
least warm. It was true that he had given his consent to
David's road attack but he had made no comment on it.
Indeed, neither Hackett nor David had any idea of his opinion
of the S.A.S.

However, once David had departed Montgomery became
less restrained. He referred to David as ' the boy Stirling.'
" The Boy Stirling," he informed the officers gathered round
his dinner table, " is mad. Quite, quite mad. However in war
there is often a place for mad people. Now take this scheme
of his. Penetrating miles behind the enemy lines. Attacking
the coastal road on a four hundred mile front. Who but the
Boy Stirling could think up such a plan? Yet if it comes off I
don't mind saying it could have a decisive effect, yes, a really
decisive effect on my forthcoming offensive."

Hackett was present at this dinner, and was so pleased at
praise from Montgomery's lips that he signalled David,
" Army Commander feels your activities could have decisive
effect on course of battle."

David read this signal in Paddy Mayne's presence, then sent back the following reply, " Congratulate Army Commander on perspicacity."

The end of the story may be apocryphal. It goes like this. Somehow David's telegram was brought to Montgomery's notice. The latter was pleased at its agreeable tone, but it made no sense to him; what was the Boy Stirling referring to? He asked to see the original message. When a rather embarrassed A.D.C. produced it, the general made no comment.

* * *

The evening that David and Paddy sat around the camp fire at Bir Zalten, making final plans for their attack on the road, was 29th November, 1942. On this same date the road was receiving the attention of still another band of men. When the moon rose our old friend Lieut. Timpson of the Long Range Desert Group, now recovered from his injury in the Sand Sea, established a night and day watch within a few yards of the road in the Nofilia area.

Timpson was relieving another patrol. He continued his watch for the fourteen days preceding the Eighth Army's attack. Every vehicle that passed over the road was recorded and wired back to Eighth Army. Thus when Montgomery opened his offensive, he had exact knowledge of the enemy's strength and reinforcements.

This particular road watch was regarded by the Long Range Desert Group as the most valuable intelligence job performed during the African campaign. It was carried out under the very nose of the enemy, and bristled with frightening and dramatic moments. Timpson kept a diary and his account gives such a vivid picture of the atmosphere of ' the road,' which was so soon to receive the fire of the S.A.S., that the reader must forgive a brief digression.

Timpson left Kufra on the eight hundred mile drive to the coastal area with twenty men, five trucks and two jeeps. During the journey he was engaged by enemy armoured cars and lost half his patrol. He arrived in the vicinity of Nofilia with ten men, one jeep and two trucks, both of which had suffered from the journey and were in bad running condition. He had petrol for another five hundred and fifty miles, and water rations for three weeks.

He decided to establish a rendezvous twelve or thirteen miles from the coast. This meant that the ' watchers ' would have a long walk home, but Timpson felt it wise to play safe until he was more familiar with the country.

He and a soldier named Welsh undertook the first watch. The jeep drove them within four miles of the road, then returned to the rendezvous. The two men walked toward the coast until they came to a small hill which gave them a perfect view of the road, four hundred yards below them.

" At dawn the traffic started," wrote Timpson, " and was fairly heavy throughout the day. Some tankers at sea passed close inshore, and we longed to call up the R.A.F. by wireless, for they were deep in the water.[1] If this continued to occur it might be possible to hide up our wireless truck close to the lookout and lay on some long distance target observation.

" That night we started back to the rendezvous. . . . After covering a mile, we came on one of the numerous native camps which stretched far inland in this area. We now had no water left and were very thirsty and tired, for we carried a fairly heavy load; waterproof greatcoats, grenades, rifle, tommy-gun and ammunition. The Bedouin was suspicious of us. They sat round us in a half circle and asked us threateningly if we were British. On assuring them we were Germans they became less menacing, but our dishevelled appearance was not calculated to arouse respect.

" In my bad Arabic and their Tripolitanian dialect, very different from the homely chatter of the Senussi of Cyrenaica, we discoursed on the close friendship between the Arab and the German races, and our common dislike of the Italians; this latter at least was a genuine sentiment. I thought fit however to enlighten them as to the course of the campaign. It was indeed going very badly for us Germans. Benghazi

[1] This showed that they were loaded to capacity.

and Agedabia had fallen; they did not know this, and
were astonished. El Agheila, too, had just been entered
by the hated British; this was not true at the time, but was
received with much clicking of tongues in sympathy. They
might easily guess we were British, in spite of our denials
at the start, so I thought it prudent to enhance British
prestige.

"They asked what type of weapon my tommy-gun was. It
was a Schmeisser. My water bottle they considered very small
for a litre. They wanted to inspect the tommy-gun, but I
held on to it firmly. When they asked me to fire it, I declined
as gracefully as I could, for I knew it was much too dirty to
function. If they knew this they might well set on us. Where
were we going? To Nofilia. We had just come back from the
front, and my trucks were due to pick me up here, having
lost me in the dark. At least I was not giving the Germans
credit for much competence. Why not get a lift from one of
those German trucks which one could see passing down the
Meduma-Nofilia track a mile away? An awkward and reasonable suggestion which was not very satisfactorily answered. At
last, however, they brought bowlfuls of goats' and sheep's milk.
They could spare no water. We drank it as slowly and in as
nonchalant manner as possible. This somewhat undignified
durbar was brought to an end by the jeep appearing on the
horizon, careering along at high speed, circling round us, but
never stopping for long enough for us to catch it. We waved
and shouted, but it disappeared again."

Timpson and Welsh finally found the camp after a twenty-
mile walk. "I immediately made out an analysis of the traffic
I had seen and sent it by wireless to Kufra. Activity on the
road was obviously increasing and its details, together with
estimates of troops seen and unit signs observed, had urgent
news value which warranted immediate transmission to Headquarters. The danger of our signals being plotted was a very
minor risk, and we invariably sent back every day an account
of the previous day's road watch.

"The procedure from now on was that the jeep left camp
every afternoon at 4 p.m. with the next pair for the watch,

together with a driver and one other man. It would halt at
the R.V. three miles from the road and about twenty-two
miles from camp, and from here, after some cold supper and
a short rest, the new relief of two men would go off on foot,
to be in position by the road at 11.0 p.m. The other two who
stayed with the jeep would await the returning watch party
who must remain on lookout until midnight. Thus, an overlap
in time of one hour between successive reliefs ensured continuity.
This was important, for gradually the amount of traffic at
night increased. Having completed the relief, the jeep would
return to camp at dawn."

*   *   *

For twelve days the eight men of Timpson's patrol took
turns keeping their night and day watch, and wirelessing the
details back to Kufra. Once they lay up within a mile of a
tented enemy camp. It rained for several days and at night
it was bitterly cold. One of the patrol was taken ill, and two
others failed to return to the rendezvous. Later Timpson
learned they had been taken prisoner. By 11th December it
was obvious that Rommell was not going to make a determined
stand to check Montgomery's imminent offensive, for the
enemy began to pull out of their defensive positions near El
Agheila, and the road was soon overflowing with retreating
forces. Timpson reported 2,000 westbound vehicles a day;
two days later, after the British offensive had begun, the figure
had swollen to 3,500.

This was the last day of Timpson's watch. Headquarters
had wired that two more patrols which had been sent out from
Kufra would be relieving him within the next twenty-four hours.
But before this happened, however, he had a harrowing experience. " The only space near the road unoccupied by the
enemy was a wadi with steep sides," he wrote. " It flattened
out close to the road where the shallow bed contained a few
thorn bushes. These were not very thick and rather short, but
grew on small hummocks which gave good observation on to
the road. During the night we sat in one of these, by the road's

edge, and moved back to one two hundred yards from the road at dawn.

" Traffic was heavy throughout the night, nearly all driving west, and at first light it grew even thicker. And then they started to pull off the road. In the first truck came the German Camp Commandant. He liked the look of the ground on the right of our bush and proceeded to allot the area to each lorry as it drew off the road. They halted all around us and drove up the wadi behind us, but luckily none were parked immediately between us and the road, which we could still observe clearly. We crawled gingerly from one side of our bush to the other as a party of Germans came up to our hide-out and decided it was an excellent place for their cooker-lorry. ' *Sie können ruhig hinein fahren* ' (' You can drive in all right '), said the man who guided the truck into position. They halted just short of our bush. Of the other lorries about six were within a hundred yards of us, and scores within two hundred yards. Our chief worry was that they would think of using the dry thorn-wood as fuel for their fires. There were only about eight thorn bushes like ours, and no other natural fuel was available.

" It did not seem very hopeful that we would see the day through undetected. Automatically we continued with our traffic census. ' West, three 3-tonners; German covered; many troops in back,' Welsh would whisper ceaselessly, while I would write. The density grew so heavy that one could not write fast enough, and it was only possible to keep the record going by quickly making a list of every ten minutes of the different classifications of vehicles, troops, stores, equipment and unit signs, and adding a mark against each type as it passed, in the manner of scoring at cricket. After a while Welsh would take over the score, and I would observe and whisper.

" And so it went on all day. Men walking between trucks would come unpleasantly close. We only heard German spoken. Our neighbours were well disciplined and cheerful. We could have assured the B.B.C. that the retreating Afrika Korps was not in the least a ' shattered remnant.' Even the

Italians, who were crowded all over many of the passing lorries, sang lustily of Napoli. At 12.30 p.m. the Germans had macaroni, gulash and gherkins for lunch. We heard the menu described, we could smell it being cooked, but we could not taste it. Nor could we move to reach our own tins of bully beef left on the other side of the bush. The repertoire of songs included chiefly somewhat out-dated American jazz numbers, but such music held little charm for us. Nor did it seem the moment to raise our own spirits with a duet in ' Land of Hope and Glory,' let alone ' Rule Britannia.' Levity in retrospect of such incidents is easy, but things were earnest enough at the time.

" The twelve hours of daylight gradually drew to a close. A number of Germans were sitting round the cooker lorry, gossiping about sergeant this and captain that, and ragging one another, much as our soldiers do. An armed sentry stood nearby. The moon was shining at intervals between the drifting clouds, which brought occasionally showers of rain. A British Beaufighter roared over at 8.0 p.m. strafing our area and the traffic on the road which was still moving densely west. Five minutes later it came back and did the same. We saw nothing hit. The Germans took hasty cover in slit trenches, but soon reassembled, laughing.

" I wanted to leave before midnight, to prevent the next relief from coming to this area. Up till now this was the only vacant stretch of ground that remained near the road. I knew they intended to make for it.

" At 9.0 p.m. we gingerly started to pick up our belongings, our tins of bully, rifle, tommy-gun, and magazines. The moon was still rising, but even when it was behind the clouds we could see, and be seen, for far around. It was no good crawling or sneaking away. We moved to the edge of the bush away from the cooker lorry and towards the road, then we stood up briskly. We at once walked off slowly, in a nonchalant way, first towards the road and then swung left in a semi-circle, in the hope of walking past the various parked vehicles, and so continue inland.

" A German sentry challenged, demanding the password. We

walked on slowly. He challenged again, in an excited voice.
I replied 'Friend' in German, but this was not of the least
use, for he fired a shot from fifty yards away, and as we continued to walk slowly past, he fired again and again. At this
rate he would hit us soon, so we started to run. Numerous
other voices all around swelled into a clamour, shots were
popping off about us. The chase was on.

"Our equipment and heavy coats did not ease the task of
our legs, stiffened from inactivity all day. We crossed the
open ground ahead of our pursuers, and reached the deep part
of the wadi, at the bottom of which flowed a torrent of water
three feet deep. Here we paused to take breath.

"The Germans could move faster than us, and some were
now rushing past along the top of the river banks, firing down
into the wadi with rifles and automatics. We stumbled on
through the water. I fell down in it several times and lost
sight of Welsh. I then doubled up the side of the wadi passing
between two parties of pursuers, who nevertheless caught sight
of me and gave chase. They were overhauling me, but just
then the moon was darkened by a cloud, and I flopped down,
very exhausted beside a minute bush of camel thorn. The pack
passed by, and I could see and hear them searching around.
When I got up, I was again seen and chased, but they again
lost sight of me when I repeated the previous imitation of a
bit of scrub.

"Leaving a standing patrol near the wadi, they eventually
went away back to camp. I heard one of them say: 'They are
probably only food thieves.' After making a detour I came
back to the deep wadi higher up. I waited there for some time
for Welsh, calling him softly. There was no sign of him, so
I walked on towards the R.V.

"Here, to my relief, the jeep, with Sergeant Ollerenshaw
and Blaney, the next relief, and Corporal Leach were waiting.
They had heard and seen the shooting and Very lights in our
direction, but in any case they did not intend to go to the
road without seeing me; for the great news had come. G.1
Patrol had established a new road watch west of Sirte yesterday.
Our watch was at an end.

" The next day I returned to the rendezvous in a jeep and succeeded in finding Welsh. He thought the Germans had hit me when he saw me fall in the wadi. He had been much concerned in trying to remember details of the previous day's traffic, since I had the notebook. He climbed into the jeep beside me, and we drove back to the main camp."

CHAPTER SEVENTEEN

ROMMEL AND THE S. A. S.

ON THE 13th of December, the day that Lieutenant Timpson arrived back at his rendezvous, the eight S.A.S. patrols of B Squadron were taking up positions along two hundred and twenty miles of the enemy's coastal road, preparing to deliver their initial assault.[1]

David had led the squadron from his meeting-place with Paddy to a second base, several hundred miles farther west, known as Bir Fascia. The trip had been one of the roughest ever taken. They were travelling farther south than usual and the ground was so rocky and broken, giving way suddenly to deep wadis, or treacherous pieces of soft sand, that the convoy took much longer to cover the distance than they had planned. Mike Sadler had drawn a route around the edge of the Wadi Tamit, since this far south it was marked ' impassable ' on the map. However the going was so bad, the officers concluded the wadi could scarcely prove worse; they decided to try their luck in crossing it.

This decision nearly ended in complete disaster. Once in the wadi they found themselves on a surface made up almost entirely of boulders. Several of the vehicles had their axles broken, and it was not uncommon to get two or three punctures within a few minutes. So many jeeps were crippled that three had to be dismantled for spare parts. There was no alternative but to leave the crews behind. They were given food, water and ammunition and told to carry out whatever attacks they could until the Eighth Army caught up with them. Before the

[1] This was the same day that General Montgomery's major offensive opened.

rest of the party could get out of the wadi they had to construct a track, which took four days.

Once released from their prison they had only one further incident. This was when they approached a cross-road and passed an Italian fort which, in the distance, looked lonely and abandoned. Unexpectedly two armoured cars appeared just below it. They came forward in a cloud of dust and opened fire. One of the jeeps was hit, caught fire and had to be left behind.

David instructed the main body of vehicles to go ahead, keeping to their course, and to pull up ten miles further on. He and Peter Oldfield and Pat Hore-Ruthven would deal with the attackers. As soon as the convoy was some distance away they opened fire. " Of course we really couldn't do them any harm," wrote David, " but our .5 Brownings made a nasty noise on the outside of their armoured cars, and if they were Italians the chances were that we might be able to scare them away. It seemed to work. They stopped in their tracks and did not approach any further. For two hours we all remained motionless glaring at each other. Finally darkness fell which gave us a chance to slip away and catch up with the others."

The following day the squadron reached Bir Fascia. The actual ' bir ' or well, was an underground cistern made by the Romans, and held a large quantity of water. A wadi ran from the bir, and offered cover in the shape of thick bushes and scrub. Sadler chose a place for the camp about three-quarters of a mile from the well itself. From now on the spot would serve as a storage depot and a rendezvous for the men when they ran out of petrol and rations. Since the squadron was nearly a week behind schedule, and due to open its attacks the following night, there was no time to lose. The men spent the day making preparations and set out that same night.

The squadron was divided down into eight patrols of three jeeps each; each jeep carried two, and sometimes three men. The patrols were assigned particular sectors of the road. This is the way they were divided: Gordon Alston and Wilfred Thesiger were given the stretch west of Bouerat; then came Captain Hore-Ruthven as far as Misurata, Major Vivian Street

Misurata to Zliten, Lieut. Martin Zliten to Toglat Oasis, Lieut. Hough Toglat Oasis to Homs, Lieut. Mather and Lieut. Maloney Homs to Tripoli. Peter Oldfield was instructed to ' rove ' in the small gap that divided A and B Squadron areas in the Bouerat area.

David briefed the men once again. Their job was to try and deliver an attack on the road once every three days; blowing up enemy transport, laying mines, cutting telephone wires. If they succeeded in doing this, their raids would amount to sixteen a week. The object was to force the enemy on to the road only by day, which would give the R.A.F. a splendid target. If they ran short of supplies they must make their way back to the dump at Fascia which would be replenished if the Eighth Army did not reach Bouerat in the next ten days. General Montgomery's attack was opening the following night, the 13th; he was expected to drive as far as Sirte, perhaps even to Misurata. This would mean that Paddy Mayne's squadron probably would be out of business before the month was over, and that the British front line might soon run through B Squadron's scene of operations.

David was due back at Headquarters. He had received a signal from Shan Hackett reminding him of his promise to return to base. Before he started, however, he could not resist a brief skirmish. Whereas most men regarded raiding as an anxious business, David appeared to look upon it as pure relaxation. " We can't leave before we've had a bit of a go," he remarked to Mike Sadler; and Mike who never said no, but could easily have foregone the pleasure, nodded in agreement.

They had a busy night. They motored to the road and shot up two lorries and a staff car. Then they mined the road and blew down the telephone poles. They made so much noise that Mike was glad to leave the spot. His heart sank when David suddenly said he had left his pipe behind; and would anyone mind if they went back to look for it? In the end they failed to find it.

Before they had done with the night's work they had destroyed a mobile workshop and a transport park, and come

across a general's tented headquarters which they swept with
bullets. Mike was fascinated by David, who seemed to regard
the whole business as a tremendous lark. At one point they
spotted a few lights in the middle of a wadi some way below
them. David thought they ought to drive down to see if it
was an enemy camp. The track was rough and precarious.
If they got into a fight at the bottom it might be difficult to
make a graceful exit. " How will we get out again? " asked
Mike. " Oh, let's worry about that when the time comes,"
replied David cheerfully. As things turned out, he was right
not to concern himself in advance for when they reached the
bottom they saw that it was only an Arab camp. They returned to the Fascia base as dawn was breaking, and a few
hours later started back to Eighth Army Headquarters.

*   *   *

The assault of Squadron B on ' the road ' did not work out
as David had hoped. He had visualised it as a relentless series
of attacks over the space of several weeks. Instead, after one
or two raids almost every patrol came to grief.

Vivian Street and Pat Hore-Ruthven were operating next to
each other in the Misurata area and agreed to combine for
the first operation. They selected a point near the town of
Misurata itself and decided to establish a rendezvous in a
secluded spot near the enemy airfield of Bir Dufan. For two
days it rained heavily, which made the going difficult but they
finally reached their hide-out and concealed themselves and
their stores. They would make their raid with three jeeps
and nine men. They left the remaining vehicles and drivers
to await their return in the morning.

" We started at 9.0 p.m.," wrote Vivian Street,[1] " and two
hours later, as we topped a rise, we saw the road about a
quarter of a mile ahead of us running like a ribbon across the
desert. It was a great moment for us all. For over two weeks
we had been travelling and had covered several hundred miles.

[1] This account was originally published in Blackwood's Magazine in March,
1947.

All the while our talk, our thoughts, and even our dreams had been about ' the road.' At times it had seemed nebulous and unattainable, and we doubted if we could ever be there by the appointed day, or even reach it at all. And now as we lay there sweeping the road with our glasses, we realised excitedly that or efforts had not been in vain and that all along the road other parties like ourselves were stealing up to strike at the enemy's supply line nearly two hundred miles behind their front.

" The moon had been hidden behind cloud, but now for a fleeting minute it came out and we saw close ahead a group of vehicles huddled together and obviously pulled in off the road for the night. There was no sign of any sentries and it was clear that the occupants had fallen asleep safe in the thought that many miles separated them from the nearest enemy. They were to have a rude awakening.

" On foot we crept up to the lorries. There were twenty of them loaded with supplies of all descriptions. Without a sound we went to each in turn and planted our incendiaries. We crept away and waited. A few minutes later the first incendiary went off, enveloping the vehicle in a sheet of flame. Then another, and another and another. Soon all twenty lorries were burning furiously, their Italian drivers scurrying round in panic with no idea of what had happened. Meanwhile others from our party had been busy mining the road and destroying the telegraph poles. This accomplished they rejoined us, and for a minute we stood and watched the great bonfire of vehicles lighting up the countryside. Then jumping into our jeeps we drove out into the desert and hurried away. As the first streaks of dawn appeared we reached our hide-out near Bir Dufan.

" It had been a night of great adventure, so easy that it seemed unreal, like some elaborate game of Red Indians. We felt there was nothing to prevent our repeating the perform-ance on the main square of Tripoli. We were very tired, but before we crept under the bushes to snatch some sleep we pulled out our last bottle of rum and drank to further successes against ' the road.'

" We did not remain undisturbed for long. Soon after light an aircraft passed low overhead, wheeling and turning up and down the wadis. It was clear that the search was on and that our activities of the previous night were not to pass unnoticed. At frequent intervals all that day we saw aircraft searching for us, but our hide-out was a good one, and at dusk when we crept out to stretch our cramped limbs we were still undetected.

" We lay hidden for two days. Pat Ruthven left with his three jeeps and six men for his area south of Misurata; and I set forth to try my luck near Zliten at the other end of my sector. The country here was thickly interspersed with little white Italian houses, established in the thirties as ' colonies.' It was plain fresh tactics were required. We drove to within three miles of our objective and made a small dump. The jeeps then returned to our hide-out, leaving four of us to operate on foot for a few days. It was nearly midnight when we set off to walk to the road with blankets draped round our shoulders to give the impression of Arabs to anyone who spotted us in the moonlight.

" Two hours' walk brought us to the edge of the Italian colony flanking the road, and to our dismay we found it to be full of Italian soldiers. Before we knew what had happened we walked on top of two prowling Italian sentries; fortunately they had their backs towards us, and we slunk into the shadows, where we were forced to remain until the setting of the moon gave us the opportunity to move on again. We had lost much valuable time and there was barely half an hour of darkness left after we had made our way through the colony. Obviously no action was possible that night, so we crossed the road and headed for the sandhills, which ran close to the sea. Here we hoped to lie up and remain unobserved until dark.

" An hour after light two Italian soldiers patrolling the seashore saw us and walked up to the spot where we were, their rifles slung on their backs and their hands in their pockets. They were as surprised to see us as we were to see them, and appeared to think we were Germans. We encouraged them in their mistake, and they soon moved on, apparently quite unsuspecting. It was clear, however, that we could not remain there.

" Directly the Italians were out of sight we hurried back across the road, and into the Italian colony through which we had passed the night before. It was broad daylight and on every side soldiers were cooking their breakfasts and shaking themselves out in the early morning sun. With three weeks' growth of beard on our chins, and in our tattered and sandy battledress we must have looked a queer little party, but by walking along quite openly as if we had been there all our lives, we attracted no attention and reached the open desert unnoticed. Ahead of us was some broken ground which we made for, hoping to find some cover to conceal ourselves.

" Suddenly there was a burst of firing from behind, and on looking round we saw three groups of men advancing towards us, gesticulating and shouting wildly in true Italian style, stopping now and again to take erratic pot-shots at us with their rifles. The four of us paused a minute. What could we do with our miserable pistols against fifty rifles? The open desert lay ahead of us and there seemed not the remotest chance of escape. " We'll make a run for it," we said to each other, and took to our heels, two of us going to the left and two to the right. Any minute we shall be bowled over like a couple of shot rabbits, I thought, as I panted along, but the shooting of those Italians was unbelievably inaccurate, and with lungs nearly bursting we reached some dead ground. Here, to our surprise, we found two newly-dug holes about three feet square and two feet deep.

" In a flash we each jumped into one of them and lay curled up with our knees to our chins, expecting to be discovered at any minute. We could hear the Italians getting nearer and nearer, but when only a few yards away they stopped. They were clearly quite unable to understand our apparent disappearance into thin air. Eventually they moved on and we were left undisturbed all that day. At dark we crept out of our holes and stretched our aching limbs. There was nobody about as we started off to walk the twenty-five miles back to the Bir Dufan hide-out. Reaching there tired and hungry, the following evening, we found the other two, who had likewise managed to get clear after adventures somewhat similar to ours.

" Next day two enemy patrols passed close by us without detecting our hide-out. It was clear that the enemy were making a thorough search of the whole area. Our petrol and food were running short, so at nightfall we decided to move south to our rendezvous at El Fascia in order to replenish from the dump and allow the hue and cry to subside before we undertook any further operation."

*   *   *

Vivian Street gave the order to return to El Fascia on the day before Christmas. He was not the only one who decided to make for this spot at this particular time. On 24th December Field Marshal Rommel motored to El Fascia. He was disturbed by reports of British ' sabotage raids.' They were growing so numerous and daring that now he was forced to divert armoured patrols, badly needed at the front, to hunt down the marauders. His intelligence was good, for he wrote in his diary that the raids were conducted on a well thought-out plan. " They succeeded again and again in shooting up supply lorries behind our lines, laying mines, cutting down telephone poles and similar nefarious activities."[1]

The name of David Stirling was well known to Rommel. It had almost become a bugbear, for the field marshal refers increasingly to his startling tactics. Once the attacks on the road had begun he was not slow to attribute them to Stirling's fertile brain. " On the 23rd December," he wrote, " we set off at 07.00 hours on a beautiful sunny morning to inspect the country south of our front. First we drove along the Via Balbia and then—with two Italian armoured cars as escort—through the fantastically fissured wadi Zem-Zem toward El Fascia. Soon we began to find the tracks of the British vehicles, probably made by some of Stirling's people who had been round there on the job of harassing our supply traffic.

[1] *The Rommel Papers:* Once again Rommel confused the L.R.D.G. with the S.A.S. He seemed to think they were part of the same organisation and some-times referred to both of them as ' commandos.'

The tracks were comparatively new and we kept a sharp lookout to see if we could catch a ' Tommy.' Near El Fascia I suddenly spotted a lone vehicle. We gave chase, but soon found that its crew was Italian. Troops from my *Kampfstaffel* were also in the area. They had surprised some British Commandos the day before and captured maps marked with British store dumps and strong points. Now they were combing through the district also hoping to stumble on a Tommy." [1]

*   *   *

The ' Tommy ' they hoped to catch nearly turned out to be Vivian Street. Unsuspectingly Vivian's patrol approached El Fascia on Christmas Day. " As we came over a rise," Vivian wrote, " we found ourselves face to face with an Italian armoured car. We wheeled about and beat a hasty retreat, and then approached the oasis from a flank, only to find that there were picquets on every side. It was apparent that the enemy had driven us off our dump and had themselves occupied Fascia.

" We had petrol only for twenty miles, and two days' food at quarter rations. Our sole chance was to make back for Bir Dufan and then to the rendezvous that we had arranged for New Year's Eve with the troops operating in our neighbouring sector. So we started on the journey back. After twenty miles we ran out of petrol as we had feared, and were forced, after concealing our jeeps to continue the remaining sixty miles on foot. Three long and painful days of trekking brought us to the Bir Dufan wadi very exhausted and with no food left except a few dates. It was three in the morning and we concealed ourselves carefully, intending to lie up until the following evening, when we would cover the last few miles to the rendezvous.

" When daylight came we found to our dismay that the whole wadi in which we were concealed was picqueted with posts of Italian soldiers every three hundred yards or so. This was no place to remain in, but we could not move in daylight, so there was nothing for it but to lie hidden and hope to slip

[1] *The Rommel Papers:* Edited by B. H. Liddell Hart.

away later under cover of darkness. Unfortunately, some passing Arabs saw us and warned the neighbouring Italian post. A few minutes after a party of soldiers started moving towards the very spot where we lay hidden, while to a flank a machine-gun opened up, spraying the bushes. Behind us we saw another party systematically searching the wadi towards us.

"I looked round at the weary, half-starved faces of my companions, each armed with only a pistol, and realised how slim were our chances against so many. In vain we sought an opening in the net that encircled us, but this time there was no escape. Through my mind flashed the picture of five Englishmen fighting to the death against impossible odds in the true story-book manner, but a couple of hand-grenades landing near us soon banished these mock heroics, and with the enemy only twenty yards away we were forced to accept the inevitable and held up our hands in surrender." [1]

*   *   *

In the meanwhile Gordon Alston and Thesiger were carrying out a successful series of raids in the area west of Bouerat. Their sector was the closest to the Fascia base. They were able to lay their mines and return to the rendezvous the same night. They attacked three or four times, destroying telephone wires, shooting up lorries, and once driving slap through a Divisional Headquarters with all guns firing.

Each time they got back to Fascia safely. The wireless truck was hidden there, as well as a supply of food and petrol. They received messages from Headquarters and learned that the attack which had opened on the thirteenth was going well, and that the Eighth Army was advancing toward Sirte. They were almost beginning to feel settled in their strange new routine, when early one morning a few days before Christmas,

Vivian Street did not remain in captivity for long. He had one of the most remarkable escapes of the war. With ten other prisoners, of all nationalities, he was transported across the Mediterranean in an Italian submarine. *En route* the submarine was spotted by British aircraft and destroyed by depth charges. Miraculously the prisoners got out, and seven were picked up from a rough sea by a British naval vessel. Street was one of them. He was taken to Malta and flown back to Cairo where he rejoined his unit.

Alston took a jeep and driver and travelled the three-quarters of a mile to the well to have a bath. He was just removing his clothes when he heard the sound of engines. He hastily pulled on his trousers, jumped into the car and drove toward a thick undergrowth a hundred yards away. A German plane was approaching, flying very low. Alston decided that it was better to stop in his tracks than continue moving toward the cover. Although the jeep was in full view the plane did not spot him. As soon as it had passed he drove the jeep headlong into a large bush. " Hardly had I done so," he wrote, " when the plane came back and flew over the wadi again. By this time I could hear the noise of armoured cars, though none had come into sight."

For the next few hours Alston and his driver had an unpleasant time. Soon armoured cars were swanning all around them. Every moment they expected to be discovered, but by noon the vehicles began to move away. He decided to leave his jeep and driver hidden in the bush and to try and get back to the wireless truck and destroy the cyphers. Each time he began to walk an armoured car seemed to appear from nowhere and he had to dive for cover again. In the middle of the afternoon he heard a furious burst of shooting in the direction of the truck, and soon after more shooting from the place he had left the jeep. " I began to think I would have to walk back to the Eighth Army," he wrote. " I extricated the silk map of Libya I had sewn in my shirt and wondered how long it would take. I also realised I was wearing sandals and not boots. I decided to have a look at the wireless truck, however, and as dusk fell I crawled up to it. To my surprise I heard French. I found that both the truck and the crew were safe and had been lying low all day. The firing I had heard had been armoured cars chasing a jeep manned by Lieutenant Martin, a Free French officer of the S.A.S. and two French soldiers. Martin had escaped and without realising it had driven into a bush very close to the wireless jeep.

As soon as it was dark my driver brought my jeep in too. The firing behind me had been some other unfortunate being chased. Meanwhile some of the enemy armoured cars had bedded down for the night on some rising ground about five hundred yards to the south of our hiding-place, and the Feisler Storch plane had landed on a smooth piece of sand alongside, and was obviously going to remain there for the night."

Martin and Alston had a long discussion as to what the next move should be. Martin had succeeded in doing a good deal of damage in the last week; he had shot up enemy transport, planted dozens of mines and blown up hundreds of feet of telephone wire. He had narrowly escaped capture several times and reported that the enemy appeared to be organising considerable forces to try and round up the raiders. From the gun-fire he had heard he feared that a number of the S.A.S. patrols had run into serious trouble.

The officers finally decided that the best course was to move south. If the enemy were sending out counter-patrols, it would become increasingly impossible to operate near the coast on that sector.

When darkness fell the men loaded their vehicles, and started to drive out of the bushes. They travelled until day-break, when they came to a valley about a quarter of a mile wide, with steep sides, and a profusion of long bushes which offered good cover. Here they camouflaged down. They were anxious not to be detected by the local inhabitants, but soon after their arrival an Arab shepherd playing a pipe wandered into the ravine and spotted them. The raiders were not too happy at this. They knew that Tripolitanian Arabs often collected rewards for reporting British soldiers to the enemy.

However, Wilfred Thesiger the Arab expert, knew the ceremonial way to offer tea. He carried an enamel tea-pot and little cups expressly for this purpose. The shepherd seemed friendly enough, and the men were having a discussion whether or not they should move, when a second Arab appeared. This one was more important, for he was dressed in white and rode a donkey. He had a goat on a lead. " He presented the goat to us," wrote Alston, " and Wilfred whispered to me that it should be killed there and then, cooked and eaten and the

best bits given to our guest. This would then render us safe
for at least forty-eight hours. I looked around in despair but
luckily one of the French soldiers did the necessary with a knife
and cut the wretched animal up."

They decided to take a chance and remain where they were.
During the next few days they occasionally heard enemy cars
rumble by on the plain above, but no one molested them.
Indeed, they spent a fairly pleasant Christmas in their little
valley.

*　　　　*　　　　*

As things turned out these three men were the only officers
in B Squadron to avoid capture. The other patrols met with
a similar fate to that of Vivian Street. David did not learn
what had happened to them for several weeks. He was at
Headquarters planning his next operation. Montgomery's
offensive had taken the Eighth Army from Agheila to a point
just short of Bouerat. This was the stretch along which Paddy
Mayne's A Squadron was operating. The advance was so
rapid that Paddy's men were able to launch only one or two
assaults against the road before being instructed by H.Q. to
' lay off '; there was no point in blowing up installations and
damaging communications that would soon be British. By
Christmas almost the whole area had become ' home territory '
and David ordered him to take his men back to Kabrit and
prepare for the move to the Lebanon.

In the early days of January news came trickling in about
B Squadron, most of it picked up from the German wireless.
Pat Hore-Ruthven had been killed, and Carol Mather, Peter
Oldfield, Vivian Street, Geoffrey Keating, Hough and Maloney
had been taken prisoner.

However, all of them had made one, and many of them two
or three, attacks on the road. There was no doubt that they
had caused Rommel serious unquiet. They had forced him
off the highway for several nights at a crucial point in the
battle. As David had foreseen, this had enabled the R.A.F.
to take an unusually heavy toll in the daytime. And the fact
that they had also compelled Rommel to send special ground

patrols to round up the raiders, and to man keypoints with
extra guards, was an added contribution. Eighth Army
Intelligence intercepted a number of reports which showed
that the S.A.S. not only caused the enemy serious concern,
but had succeeded in rattling a number of Rommel's sub-
ordinates.

Indeed, Peter Oldfield was nearly put in front of a firing
squad. He had done a great deal of damage. He had mined
' the road ' in several places, set fire to a number of lorries,
shot up a German Headquarters, and destroyed several fighter
aircraft on Turogo airfield. He finally attacked a convoy of
lorries, and, along with his driver, was seriously wounded and
taken prisoner. The authorities were so unnerved and angry
that when the two men were brought into the hospital they
gave the order that they were to be shot. Peter was saved by
a strange twist of fate. The surgeon looking after him was a
friend of Baron von Lutteroti, the German doctor who had
been captured by the S.A.S. and later escaped. Oldfield's
doctor thought it wrong of his superiors to execute badly
wounded men; besides, he said, the S.A.S. had treated
Lutteroti well enough. So in the middle of the night he
smuggled Peter into a lorry and sent him to a hospital in
Tripoli. He survived the war.

Despite the S.A.S. accomplishment it had not suffered such
a serious loss in personnel since its first abortive effort fourteen
months previously. David attributed it to two factors; first,
that B Squadron was operating in a much more populated and
built-up area than ever before; second, that the Arabs were
hostile; and third, that so few of the men had had practical
experience. This last point seemed to be emphasised by the
fact that the sole member of Hore-Ruthven's patrol to get
back to the British lines was that wily desert fox Sergeant
Seekings; and that out of the three officers to avoid capture
—Thesiger, Alston and Martin—the last two were old hands.

These survivors had continued to find their valley a safe
hiding-place. They emerged from it at night and carried out
several more raids on enemy communications. They still had
the wireless truck with them and were able to keep in touch

with David. On the 5th of January they signalled him that they were running low on petrol. He instructed them to proceed to a rendezvous in the Bir Guedaffia area, about twenty miles from their present position. They were to remain there until he arrived with fresh supplies. A new operation was under way.

CHAPTER EIGHTEEN

TO THE FIRST ARMY

DAVID HAD worked out four daring tasks for the S.A.S. The Eighth Army's next offensive was scheduled for the 15th of January and it was hoped that the troops would reach a point well beyond Tripoli. Two of David's missions would tie in with the coming attack; the other two would bear on the final phase of the campaign.

The plan was this. One group, composed of three French patrols under Captain Jordan, would raid the enemy's lines of communication between the coastal town of Sfax and Gabes in Tunisia which were now supplying the main bulk of the Afrika Korps. A second group (at the special request of General Montgomery) would make a demonstration of strength on the west side of Tripoli while the Eighth Army was attacking from the east and south, to try and panic the enemy and prevent him from carrying out an orderly destruction of the port installations. A third group would move as close as possible to the Mareth Line and observe what preparations were being made. And a fourth group, led by David, would reconnoitre the territory in Northern Tunisia and join up with the First Army which had landed in Algeria in November.

David's trip sounded unusually rash. He had been told that General Freyberg was considering an outflanking movement of the Mareth Line, but that the maps were so bad Army Intelligence could not decide whether the plan was feasible. He was certain that he could provide the general with useful information.

He had another purpose, which he did not disclose, for

wishing to make the trip to the First Army. He had decided to try and secure brigade status for the S.A.S. "My plan," he wrote, "was to bring in my brother Bill's 2nd S.A.S. Regiment, and to divide down my own regiment, which had grown far beyond the official establishment of a full regiment into the nucleus of a third one. This would enable me to keep one regiment in each of the three main theatres—the Eastern Mediterranean area, the Central Mediterranean—Italian area, and the future Second-front area.

"I felt it was vital to get intervention and support from a more important formation than Middle East Headquarters. The first step in this plan seemed to be to acquire the sympathy of the top brass of the First Army, and to consult my brother Bill, who had recently arrived on the First Army front, with the 2nd S.A.S. Regiment, as to the state of the game at the War Office. I was conscious that the reputation of the S.A.S. would be greatly enhanced if it could claim to be the first fighting unit to establish contact between the Eighth and First Armies. A little additional prestige would come in handy in getting across my brigade proposition.

"What I did not know at this time was that Antony Head, on loan from Bob Laycock and Mountbatten of Combined Operations, was already on his way to the Middle East to investigate the whole position of raiding forces and the S.A.S. role in relation to future planning in each theatre. He was to discuss the position with Shan Hackett and myself before submitting proposals to Eisenhower and Sir Alan Brooke. Events, if only I had realised it, were for once playing for our side. Antony arrived in Cairo about four days after I had left. If only we had met I am quite certain that he would have consented to become a key agent in bringing about the plans which I have sketched."

*   *   *

David assembled his men and vehicles at Eighth Army Headquarters. He would take Mike Sadler with him; if anyone could navigate the patrol through the unknown territory of Algeria it was the brilliant Rhodesian. He would also like to take McDermott, the daring Irishman who had succeeded in capturing an enemy railway station in September. However, McDermott was a member of Paddy's squadron, and it was not until a good deal of arguing had taken place that David was allowed to ' borrow ' him. Of course the indispensable Cooper would go with him, but Seekings, alas, was not back. from the raid on ' the road.' It was at this point that David signalled Thesiger, Alston and Martin and told them to proceed to the designated rendezvous and wait for him. Captain Jordan, he said, would be joining them, coming straight from Kabrit with three French patrols.

*   *   *

David's party set forth on 10th January. The rendezvous was in the vicinity of Bir Guedaffia. It lay about forty miles behind the lines on which the enemy was now standing. It was on a direct route to Ghadames, which was David's next staging point because of food and water and in order to give enemy patrols a wide berth. Lieut. Harry Poat, who had recently transferred to the S.A.S. from the King's Own Scottish Borderers, was in charge of the raid on Tripoli. He accompanied the party as far as the rendezvous then turned off to carry out his task.

Captain Jordan had already reached Bir Guedaffia and joined forces with three officers when David's group arrived. After much discussion about routes and petrol Stirling decided to divide his men into two sections. Although all of them would be heading in the same direction it was safer to travel in smaller numbers. He would establish a rendezvous in Northern Tunisia in the area of Bir Soltane. The French patrols under Jordan, and the British patrols under himself, would travel to this area independently. Soltane would provide a convenient base for all the operations taking place. It was only 30 miles from the Mareth Line. Alston and Thesiger could establish themselves here for their observation work on the Mareth fortifications. Secondly, it was in the heart of the country which David wanted to reconnoitre for Eighth Army Intelligence. Thirdly, it would make a good jumping-off point for Jordan's dangerous passage through the narrow Gabes Gap—a stretch of land, only five miles wide at its narrowest point, wedged between the Mediterranean on one side and salt lakes on the other. The Gap offered the only direct route to the coastal sector which Jordan would attack.

The two sections set forth the following day. David had attached the Frenchman, Martin, to his own party, and had a total of about twenty men and seven or eight jeeps. Mike Sadler was navigating and took them on a straight course to Ghadames. At first the going was rough, but as they moved farther south the ground became flat and smooth; for a long stretch the vehicles cruised in formation, at fifty miles an hour, like super-fast destroyers on a calm sea. When they reached Ghadames they discovered that General Leclerc's Free French forces were at that very moment only seventy miles distant, on their way from Lake Chad—to deliver an attack on Rommel's flank. They were expected within the next forty-eight hours. Martin and his Frenchmen enjoyed themselves by writing rude and humorous messages on the walls asking them why their journey was taking so long.

From Ghadames David drove due north. The trip was a nightmare. The patrol had to pass through the ' Grand Sea Ergh ' the most difficult ground that David had ever tried to manœuvre across. " The waves or dunes of the Grand Sea Ergh were short and choppy like a rough Mediterranean sea," he wrote, " in contrast to the sand sea south of Siwa, which was more like the long Atlantic rollers and easier to negotiate."

As David approached Bir Soltane he branched off and spent twenty-four hours doing a thorough reconnaissance of the country on the Mareth flank. He had been keeping in fitful wireless touch with Jordan. The two men were travelling not far apart, and frequently signalled each other their positions. David had told Jordan that as soon as he set up a rendezvous he would wire him a map reference, but when the time came he was unable to get through to him. As luck would have it one of David's officers ran into Jordan by accident three kilometres from Bir Soltane and guided him to the base.

It was a fortunate encounter as David had been trying to

contact Jordan for other reasons as well. He wanted to tell him that Gafsa had fallen to the Allies, and that Tripoli was in British hands. Even more important, he had received a message from Headquarters stressing the urgency of carrying out raids on the roads and railway lines between Sousse, Sfax and Gabes as rapidly as possible. Part of this sector, of course, had been Jordan's objective ever since he started. Now Headquarters was emphasising the necessity of speed. Rommel's supply position was desperate; if his lines of communication could be disrupted it would be of the greatest assistance to the Eighth Army's advance. It might even prevent him from making a determined stand on the Mareth Line.

There was no time to lose. Jordan must leave at once with all of the French patrols; his own, Klein's and Martin's. They must try to get through the Gabes Gap and be ready to operate the following night. The distance to the Gap, taking detours into account, was nearly a hundred miles; if Jordan set off at 4.0 p.m. and averaged six miles an hour he would be safely through it by early morning.

David's own schedule would be altered as a result of the Headquarter's request. There were two routes to the First Army. The safest but longest way was to head west and skirt the southern edge of Lake Djerid, then swing north to Tozeur and Gafsa. The quickest and most dangerous way was to move through the Gabes Gap. David had planned to follow the first route, but now that the need to attack the coastline was becoming increasingly urgent, he decided to finish his reconnaissance on the Mareth flank in the next twelve hours, then proceed through the Gap on Jordan's heels. He would travel to Sousse and deliver an attack before trying to contact the First Army. He was running short of petrol and would have to rely on capturing an adequate supply when he carried out his raid.

This was a startling schedule, the success of which depended on almost every detail going right. But it did not strike David as over-optimistic. After months of raiding he regarded it as routine work. However, he instructed Alston and Thesiger not to abandon the Bir Soltane rendezvous for ten days. He

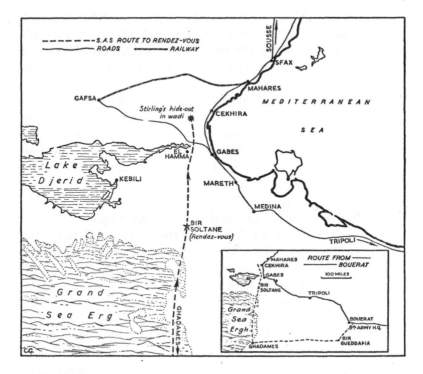

Passage through the Gabes Gap en route to the First Army

would leave the wireless truck with them, and if any of the
patrols got into trouble on the Tunisian coast and could not
reach the First Army, they could make their way back to it.
Then he emphasised the necessity of Jordan's patrols slipping
through the Gap as quietly as possible. " No matter how
delectable the targets don't shoot until you reach your area.
Go through as softly as church-mice, because we'll be close
behind you."

Jordan attached a French soldier named Taxis, who spoke
perfect Arabic, to David's patrol as a parting gesture. At four
o'clock the Frenchmen set off.

*   *   *

They left the rendezvous with nine jeeps, one of which was

a wireless car. They consisted of three patrols; Klein's, which would raid the stretch between Sfax and Mahares, Jordan's between Mahares and Cekhira, Martin's between Cekhira and Gabes. Until the moment came to split up they were under Jordan's command.

David had been more than sanguine when he reckoned that they could average six or seven miles an hour. They ran into a large area of undulating sand, and found themselves bogged down time and again. At the end of five hours they had travelled five miles. Jordan told the wireless operator to signal David: "Retarded by sand. Cannot make objective to-night. Accomplish to-morrow." The operator reported that he was unable to establish contact with Colonel Stirling.

The patrols drove all night and continued until noon the following day. The closer they got to the Gap the worse the country seemed to become. If they were not travelling across sand they found themselves trying to descend steep ravines blocked by boulders or moving along tracks that suddenly petered into nothing. They had one good piece of going where they covered fifteen or twenty miles; then they went back to an average of a mile an hour.

At five-thirty in the afternoon of the 22nd, just twenty-four hours after they had left David, Jordan assembled the three patrols and warned them that during the night they probably would pass very close to the enemy. They were moving into a 'built-up' area as they neared the Gap. They knew there were heavy concentrations of troops, and that the tracks had much traffic on them. Jordan told the men that it was of the utmost importance that they should pass through the Gap undetected. Other S.A.S. patrols would be following them; perhaps within a few hours. No one must show a light at any cost; no one must 'rev up' his engine or even change gears in a noisy way. There was to be no firing unless he himself gave the signal.

The patrols had to cross a steep wadi. At the bottom the track ended, and it was so rough they had to stop and wait two hours until the moon rose sufficiently to give them enough light to thread their way through the ravine.

On the other side, the going was reasonably good. They averaged four or five miles an hour for the next five hours. About 3.15 in the morning the jeeps were travelling in single file along a narrow track, bordered on either side by soft shoulder of sand. Jordan rounded a bend and suddenly found two powerful headlights bearing down on him. He tried to turn on his own lights but they did not work. " In a few seconds," he wrote, " I found myself level with a German armoured car. It was followed by several other vehicles all of which had their lights on; another armoured car, two lorries, then a third armoured car. The last vehicle blinded me and as it did not keep to the right it edged me off the road into the sand. For a brief moment I found myself at a stop, within a foot of the German car which also had stopped. The Afrika Korps navigator put his head out of the turret and stared at me with interest. I do not know who he thought I was, and I did not wait to find out. I accelerated and to my infinite relief the tyres gripped and the jeep leapt forward. I looked back and saw that the other jeeps were following.

" At first I thought we had got away with this unfortunate encounter. Then the eighth jeep came racing up to me, and reported that jeep No. 9, the last in line, had been cut off. One of the armoured cars had suddenly decided that it had a suspicious look about it, and had driven across its path. " A moment later we heard loud bursts of machine-gun fire. There was nothing the rest of us could do but continue on our way hoping that our comrades would manage to escape on foot. We spread out as much as possible, in case we were pursued and attacked again, and in doing so Martin and his two jeeps became separated from us. We did not see him again."

Jordan now had only six jeeps and the wireless car left. He travelled along undisturbed for the next hour. By this time he was close to the village of El Hama which was only five miles from the narrowest point in the Gabes Gap. As he neared the outskirts he heard the noise of engines somewhere in front of him, and in the moonlight soon made out the shape of three lorries moving towards him. He had to take a quick decision.

Should he pass them quietly or open fire? He decided that since surprise had been lost in the fighting an hour before there was no longer any point in allowing worth-while targets to pass unmolested. The jeeps stopped and spread out; and when the trucks were within point-blank range they opened fire. An enemy gunner answered back. One of the jeeps was hit and had to be left behind. Jordan kept firing until all three trucks were put out of action.

During this skirmish the remaining five jeeps again got separated. The wireless car had disappeared down the road. Three vehicles had gone after it thinking they were following Jordan. The remaining jeeps searched for them for half an hour and found only two of them. Also the wireless car was still missing. Eventually it was discovered lying in a pool of oil with its sump broken. Its occupants were nowhere to be seen. All this took place in the jaws of the Gap itself. It was essential to get clear of the dangerous trap before light came. Jordan had only four jeeps left; a short while later the engine of his own vehicle seized and he was down to three.

At five in the morning his little group was relieved to see the Gabes-Gafsa road stretching out in front of them. This marked the end of the bottle-neck. They crossed it and halted as dawn began to break. Jordan decided that they must lighten their load. It was difficult to know what could be spared; finally some of the rations were dumped off; and blankets, tarpaulins and camouflage nets were discarded.

They remained hidden all day. At one point, however, they were discovered by a group of Arabs who mistook them for Italians and came forward professing great admiration for Signor Mussolini. One of Jordan's sergeants spoke perfect Italian so he accepted their compliments gracefully, taking pains not to enlighten them.

Jordan told the men that with luck they would reach the coast and be able to mine the Sfax-Gabes railway line that night. However, when they set out again after dark, they found themselves moving through an increasingly cultivated and populated area. It was dotted with orchards and clusters of white houses, originally built as ' colonies.' They had to make so many detours that the attack was postponed until the following night.

In the early morning of 25th January they saw one of their objectives, Cekhira, in front of them. They hid themselves on top of a wooded hill from which they could clearly observe the railway line and road. In the afternoon, several lorries and two goods trains passed.

The raid that night was successful. The Frenchmen laid twelve charges on the track and started back to their hide-out without encountering opposition. On the way home, however, they passed a lone vehicle parked by the road. Jordan thought it might prove a good opportunity to pick up some petrol. As he came alongside, he saw that it was a Red Cross van. Inside an orderly was sleeping. Jordan woke him up and asked him in German if he had any ' benzine.' The man scarcely bothered to open his eyes. He had run out of petrol himself, he mumbled, and dozed off again. It tickled Jordan's fancy to think that he would never know whom he had spoken to.

Soon after this encounter the patrols heard distant explosives and knew that their work had been well done. A half an hour later they approached a level crossing. There were several military tents nearby and a dozen stationary lorries. Just as they were moving over it a sentry shouted, and fired a rifle shot into the darkness. It was plain that news of S.A.S. activities was spreading.

The patrols accelerated and sped on as fast as possible. They stopped a quarter of a mile away and listened; no one seemed to be following. After a bit they decided to remain where they were and go back to the railway crossing on foot and lay more charges. The camp appeared to have gone to sleep again, for everything was still, not even the sound of a guard's footsteps. They accomplished their task quickly and efficiently, each patrol laying four mines. Once again they got away without detection.

Jordan felt that they were on to a good thing. He decided to return at once to the level crossing—this time in jeeps—and shoot up the stationary lorries. The men approached the track as silently as possible. Suddenly an armoured car seemed to appear from nowhere and took up a defiant position in the middle of the track. A moment later the air was torn by fire. Germans had manned the trucks, and there was a general free-for-all in the darkness. The three French jeeps scattered into the night and escaped unhurt. However, they were now separated and the jeep containing Jordan, Klein and Melis could not find the other two again.[1]

Now Jordan was alone with one car and two men. He decided that the time had come to head for the Allied lines. During the next two days he travelled without incident over rough, hilly country. On 28th January, just before dusk, he was passing through a small wadi. Midway he met an Arab shepherd. He drew up and asked the man if there were any enemy troops in the vicinity. The shepherd did not reply. He merely raised his eyes to the brow of a hill a few hundred yards away. Jordan looked up and to his consternation saw that he had driven into a trap. Lining the top of the hill was an Italian company with machine-guns trained on his lone vehicle. His own machine-gun was out of action; he had only revolvers and grenades. There was nothing to do but surrender.

*   *   *

Now to get back to David. He completed his reconnaissance the day after Jordan had departed, and the following morning started for the Gabes Gap. His party consisted of about 5 jeeps and 14 men. " We found the lie of the land over which the Eighth Army might make its out-flanking movement reasonably good," he wrote, " but as we travelled farther north the going became atrocious. It was hilly with many ravines, and when it became flat it was laced with bogs and marshes."

He neared the hills south of El Hama, where the French patrols had run into the armoured cars, just twelve hours behind them. Jordan's encounter had taken place at three in

---

[1] These two jeeps managed to join up together. A short while later they drove into a bog from which it took several hours to extricate themselves. They finally managed to get out and hid the next day in a cornfield. They were betrayed by Arabs and captured by the Germans.

the morning and it was now three in the afternoon. Two hours later, as dusk was gathering, the men saw two German reconnaissance planes appear on the horizon. They hurried for cover and watched the planes scouring the ground at a height of a hundred feet. " Despite our camouflage they spotted us just before dark," wrote David. " It was too late for them to attack us but we knew that they would alert the ground forces in the Gap. It was obvious that the French patrol must have bumped into the enemy, or begun its operations on the Gabes sector."

Although no one had had any sleep for forty-eight hours David decided that they must press ahead and get through the Gap before morning. Once they crossed the Gabes-Gafsa road, and were out of the bottle-neck, they could lie up and get some sleep. The drive was a nightmare of deep ravines and rocky tracks. One of the jeeps went into a bog and took several hours to extricate. However, they did not encounter the enemy, and by first light were on the edge of the Gafsa road. Enemy traffic was running along it and they had to wait an hour until there was a brief lull, and they could make a dash across it. They drove another twenty miles northward. Then they found a deep wadi which seemed to offer perfect cover. It had plenty of inlets and bushes and they decided to hide there for the day.

Once the vehicles were thoroughly camouflaged Sadler and Cooper climbed to the top of the wadi to have a look around. They were surprised to discover a road, not a mile away, on which a steady stream of enemy traffic could be seen. The road was not marked on their maps, but apparently they had been travelling parallel to it for some time. They watched for a few minutes and saw several trucks draw up and unload; it must be some sort of junction. There was no hope of moving now; they were lucky not to have been seen as it was. David was unperturbed, and insisted that the best thing everyone could do was to get a good sleep. They would raid the Sousse road and railway that night and it was important that the patrol should be thoroughly rested. His decision was perfectly correct. The enemy had no idea of their presence and if Fate had not intervened, their schedule would have moved according to plan.

Indeed, this is what happened. Sadler and Cooper were near the entrance to the wadi. Across from them was the French soldier, Taxis. It was a cold clear day and the men dropped asleep almost at once. Sadler and Cooper were so tired they did not even take off their boots. About three in the afternoon they were awakened by a steady crunch, crunch, against the rocky surface. Both men opened their eyes and found themselves staring up into the faces of two fully armed German soldiers. They sat bolt upright and opened their mouths to speak. To their astonishment the soldiers motioned them to lie down and be quiet, then continued on their way through the wadi.

Taxis was now awake too. The three men leaped out of their sleeping-bags and ran up the wadi as fast as they could go. They made the hundred yard climb with bursting lungs and flung themselves into a narrow gulley.

*   *   *

David, in the meantime, woke up to a barking command in German. He and McDermott were sleeping side by side in a shallow cave. They opened their eyes to see a small, red-faced soldier standing over them with a drawn revolver. He began to shout his orders, his gun weaving dangerously. The two men disentangled themselves from their sleeping bags, rose to their feet and held up their hands. David's experienced glance took note of their captor's over-excited manner and unsteady hand. Obviously he was a raw recruit; if this was the type of opposition with which they had to deal they need not take their predicament too seriously.

The German backed out of the cave, his gun still levelled at them, motioning them to follow him. Still backing, he moved down the wadi. David and McDermott scowlingly advanced toward him, their eyes strained to any move that would give them the opportunity to make a break. The German marshalled them round a bend, where an overwhelming sight met them. There at the mouth of the ravine stood a fantastic array of guns trained down the wadi. A company of at least five hundred men was engaged in the business of rounding them up.

David learned afterwards that this company had been specially imported from Germany to track down the S.A.S. It had no idea of the latter's whereabouts, but was on a training course, and out of the dozens of surrounding wadis had happened to pick on this particular one for an exercise! It had sealed both ends of the ravine, and sent a patrol through. " I learned afterwards," said David in disgust, " that the man who captured me was the unit's dentist! "

*   *   *

The prisoners were herded together and searched. They did not find the tiny compass David was wearing as a button, nor the silk map of Africa sewn inside McDermott's coat. Most of the S.A.S. were bootless. The officer in charge finally allowed one of David's sergeants to go back to the wadi with an escort and pick up personal belongings such as shoes, blankets, mess tins and the like.

The men were led to a small hill about a hundred yards away and put under heavy guard. In the meanwhile a patrol went through the wadi, pulling the camouflage off the jeeps, and collecting the weapons. The vehicles were driven out, and another squad of soldiers walked the length of the ravine spraying the area with machine-gun bullets to make sure no one was left behind. They had seen some of the men run over the top, so they searched the high ground as well, shouting to each other and firing into any scrub which might serve as a hiding-place. David wondered anxiously whether they would stumble across Sadler and Cooper.

While this was going on he pondered the best method of escape. His impulse was to make a break for it then and there. The Germans looked green and badly organised; nevertheless they had weapons and in the broad daylight the chances of getting clear were slim. Obviously it would be wiser to wait until dark.

At the end of two hours the Germans motioned their

prisoners toward a lorry. The sun was sinking but it was still too light to attempt escape. Eight armed guards stood in the back of the truck, and two rode in the driver's seat. The vehicle took its place in the middle of a convoy. It bumped along the road that Mike Sadler had observed from the wadi until it reached the coast road, then turned south. It was dark now, and the men could no longer see their surroundings. After a two-hour drive, which David reckoned must mean they were somewhere in the vicinity of Medina, the truck drew up before a large building that looked like an empty garage.

The room was bare save for a few benches against the wall and a couple of chairs near the door. It had an asphalt floor and windows so high that it was impossible to see out. The guards pushed their captives in roughly, and soldiers from the other trucks crowded into the room. They were jubilant with success, and David guessed that they had been through the papers which they had found in his jeep, and had discovered who their victims were. One of the Germans, who spoke English, approached them menacingly. " Don't be disappointed," he said, " if you get very little to eat. It would only be a waste of food, as we're going to shoot you. We have orders to execute all saboteurs, as an example to others who might be foolish enough to follow in your footsteps."

David did not take this speech too seriously. He was certain that he was in the hands of raw troops, and he knew they would not dare to carry out their threat unless they were authorised to do so from above.[1] Nevertheless it was an uncomfortable period. The men put their blankets on the stone floor and tried to sleep. In the end they were given a little soup and bread.

David and McDermott bedded down next to each other and discussed the situation in low voices. There were at least ten guards in the room. Some of them sat on a bench at the far corner; others were clustered near the door. The window was too high to get at. There was no obvious way to make a break. They decided that the best thing to do was to behave

---

[1] David knew that Hitler had issued personal instructions that all sabotage troops were to be shot on capture, but that Rommel had taken no heed of these orders.

like model prisoners and try to seduce the Germans into relaxing their guard.

The next day passed slowly. The S.A.S. lolled in groups on the floor and eyed the soldiers who clumped regularly in and out. Ten guards seemed to be the permanent establishment, for there were never less and often more. The Englishmen were very hungry. They were given only bread for breakfast, and the same soup ration for lunch as on the night before.

However, there was no more talk about shooting. Indeed there seemed to be a subtle change in the attitude of the captors. Their jubilation was now tinged with pride, which obviously meant that they had been congratulated on their accomplishment. In the middle of the afternoon one of the guards strolled over to the S.A.S. and asked if any of them spoke German. The men shook their heads and he said in English: "Too bad. To-night we are broadcasting the capture of the notorious S.A.S. leaders. We thought perhaps it might interest you."

By evening David had made up his mind that an opportunity to escape, in which skill or cunning could be employed, was unlikely. If he and McDermott wanted to get away they would just have to bolt. "During the day," David explained, "we had been allowed out, one at a time with three guards in attendance, to do the essential in the insanitary open. Although we had such a lot of guards on continuous duty McDermott and I concluded that they were all posted in the immediate area of the garage door or inside with us. We decided on a simple cut-and-run escape. After I had been escorted just after dark by the guards to the farthest point they would allow me to go, I was to give a shout and run, and at this precise moment McDermott was to jostle the guard at the door and break out himself."

The reader may feel it unlikely that such a bare-faced plan could work, yet there was no alternative. At ten o'clock David motioned to the guard and asked to be taken outside. McDermott had moved near the door and stood against the wall smoking. The soldiers escorted David twenty yards from the house. They were relaxed and unsuspecting. They chaffed a bit and one took out a cigarette and asked the other for a light. His friend transferred his rifle to his left hand and fumbled in his pocket. At this moment David gave a blood-curdling yell and ran as fast as he could. The soldiers fired furiously into the blackness and one of them ran blindly after him. At the sound of the shots more men came running out of the garage; and at this precise moment McDermott slipped through the door and also disappeared into the night.

David ran for six hundred yards, then took cover in a clump of bushes. He could hear shots still being fired but the enemy obviously had no idea where he was. He took stock of his position. He was on the outskirts of a town. Normally the towns gave way to wilderness almost immediately, but this part of Tunisia was built up, and he would have to walk rapidly to get into rough country by first light. He would head for the rendezvous at Bir Soltane, which he reckoned was about fifty miles away.

First he would like to find McDermott. He had no way of knowing, of course, whether his friend had managed to get free. They had arranged a special whistle and cautiously David sounded the notes. There was no response. He consulted his button compass and began to walk. Every ten or fifteen minutes he gave the whistle. At the end of an hour he abandoned hope of finding him.

He covered fifteen miles during the night. He was walking across cultivated land almost continuously, skirting in and out of farmyards. Twice he raised an ear-splitting commotion, begun by barking dogs, and picked up by braying donkeys and frightened sheep.

As dawn broke he found himself on a well-kept, prosperous-looking holding. The house was bigger than the normal Arab farmhouse and there was a light in the kitchen. David knew that the Arabs were apt to be hostile in this part of the world, but he was so hungry and thirsty he decided to risk it. He knocked on the door, and it was opened almost immediately by a portly Arab, fully dressed even to his burnous. He wore several gold rings which gave him an air of affluence. His wife was bending over the stove and a small child played in the corner.

David was lucky. The Arab smiled and bowed him in. He spoke English and it soon transpired that he had a grievance against the Germans. He said they had taken a piece of his land to use as a rifle range, and had not given him proper compensation.

His sharp eyes correctly assessed David's predicament. He gave him bread, tea, dates and cold meat, and told him it was not the first time he had helped a British ' airman.' Three others had come his way at various times. David did not alter his conjectures and murmured something about his plane catching fire. With much ceremony the farmer produced cigarettes and sticky sweets, and settled down to hear how the war was going. In the course of the conversation David learned that there was a large German aerodrome only five miles away; it had often been bombed by the British, which explained his host's contact with pilots.

David did not dare stay long. The farmer directed him to a barn a hundred yards away and showed him a good hiding-place where the grain was stored. Here he spent the day. In the evening the Arab came out with more dates and water, and once again David started on his way. He reckoned that the Bir Soltane rendezvous was about thirty miles away. If he could do twenty miles through the night, he would probably reach it the next evening.

The aerodrome the Arab had described lay not far from his course and he could not resist heading for it. By this time airfields were second nature. In little over an hour he saw a small light flickering in the distance and knew he was approaching the edge of it. As he got closer he was surprised to see that there was no perimeter wire, and only a guard post. He crept up to the edge of the field and studied the layout. He could see the shapes of many Junkers 52's. He walked down the whole length of the field, which was about a mile long. He took note of hangars, administrative buildings and repair shops. There were muffled lights but all was quiet. It was an irresistable target and he made up his mind that when he reached Bir Soltane he would bring Alston and Thesiger back with him to tackle the field as a final operation before making contact with the First Army.

His reconnaissance had taken nearly two hours. It was now half-past ten. He had only six and a half hours of darkness left. He reckoned he could walk three miles an hour and should not be far short of his twenty miles by first light. But he did not take account of the rough country. Two miles after leaving the field the ground became unbelievably rocky. At dawn he had covered only ten miles. He found a small ravine and prepared a bed for himself. He collected scrub and covered up his six foot six frame as best he could. Then he went to sleep. He did not wake until five o'clock in the afternoon. He shook the covering off him, stood up and brushed his clothes. Suddenly a voice said in broken English, " You sleep good? "

He wheeled around to see an Arab grinning at him. He was a young man; his clothes were poor and he leaned on a crook. " If you like food and water," continued his visitor, " I can show."

David decided that there was no harm in going a short way with the man to see if he meant what he said. He nodded in assent and followed him along the wadi. They had walked about half a mile when the Arab motioned to a track leading to the top. Half-way, he complained about his foot and fell behind. David strode ahead, and as he came over the top, the sight that greeted him was far from reassuring. There, only fifty yards away, were four or five lorries advancing toward the track. On both sides patrols with machine-guns were fanning out. He swung around and saw that more patrols had approached from the other side, and were descending into the wadi. The Arab had pulled out a gun and was pointing it menacingly at him. Now it was clear. The latter had been keeping watch over him while he slept. No doubt he had sent a friend to alert the enemy, in order to collect the cash award which was paid for British soldiers and airmen.

David had no option but to keep walking. The trucks pulled

up and Italian soldiers spilled out and ran toward him. Among them was the second Arab—the man who had gone to fetch the patrol. Excitedly he pointed to David to make sure there would be no argument about his reward. He made the mistake of coming too close to his quarry, for blinding anger suddenly took possession of David. Like a flash he bent forward, seized the Arab by the legs and swung him around bashing him into the ground. Oddly enough the man survived. Soldiers caught David's arms and once again he was a prisoner of war.

The Italians were overjoyed to have captured the notorious saboteur, whom the Germans had clumsily allowed to slip through their fingers, and they took no chances with him. They drove him to the village of El Hama where their garrison was stationed, and kept him under a grotesquely heavy guard; then he was sent to the main Italian Headquarters at Menzel for interrogation. Finally he was taken to the airfield which he had explored so thoroughly, and flown to Italy in one of the JU 52's he had planned to blow up

*   *   *

We must return to Sadler and Cooper and Taxis whom we left hiding in a narrow gulley while the German patrol, which had captured David and his men, searched for any strays that had slipped through their fingers. The three men could hear them hunting in lines; going up and down the hill, firing off shots and letting off grenades until dark. " Twice they passed close to us," wrote Sadler, " their footsteps were only a few feet away and we wondered when the strategic moment would occur to stand up and shout ' *Kamerad*.' I had some signals in my pocket which I buried in the side of the ditch.

" At last it got dark and finally we heard them driving away. Then we had to decide what to do; whether to go west to Gafsa or to go around the northern edge of the salt lakes. We settled on the latter. We had nothing with us; no compasses, water bottles, weapons, maps or food. We walked all the first night. The following day we lay up in a cave which was shown to us by some natives. Taxis was invaluable because of his knowledge of Arabic. We were very thirsty and the Arabs told us there was water five miles away. We started off at dark and found the well. We gulped it down only to discover that it was brackish and quite undrinkable.

"Again we walked all night. The second day, soon after light, we were still plodding along when five or six Arabs came up to us and asked who we were. They invited us to their tent but Taxis said he did not like the look of them. We told them that we were in a great hurry and headed for the mountains. That was about noon. We went to sleep in a cave; several hours later we were woken up by the same Arabs. They had looked reasonably respectable in the morning but now they had changed into their poorest clothes—which they reserved for fighting. We asked them what they wanted and they replied, ' Everything you have.' They were common-or-garden robbers. We tried to stave them off by smiling and handing them something. I chucked over my battledress jacket. Then they said, ' Give us more! You won't need anything because we are going to kill you.'

"It was a strange declaration but we decided not to wait and see, but to make a break for it, and ran as fast as we could. They picked up stones and hurled them at us. Suddenly I heard Cooper cry, ' Help, I'm blinded.' We turned round and saw blood pouring down his face. I thought they had put his eyes out. Taxis and I ran back and took him in one hand each and we ran as fast as we could. They followed us for a time then gave it up. Cooper was not badly hurt; only a gash on the forehead.

"We walked for the rest of the day, all that night, and the morning of the third day. About midday we met a very dignified Arab grey-beard on a donkey with a slave in attendance. He gave us a drink of water and some dates. After we had left him he sent his slave to catch us up with a terrible old goatskin bag and instructions as to where we could find water. He also said, ' Be careful. There are very bad Arabs ten miles farther on.'

"We found the spring. Two girls were drawing water.

When they saw us filthy and unshaven, and Cooper covered with bloodstains, they gave a scream and ran away. We drank our fill and left with the goatskin bulging. A little later a horde of Arabs began to collect behind us—about twenty of them. Taxis said they were arguing among themselves whether to fight us. We were walking as rapidly as possible, trying to give the impression of being Germans, and could not hear the controversy develop. Finally they drifted away.

" That night we lay up again. The next morning we were weak from lack of food and for a while Taxis felt he could not go on. We walked very slowly, perhaps for three miles, then came in sight of the outskirts of a town. We could see it through the trees. Then we heard crying going on. Suddenly we wondered if the place had been captured by the Germans and we had arrived on the wrong day. At any rate we were so whacked we had no alternative but to risk it. We walked into the town, and suddenly found ourselves surrounded by Frenchmen. Oh, the joy of that moment! A French colonel came out to greet us; and we were taken inside a house serving as headquarters and given all the food and water we could drink while they listened to our story. Then the colonel told us he would have to hand us over to the Americans as they were in command of the sector.

" Our treatment by the Americans was quite different. They were suspicious of us and we suddenly found ourselves under armed guard. Finally an officer appeared and said: ' I'm the colonel. So what? ' He was gruff and unfriendly. We told him our story, but he obviously did not believe us. Although we were dead tired, we were piled into an ambulance, again with an armed guard, and taken to Gafsa where a more senior officer could decide what to do with us. At Gafsa we were checked on still further; signals flew back and forth between Eighth and First Army. At last we were cleared.

" I was flown to Algiers, then back to the Eighth Army to act as honorary guide to General Freyberg's New Zealand Division, which, in fact, did outflank the Mareth Line. Thus I passed for a second time over the same territory that I had reconnoitred with David, but in far more comfortable con-

ditions. It was good to know that the original journey had
not been in vain."

*   *   *

The same day that Sadler reached the First Army Lieut.
Martin and his three men reached allied lines at the railway
station of Zenouche. Thus seven members of the S.A.S.,
British and French, linked the First and Eighth Armies
together in the early days of 1943. They were the first men
to do so.

AFTERWARDS

DAVID WAS an unruly prisoner. He was sent to Gavi, an Italian punishment camp, and managed to escape from it four times. Once he was out for five days and another time for eleven. Because of his unusual height, however, he was always caught and brought back. Finally he was transferred to Colditz in Germany.[1]

Immediately after his capture, confusion reigned at S.A.S. Headquarters. David alone had known where everyone was, what they were doing and what they would do in the future. When Harry Poat appeared from a successful diversionary raid on Tripoli he was asked where he had been; and Alston and Thesiger were summoned home to find out what their mission was.

Few officers in high places could fail to salute the work accomplished by the S.A.S. in the fifteen months before David Stirling's capture. Over two hundred and fifty aircraft had been destroyed, dozens of supply dumps wrecked, road and railway communications disrupted, and literally hundreds of enemy vehicles put out of action. All this had been accomplished at an astonishingly small cost of life. Except for the initial assault in November 1941, which failed, and the attack on the road in December 1942 which ended in the capture of

---

[1] McDermott was also recaptured and spent the remainder of the war in a German prison camp—a different one from that which Stirling was in. The latter tried to get in touch with him after the armistice but failed to find him. In fact the two men have not seen each other since the night of their African escape.

seven patrols, the tactics of the S.A.S. were brilliantly successful.

As for David himself he had become a well-established legend. The courage and modesty, the enterprise and restraint that were rolled into one made him a fascinating and unpredictable character. His admirers found it highly amusing that he should end the war with a D.S.O. and nothing else. In 1954 Major-General Laycock, who succeeded Mountbatten as head of Combined Operations, described him as " a leader of quite exceptional resource and one of the most underdecorated soldiers of the war. More than once he would have won the highest military order that a Sovereign can bestow, were it not for the rule that a senior officer must be present to vouch for the circumstances of the citation—and senior officers were never well placed to witness Stirling's raids behind the lines." [1]

The sudden removal of David's forceful presence resulted in many difficulties for the S.A.S. Paddy Mayne, who had destroyed more aircraft with his own hands than any man alive, took over command.[2] He was outstandingly able and energetic but it soon became apparent that the welding together of the organisation had stemmed from David's personality. Bits of the regiment began to break away. The Special Boat Section regained separate identity under Lord Jellicoe; the French sections formed into units of their own; and the Greek Squadron was never put to the use originally intended.

For the next two years many battles were fought by Paddy Mayne and by David's brother, Bill, to ensure that the S.A.S. was used in its correct role. Bill finally resigned from the command of the 2nd S.A.S. because of disagreement over the policy. Nevertheless, the two regiments, led by Paddy Mayne and Bryan Franks, figured in daring and successful exploits in Sicily, Italy, France and Germany. The battle order for D-day included the following:

[1] *Commando Extraordinary:* Charles Foley.
[2] By May, 1945, Paddy Mayne had been awarded the D.S.O. and three bars and was the most decorated soldier in the British Army.

H.Q. S.A.S. Brigade
(plus F Squadron Phantom)
1st S.A.S. Regiment   2nd S.A.S. Regiment
3rd S.A.S. (French) Regiment   4th (French) Regiment
1st Belgian (Independent) Squadron

*   *   *

When the European War ended David flew home. He was sent for by the War Office and asked if he would take a force to the Far East to fight against Japan. He accepted, but before he left England the atom bomb brought the conflict to an end.

David did not wait to be demobilised. He packed up and went to Rhodesia to seek his fortune in industry. At the end of three years he found that he was more absorbed by politics than business. In 1948 he formed the Capricorn Society whose aim was, and is, to establish a *modus vivendi* by which all races, colours and creeds in Africa can live in harmony.

In 1945 the British S.A.S. was disbanded. It was not until Churchill became Prime Minister again that it was revived. Two S.A.S. regiments are now in being; one is serving in Malaya and the other stationed in England. On the continent they continue to flourish as well. When Stirling was in Europe a short while ago he called on General Gruenther at N.A.T.O. Headquarters in Paris. Outside the general's office a Belgian sentry stood on duty. He stopped to admire the badge on the man's chest. It was a winged dagger and underneath were the words: " Who Dares Wins." Not every young man can claim to add a permanent regiment to the British Army; even fewer to the French and Belgian armies as well.

*   *   *

This, however, was not Stirling's main purpose. He had an understanding of the speed and movement of modern war which many military minds failed to grasp. He believed that as weapons increased their explosive power, the role of the soldier was bound to undergo a revolutionary change. Just as on the factory floor man-power was giving way to automation, he felt that small, highly-skilled regiments would soon be able to do the work of whole divisions.

His theory is slowly being accepted. It was a deep disappointment to him, however, that it was not put into practice at the time of Suez. More than one enlightened military mind tried to persuade the staff officers concerned not to use bombers to destroy the gun installations and airfields in Egypt, but to employ the S.A.S. instead. Twenty-five men, they argued, could do the task of a hundred bombers, and could do it much quicker. Instead of taking ten days they could accomplish the task in the space of one night.

The conventional thinkers rejected the suggestion. When one considers to-day what the outcome of Suez might have been had world opinion not been aroused by ten days of bombing, it seems tragic that more enterprising minds did not dominate the planning. Perhaps it is a British failing that although it encourages individuality in time of war, it is slow to learn the lessons in time of peace. That the S.A.S. sprang into being at all is a tribute to the inventiveness of the national character. It is inconceivable that this type of organisation could have flourished in any other army in the world. It was British to its fingertips. It was in the classic tradition of high-spirited boldness which has often brilliantly stamped the pages of English history.

If David had not been captured he might have seen the S.A.S. fulfil all that he had hoped. He wanted to continue operating in small groups of four or five men, but he wanted to strike on a far wider front. He believed that his men should be trained to move behind the enemy lines by sea, air or land, and should be used to attack repeatedly on a wide range of targets, not to be geared to special, isolated operations.

With the development of atomic weapons Stirling's conception of the way military man-power should be used is more valid than ever. With a drastic reconstruction of the British Army taking place, it may well be that in the next few years his ideas will come into full power. Perhaps one day several thousand men will wear the insignia: " Who Dares Wins."

APPENDIX

THE READER may be interested to know what happened to some of the men mentioned in this book. Most of them survived the war. Paddy Mayne, however, was killed in a car crash a few years ago. Fitzroy Maclean is a distinguished writer and Member of Parliament; Randolph Churchill is a prominent journalist and the Chairman of Country Bumpkins Ltd.; Lord Jellicoe is in the Foreign Office and is the British representative on the Baghdad Pact; Vivian Street, Carol Mather and Mike Sadler are in the regular army; Sandy Scratchley lives in the country and breeds blood-stock; Gordon Alston is Civil Assistant at the War Office; Steve Hastings represents a business firm in Paris; Peter Oldfield is a partner in the real estate firm of Knight, Frank and Rutley; Harry Poat runs a tomato farm in the Channel Islands; Bill Cumper died in Africa after the war. Among the Frenchmen, Lt. Martin was killed in 1944; Captain Jordan has the rank of Minister in the French Foreign Office; Colonel Bergé is in charge of France's helicopter forces, and took part in the Suez operation with the parachute troops.

Among the soldiers whom I have referred to or quoted from, Seekings is farming in Africa. Cooper, who became a commissioned officer, is with the S.A.S. in Malaya, and so also is Sgt. Lilley. Sgt. Du Vivier works at the Prestwick Airport Hotel in Scotland, Sgt. Major Bennett is in the S.A.S. Regiment in England, Sgt. Major Riley rose to the rank of captain and runs a pub in Essex.

The following list contains the only names that have been preserved of the officers and men who took part in some of the raids described. It does not pretend to be complete.

CHAPTERS 2 AND 3

The original Establishment of 'L Detachment,' S.A.S., most of whom took part in the *Timini-Gazala raids:* Lts. Lewis, Fraser, McGonigal, Mayne, Thomas and Bonnington. N.C.O.s: Yates, Riley, Cheyne, Lezenby, Stone, Almonds, Tait, Du Vivier, Badger, Monachen, Kershaw, White, McGinn, Gryne, Orton, Storrie, Leitch, Hildreth, Walker, Evans, Smith, Rose, Arnold, Cattell, Kendall, Bennett, Brough, Kaufman, MacDonald, Lilley, Cooper and Seekings. Ptes.: Cockbill, Keith, Warburton, Phillips, Davies, McKay, Westwater, White, Harvie, Trenfield, Morris, Hill, Sadler, Carrington, Bolland, Keenan, Bridger, Baker, Chesworth, Leadbetter, Rhodes, Austin, Hawkins, Blakeney, and Robertson.

CHAPTER 4

The Agheila raid: Lts. Lewis and Fraser. N.C.O.s: Almonds, Kershaw, Lilley, Rose, Bennett. Ptes.: Storey, Warburton, Phillips, Baker and Rhodes.

The Sirte and Tamit raid: Capt. Stirling, Lt. Mayne. N.C.O.s Brough, MacDonald, Seekings, Cooper, Cattell, Burns, Chesworth, White and Hawkins.

The Agedabia raid: Lt. Fraser. N.C.O.s Tait and Du Vivier. Ptes. Phillips and Byrne.

CHAPTER 5

The Sirte raid: Capt. Stirling. N.C.O.s Brough, Cooper, Cattell and Seekings.

The Tamit raid: Lt. Mayne. N.C.O.s MacDonald, Bennett. Ptes. White, Chesworth and Hawkins.

The Nofilia raid: Lt. Lewis, N.C.O.s Almonds, Lilley. Ptes. Storey, Warburton and White.

The Marble Arch raid: Lt. Fraser. N.C.O.s Tait and Du Vivier. Ptes. Phillips and Byrne.

CHAPTER 6

The Bouerat raid: Capt. Stirling, Lt. Duncan, Flying Officer Rawnsley, N.C.O.s Riley, Badger, Bennett, Brough, Seekings, Cooper. Ptes. Kershaw, Cattell, Rose, Austin, Rhodes and Baker. Also S.B.S. party under Lt. Duncan and Cpl. Barr.

APPENDIX

311

CHAPTER 7

The Benghazi Harbour raid: Major Stirling, Cpls. Seekings and Cooper. Also S.B.S. party consisting of Captain D. Sutherland, Captain Allott. Sgt. Moss, Cpls. Sinclair and Pomford. Misc. Capt. Alston, I.O. Capt. R. Melot, and 2 Arab guides.

The Berka satellite raid: Capt. Mayne. Cpls. Rose and Bennett. Pte. Bryne.

The Barce raid: Lt. Fraser. Sgts. Badger, Kershaw, MacDonald. Ptes. Phillips and Chesworth.

The Slonta raid: Lt. Dodd. Sgts. Riley, Du Vivier and Brough. Cpl. Cattell. Ptes. Warburton and Storey.

Second attempt on Benghazi Harbour: Major Stirling, Capt. Churchill, Lts. Maclean and Alston. N.C.O's Rose, Seekings, Cooper and Bennett.

CHAPTER 8

Derna-Martuba raids: Lt. Jordan, Capt. Buck. Sgt. Gillet, Cpls. Tourneret, Royer Georges, de Bourmont and Vidal. Chasseur Drezen, Jouanny, Le Goff, Geiger, Logeais, Royer, Jean, James, Prados, Guichaoua, Pte. Hillman.

CHAPTER 9

The Benina raid: Major Stirling. Cpls. Seekings and Cooper.

The Berka raid: Captain Mayne. Cpls. Lilley, Warburton and Storey.

The Benghazi raid the night after: Major Stirling, Major Mayne. Cpls. Lilley, Storey, Cooper, Seekings and Karl Kahane.

The Barce raid: Sub.-Lt. Jaquier. Sgt. Martin. Cpl. Lageze, Chasseur Boutinot.

The Berka satellite raid: Aspirant Zirnheld, Sgt. Bouard, Cpls. Fauquet and Itturia, Chasseur Le Gall.

The Crete raid: Commandmant Bergé, Captain Lord Jellicoe. Sgt. Mouhot, Caporal Chef Sibert, Cpl. Leostic.

CHAPTERS 12 AND 13

The raids in the Fuka area: Major Stirling, Captain Mayne, Captain Jordan, Flying Officer Rawnsley, Lts. Bailey, Fraser, Scratchley, Hastings, Mather, Lord Jellicoe, Sadler, Russell,

Le Grand, Zirnheld, Martin, Harent, Klein. N.C.O.s Seekings, Cooper, Rose, Bennett, Riley, Almonds, Kershaw, White and Tait. Cpls. Lilley, Stone, Badger, Lambie, Down, Guegan, Le Gall, Boven, Hurin, Fouquet, Lageze, Chasseurs Boutinol and Leroy.

CHAPTER 14

The Big Benghazi raid· Major Stirling, Captain Mayne, Captain Maxwell, Captain Cumper, Captain Melot, Lts. Scratchley, Maclean, Bailey, Hastings, Mather, Sadler and Flying Officer Rawnsley. N.C.O.s Seekings, Cooper, Bennett, Rose, Riley, Almonds, Lilley, Tait, White, Kershaw, Phillips, Badger, Brough, Cattell, Lambie, Henderson, Laird, Bunfield, Adamson, Sturmey, Reddington, Milne, Ward, Burgess, Huckle, Miller, Leadbetter, Wortley, Caton, Downes, Kennedy, Belsham, Taylor, Fitch, Hindle, Sharman, Wall, Cooper, Wilson, Dronjin, Maynell, Roberts, Allan, Hill, Shaw, O'Dowd, Hutchinson, Johnson, Hall, Cunningham, Arnold, Moore, Ridler, McKinlay, Kennedy, Bull, Biard. A group of French officers and soldiers took part but their names have not been preserved.

CHAPTER 15

A Squadron: Major Mayne, Captains Fraser and Cumper, Lts. Lord Charlesworth, Wiseman, McDermott, Kennedy and Marsh. N.C.O.s Lilley, Phillips, Sturmey, Henderson, Maier, Leadbetter and Hindle. Cpls. Leigh, Kendall, Downs, O'Reilley, Donoghue, Ward, Allen, Swan, McDiarmed, Belsham, Finlay, Sharmon, Adams, Fitch, Kerr, Gladwell, Wall and Wortley. Ptes. Moore, O'Dowd, Allen and Sillito.

CHAPTERS 17 AND 18

B Squadron: Colonel Stirling, Major Street, Captains Hore-Ruthven, Morris-Keating, Galloway, Sullivan, Lts. Mather, Hough, Maloney, Martin, Sadler and Lalherahl.,

AFTERWARDS

Colonel Stirling, Captains Jordan and Poat, Lts. Alston, Thesiger, Sadler, Martin, Klein, Harent, McDermott, Le Grand, and Sgts. Taxis, Cooper and Seekings.

INDEX

Abassea, 37

Agedabia, 55-56, 57, 67, 69-70, 73, 113, 257

Agheila, 18, 57, 67, 73, 74, 77, 84, 107, 253, 255, 258, 261, 262, 279

Alamein, 135, 167, 169, 186, 188, 220, 221, 226, 245, 248, 249-253

Alanbrooke, Field Marshal Viscount (General Sir Alan Brooke), 230, 283

Alexander of Tunis, Field Marshal the Earl, 230, 231, 243, 253, 254

Alexandria, 12-16, 19-24, 90, 168, 169, 226

Allott, Captain Ken, 115, 117-119

Almonds, Sergeant Jim, 69, 80, 215, 237

Alston, Lieutenant Gordon, 268, 284, 300, 286, 305, 309; in Benghazi raid, 114, 115-120, 124-131; nearly captured, 276-279, 280

Auchinleck, Field Marshal Sir Claude, 91, 107, 167; succeeds Wavell, 19; difficulties with Churchill, 22, 132-136; supports Stirling, 22-23, 48, 86-88; plans to relieve Tobruk, 39, 49; consolidates at Gazala, 112; and Malta, 134-135; relieved of command, 230

Bagnold, R. A., 53-54

Bagush airfield, 170, 174, 176-180, 215

Bailey, Lieutenant Chris, 191, 220, 222, 238

Baltel el Zalegh, 145

Barce airfield, 113, 120, 136, 152, 161, 227, 229, 232, 242

Barr, Corporal, 93, 98, 103

Benghazi, 55, 87, 107-108, 112, 113-131, 136, 147-166, 226, 227, 229, 230-239, 246

Benina airfield, 113, 120, 146-151, 156, 166

Bennett, Air Vice Marshal Bruce, 219, 231

Bennett, Sergeant Major, 24, 65, 107, 111, 217, 309

Bergé, Colonel, 90, 136, 161-166, 309

Berka satellite airfield, 113, 120, 151-152, 166

Bir Chalder, 174

Bir Dufan airfield, 270-271, 273-274, 275-276

Bir Guedaffia, 281, 284
Bir Soltane, 284, 285, 286, 298, 299
Bir Zalten, 256, 257-259
Blaney, Sergeant, 265
Bonnington, Lieutenant, 24, 41, 47-48
Bouerat, 87-88, 91-92, 93-108, 113, 258, 268, 269, 279
Bourmont, Corporal, 143-144, 145
Brooke, General Sir Alan (Viscount Alanbrooke), 230, 283
Brough, Sergeant, 62-65, 74
Brückner (German p.o.w.), 138, 140, 141, 143, 145-146, 151
Buck, Captain Herbert, and Special Interrogation Group, 137-145, 222, 240
Bulgaria, 18
Byrne, Private, 80-85

Cairo, 12, 86-93, 113, 134, 139, 167-168, 169-170, 219, 226-233, 244
Campbell, Major, 240
Cekhira, 288, 291
Churchill, Sir Winston, 18, 107, 168, 253, 307; disagrees with Auchinleck, 22, 132-136; anxiety over Malta, 133-135; Stirling meets, 230-231; on Alamein, 250n; enthusiasm for S.A.S., 254
Churchill, Randolph, 124-131, 309
Clarke, Brigadier Dudley, 23
Colditz, 305
Collins, Lieutenant Ian, 32

Cooper, Major, 65, 156, 172, 177, 213, 309; joins S.A.S., 24; on Sirte raid, 73-78; on Bouerat raid, 96, 102, 106, 110; on Benghazi harbour raids, 117-120, 123-131; on Benina airfield raid, 147-151; in jeep attack on airfield, 202; reaches First Army, 284, 293-294, 295, 301-303
Costi (Greek guide), 162, 164-165
Crete, 18, 19, 20, 23, 136, 161-166
Cripps, Sir Stafford, 134
Cumper, Captain Bill, 90, 112, 237, 309
Cunningham, General Sir Alan, 49-50

Derna, 136, 141, 143-145, 229
Dobbie, General Sir William, 134
Dodds, Lieutenant, 113, 120
Down, Corporal, 222
Duncan, Captain, 93, 97, 98, 102-105
DuVivier, Sergeant, 80-85, 309

Eason-Smith, Jake, 46-47, 242
Eisenhower, General, 283
El Daba airfield, 170, 174, 184, 186, 191-192, 250, 251
El Fascia, 267, 268-270, 274-275, 276
El Hama, 289, 292, 301
Es-Sherif, 109
Esser (German p.o.w.), 138, 140

Franks, Bryan, 306
Fraser, Captain Bill, 57, 70, 86, 172, 183; joins S.A.S., 24-25; on Timini-Gazala raids, 41, 46-47; on Agedabia raid, 67, 69-70, 71, 79; 200-mile desert march, 80-85, 86n; raids Barce, 113, 120; attacks Fuka airfields, 191, 192
Freyberg, General Sir Bernard, 282, 303
Fuka airfield, 170, 174, 176, 191

Gabes, 282, 286
Gabes Gap, 285, 286-290, 292-294
Gafsa, 286, 290, 293, 303
Galloway, Captain, 256
Gavi, 305
Gazala, 49, 55, 58, 73, 108, 111n, 112, 133, 136
Geneifa, 22, 24-25
Ghadames, 284, 285
Gibson, ' Flash ', 105, 106, 107n
Grand Sea Ergh, 285
Greece, 18, 23
Grüenther, General Alfred, 307
Guild, Captain, 139
Guingand, General Sir Frederick de, 247
Gurdon, Lieutenant Robin, 125, 129, 156, 160, 161, 170-175, 183-184, 186, 192, 196

Hackett, General Shan, 244-247, 255, 256, 258, 269, 283
Haselden, Colonel John, 227-229, 240, 241
Hasselet, 81

Hastings, Lieutenant Stephen, 191, 192, 196-198, 202, 206-208, 209-212, 213, 309
Head, Antony, 283
Heliopolis aerodrome, 36-38
Heraklion aerodrome (Crete), 136, 162-165
Holliman, Captain Gus, 57-62, 64-65, 71, 72-78, 193
Homs, 269
Hore-Ruthven, Captain Pat, 256, 268, 270-272, 279, 280
Hough, Lieutenant, 256, 269, 279
Hunter, Captain Antony, 93-109

Jackson, Sergeant, 67
Jaghbub, 52
Jalo, 51, 52-57, 67, 71-72, 78, 93, 107, 108-110, 115, 227, 229, 232, 235, 239
Jaquier, Lieutenant, 136, 152, 161, 166
Jellicoe, Captain Lord, 172, 174, 184, 191, 192, 218-219, 256, 309; on Crete raid, 162-165; in jeep attack, 201, 209, 212; and Special Boat Section, 306
Jordan, Captain Augustin, 90, 183, 191, 197, 220, 222, 282, 309; on Derna-Martuba raids, 136, 139-145, 161; leads patrols through Gabes Gap, 284-292; captured, 292

Kabrit, 39, 49, 86, 88, 90, 92, 111-112, 123, 136, 221, 254,

256, 279; S.A.S. camp and training at, 26-38
Kahane, Karl, 156-157, 160
Keating, Captain Geoffrey, 279
Klein, Lieutenant, 286, 288, 292
Kufra, 167, 169, 188, 232, 233, 239, 248, 259

Laird, Corporal, 238
Lake Djerid, 286
Lambie, Corporal, 223
Lampson, Sir Miles, 230-231
Langton, Lieutenant, 240
Laycock, Sir Robert, 17, 19, 20, 283, 306
Leach, Corporal, 265
Leclerc, General, 232, 285
Leostic, Private, 162, 165
Lewis, Lieutenant Jock, 20, 25, 41, 46-47, 86; joins S.A.S., 24, 30; invents 'Lewis bomb', 32-35; on Agheila raid, 57, 67; raids Mersa Brega roadhouse, 67-69, 77; on Nofilia raid, 71-72, 79-80; death of, 78-80
Lilley, Sergeant, 24, 156-157, 160, 309; on Mersa Brega raid, 68-69; on Nofilia raid, 79-80; on Berka satellite raid, 151-155
Lloyd-Owen, Colonel David, 189
Lovat, Lord, 16
Lutteroti, Baron von, 216, 217-219, 280

McDermott, Lieutenant, 249, 284, 294-298, 305n

McGonigal, Lieutenant, 24, 25, 41, 47, 111
Maclean, Brigadier Sir Fitzroy, 91, 122-131, 189, 230, 233, 235-239, 309
Maddalena, 49
Mahares, 288
Maloney, Lieutenant, 256, 269, 279
Malta, 132-146, 163, 166
Marble Arch aerodrome, 71, 78-80
Mareth Line, 282, 284, 285-286, 303
Marriott, General Sir John, 50-51, 55, 70, 86, 113-114, 230
Martin, Lieutenant, 191, 192, 197, 213-214, 256, 269, 277-278, 280, 284, 285, 286, 288, 289, 304, 309
Martuba, 136, 143, 145
Mather, Major Carol, 169-170, 172, 191, 192, 196-198, 201, 220, 222-225, 256, 269, 279, 309
Mayne, Captain Paddy, 41, 47, 86, 166, 172, 174, 189, 207, 216, 219-222, 255, 256-259, 267, 269, 284; joins S.A.S., 25; raids Heliopolis, 36-38; raids Sirte and Tamit, 57-62, 64, 65-67, 71-72, 73, 74, 75, 78; trains recruits at Kabrit, 92-93, 111; builds giant bed, 111-112; raids Berka satellite airfield, 113, 115-116, 120-122, 150, 151-161; raids Bagush airfield, 176-182; raids

Fuka, 191-192; through Qattara Depression, 192-195; raids coast road, 248-249, 279; takes over command of S.A.S., 306; death, 309

Melot, Captain Bob, 115-116, 235-236, 238

Mersa Brega, 68-69, 84, 107

Mersa Matruh, 20, 24, 170

Merton, Arthur, 131

Misurata, 268, 269, 270, 272

Mo (Arab servant), 88-89, 169-170

Montgomery, Field Marshal Viscount, 253, 269, 279, 282; takes command of Eighth Army, 230; refuses men to Stirling, 244-247; approves his plan for coast road assaults, 255, 258-259

Morris, Lieutenant, 68, 71, 77, 78-79

Moss, Sergeant, 116

Mouhot, Private, 162, 163, 165

Mountbatten, Admiral Earl, 283, 306

Nofilia, 71, 78, 79, 259, 261

Nye, General Sir Archibald, 134

Oldfield, Major Peter, 91-92, 93-95, 100, 108, 256, 268, 269, 279, 280, 309

Olivey, Lieutenant John, 115-117

Ollerenshaw, Sergeant, 265

Peniakoff, Lieut.-Colonel (Popski), 189, 228-229, 241

Phillips, Private, 80-85

Pleydell, Malcolm, 179-180, 190, 196, 217-218

Prendergast, Colonel, 54

Poat, Lieutenant Harry, 284, 305, 309

Qattara Depression, 167, 169, 171, 172, 188, 193-195, 223-225, 232, 248, 250

Rawnsley, Derek, 93, 109, 172, 186

Regima, 117

Reid, General Denys, 51, 52, 55, 57, 70, 86, 113

Rhodes, 17, 19

Riley, Captain, 99, 101, 102, 103, 112, 309

Ringway aerodrome (Cheshire), 30, 31, 112

Ritchie, General Neil, 15-16, 17, 22, 35, 48, 49-50, 230

Rommel, Field Marshal Erwin, 39, 70, 103, 132, 226-227, 244, 255, 285, 286, 296n; tribute to Stirling, 11; defeats Wavell, 18; penetrates into Egypt, 49; in retreat, 55, 58, 73, 74, 113; regains Cyrenaica, 107-108, 112, 133; reaches Alamein, 135; captures Tobruk, 167; on Stirling's raids, 188, 241; tactics against raids, 198-199; and the S.A.S., 274-275, 279-280

Rose, Sergeant, 24, 103, 124-127, 129-131

Royer, Corporal, 143

Russell, Lieutenant David, 137, 191, 220, 222

Sadler, Major Michael, 201n, 248, 256, 283, 309; on Sirte raids, 58-61, 67, 74; reputation as navigator, 72, 190; on Buerat raid, 93, 97, 98; in jeep attack, 202-204, 214-215; in coast road assaults, 267, 268-270; reaches First Army, 285, 293-296, 301-304
Sand Sea, 232, 233-235, 242, 248-249
Schott, Lieutenant, 174, 183
Scott, Flying Officer, 240
Scratchley, Lieutenant Sandy, 172, 184, 191, 193-195, 207-208, 209, 212, 218, 223, 239, 250-253, 309
Seekings, Sergeant, 24, 172, 237, 280, 284, 309; on Tamit raids, 65-67, 73-78; on Bouerat raid, 95-96, 102-110; on Benghazi raids, 117-120, 123-125, 177; on Benina raid, 147-151, 156, 158, 160-161; in jeep attack, 202, 211
Sfax, 282, 286, 288
Sharpe, Arthur, 183
Shaw, W. B. Kennedy, 54-55
Sibert, Private, 162, 165
Sidi Barrani, 174, 183
Sidi Haneish airfield, 199-208
Sillito, Lieutenant David, 249-250
Sinai Desert, 53, 55
Sirte, 57, 59, 61, 62-67, 71, 74, 75, 78, 269, 276

Siwa Oasis, 39, 49, 52, 53, 115-116, 124, 131, 134, 161, 167
Slonta airfield, 113, 120
Smuts, Field Marshal, 231
Sollum, 18, 170
Sousse, 286, 293
Steele, Major Don, 52-53, 55, 57
Stirling, Bill, 16, 255, 283, 286
Stirling, Colonel David: Rommel's tribute to, 11, 188; achievement of, 11-12, 86, 220, 243-244, 305; submits plan for private army to Middle East H.Q., 12-16, 21-24; career of, 16-17; in Layforce, 17-19; idea of special operations, 19-21

Recruiting for Special Air Service, 23-25; sets up camp at Kabrit, 26-38; training course, 29-31, 35-38, 111-112; plans operations, 31-35, 39 et seq; fails in attack on Gazala-Timini area, 39-48; attached to Reid at Jalo, 50-52, 55 et seq; co-operates with Long Range Desert Group, 53, 55 et seq; action against Sirte airfield, 57-67, 71, 72-78; seeks more men and supplies, 86-88; plans attack on Bouerat, 87-93; promoted to Major, 88; recruits Free French parachutists, 90, 112, 254; institutes S.A.S. insignia, 90-91; raids Bouerat, 93-107

Returns to Kabrit, 111; plans raids on Benghazi har-

bear, 117-120, 124-131; plans
raids on airfields attacking
Malta convoys, 136-138; co-
operates with Special Interrogation Group, 137, 139;
raids Benghazi airfields, 147-
151, 155-161; assembles force
for offensive against communications, 168-169; estab-
lishes desert rendezvous at
Fuka, 170-184

G.H.Q. attitude to his unit,
186-188; suggested amalgamation with Special Operations Executive, 187; legen-
dary fame, 188-190, 306; his
democratic system, 191; attacks airfield with jeeps, 199-
208, 216-217; plans operations on Alamein line, 220,
221; instructed to return
home, 220-221; sceptical of
H.Q. plan for Benghazi harbour raids, 226-227; outlines
plan to Churchill, 231

Sets off from Kufra, 232-
235; disastrous raid on Benghazi, 235-239; promoted to
Lieut.-Colonel, 243; S.A.S.
expanded into full regiment,
243; plans to harass Rommel's
lines of communication, 244-
245, 254 et seq; fails to get
trained men from Mont-
gomery, 244-248, 254; or-
ganises new force at Kabrit,
254; his plan approved by
Montgomery, 255, 258; plans
to join up with First Army,
282-283; aims at brigade
status for S.A.S., 283; route
to First Army, 284-287, 292;
captured, 294-301; escapes
four times, 305; transferred
to Colditz, 305; forms Capricorn Society in Rhodesia,
307; his conception of military
man-power, 307-308

Stirling, Hugh, 16
Stirling, Peter, 16, 88, 91, 244
Storey, Corporal, 151, 153-154,
    156
Street, Major Vivian, 256, 258,
    268, 270-274, 275-276, 279,
    309
Sutherland, Colonel David, 115-
    116

Tait, Sergeant, 44-46, 80-85
Tamit, 61-62, 65, 71, 72, 73,
    74, 75-78
Taxis, Sergeant, 287, 301-303
Thesiger, Lieutenant Wilfred,
    268, 276-279, 280, 284, 286,
    300, 305
Thomas, Lieutenant, 24, 41
Timpson, Lieutenant, 108-110,
    170, 172-174, 183, 188, 193,
    234, 259-266
Tobruk, 18, 19, 22, 24, 39,
    50, 167, 227, 228-229, 232,
    239-241
Toglat Oasis, 269
Tourneret, Corporal, 143
Tozeur, 286
Trigh-el-Abd, 45-46, 116, 235
Tripoli, 255, 256, 258, 269, 282,
    284, 305

Turogo airfield, 280

Vidal, Corporal, 143

Wadi El Faregh, 70, 82
Wadi Gattara, 159
Wadi Tamit, 73, 94-96, 267
Warburton, Corporal, 151, 153
Warr, Lieutenant, 174, 183
Wavell, Viscount, 18-19, 53, 54

Welsh, Private, 260, 263, 265, 266
Wilder, Lieutenant, 215-216

Yates, Sergeant, 44, 46, 47
Yugoslavia, 18

Zenouche, 304
Zirnheld, Captain André, 136, 152, 161, 166, 174, 184, 192, 197, 213-214
Zliten, 269, 272